A Tale of Two Factions: The US Power Structure Since World War II

By Joseph P. Raso

Second Edition

All URLs were accurate at the time of publication. Longer
URLs were shortened using TinyURL. Some individuals
may have changed positions since the time of publication.

Second edition, 2020

ISBN 9798655476752

CONTENTS

ABBREVIATIONS

ABN	Anti-Bolshevik Bloc of Nations
ACDA	Arms Control and Disarmament Agency
ACWF	American Council for World Freedom
AECA	Arms Export Control Act
AEI	American Enterprise Institute
AFC	America First Committee
AFIO	Association of Former Intelligence Officers
AFP	Americans for Prosperity
AGFC	Arkansas Game and Fish Commission
AGRA	Alliance for a Green Revolution in Africa
AIG	American International Group
AIM	Accuracy in Media
AIOC	Anglo-Iranian Oil Company

ALEC	American Legislative Exchange Council
APACL	Asian Peoples' Anti-Communist League
APLFD	Asian Pacific League for Freedom and Democracy
ARA	Analysis and Research Association
ARENA	Nationalist Republican Alliance
ASC	American Security Council
ASCF	American Security Council Foundation
BND	Bank of North Dakota
CAA	Council on American Affairs
CAL	Latin American Anti-Communist Confederation
CBN	Christian Broadcasting Network
CEIP	Carnegie Endowment for International Peace
CFF	Canadian Freedom Foundation
CFR	Council on Foreign Relations
CIA	Central Intelligence Agency

CMD	Center for Media and Democracy
CNP	Council for National Policy
COA	Council of the Americas
CPAC	Conservative Political Action Conference
CPTS	Coalition for Peace Through Strength
CSIS	Center for Strategic and International Studies
CSP	Center for Security Policy
DCF	Donors Capital Fund
DIA	Defense Intelligence Agency
DINA	National Intelligence Directorate
DT	Donors Trust
ECB	European Central Bank
EEC	European Economic Community
EPA	Environmental Protection Agency
EU	European Union
EUROWACL	European unit of the WACL

FBI	Federal Bureau of Investigation
FCC	Federal Communications Commission
FEMACO	Mexican Anti-Communist Federation
FNLA	National Liberation Front of Angola
FRC	Family Research Council
FSLN	Sandinista National Liberation Front
FWF	Forum World Features
G30	Group of Thirty
HRW	Human Rights Watch
IAS	Institute for American Strategy
IMF	International Monetary Fund
IRCA	International Railways of Central America
ISC	Institute for the Study of Conflict
ISG	Iraq Study Group
ITT	International Telephone and Telegraph

JBS	John Birch Society
JSPES	*Journal of Social, Political, and Economic Studies*
LMDC	Lower Manhattan Development Corporation
MI	Manhattan Institute
MI6	United Kingdom's foreign intelligence service
MLN	National Liberation Movement
MPLA	Popular Movement for the Liberation of Angola
MPS	Mont Pelerin Society
MRC	Media Research Center
NAFFD	North American Federation for Freedom and Democracy
NAFTA	North American Free Trade Agreement
NAM	National Association of Manufacturers
NARWACL	North American Regional unit of the WACL
NATO	North Atlantic Treaty Organization

NFF	Nicaraguan Freedom Foundation
NIEO	New International Economic Order
NOAA	National Oceanic and Atmospheric Administration
NRA	National Rifle Association of America
NSC	National Security Council
OPEC	Organization of the Petroleum Exporting Countries
OSF	Open Society Foundations
OUN-B	Organization of Ukrainian Nationalists-Bandera
PBI	Public Banking Institute
PBS	Public Broadcasting Service
PGT	Guatemalan Party of Labor
PIIE	Peterson Institute of International Economics
PNAC	Project for the New American Century
RNC	Republican National Committee

SALT	Strategic Arms Limitation Talks
SDI	Strategic Defense Initiative
SMOM	Sovereign Military Order of Malta
SPN	State Policy Network
TBN	Trinity Broadcasting Network
TCC	The Conservative Caucus
UFCO	United Fruit Company
UN	United Nations
UNESCO	United Nations Educational, Scientific and Cultural Organization
UNICEF	United Nations International Children's Emergency Fund
UNITA	National Union for the Total Independence of Angola
UPA	Ukrainian Insurgent Army
USCWF	United States Council for World Freedom
WACL	World Anti-Communist League
WEF	World Economic Forum

WLFD	World League for Freedom and Democracy
WND	*WorldNetDaily*
WTO	World Trade Organization

INTRODUCTION

The deep political history of the United States since World War II has featured two ruling factions competing for dominance in the world's most powerful country. Not simply in the formal political system, but in a broader political conception including social and economic spheres, these rival factions have shaped the destiny of the United States since the middle of last century. As a consequence of US global power during this same period, they have also profoundly affected much of the world.

Together, the two ruling factions constitute the US power structure, a *de facto* oligarchy comprised of private networks exercising control over official institutions and policymaking. Domestic and foreign policies alike are formulated through these networks of think tanks and other non-governmental organizations. These networks also produce the narratives found in the major media, thus determining the views, opinions, and ideas to which the general public is regularly exposed. By doing so, they establish the parameters for political discourse in the wider society.

Oligarchy (from Greek *oligarkhía*, "rule of the few") serves as a more accurate lens than democracy (from Greek *dēmokratiā*, "rule of the people") for viewing political developments and power relations in the United States. Democratic forms and institutions obscure the reality of oligarchy. Former US President James E. (Jimmy) Carter recently referred to the United States as "an oligarchy with unlimited political bribery."[1] In an article published in 2014, political scientists Martin Gilens and Benjamin I. Page concluded that their "analyses suggest that majorities of the American public actually have little influence over the policies our government adopts."[2] Page and co-author Jeffrey A. Winters had earlier asserted that "minority power is a fact of life in any complex society" and "it is useful to think about the US political system in terms of oligarchy."[3] Even though the authors are correct that "the existence of oligarchy need not depend upon oligarchs' holding formal government positions (indirect influence is sufficient)" and "does not require extensive political engagement by oligarchs themselves," the following investigation of the US oligarchy offers evidence of each, an oligarchy of both power and influence.[4]

Examples of oligarchy abound throughout history and the present. In Latin America, and the Global South generally, where the economy has traditionally been based on agricultural exports, oligarchy has long been associated with vast land ownership. Large landowners later became proprietors of industrial enterprises. Today, financial interests factor heavily.[5] From another part of the world, Russian oligarchs have achieved notoriety through

---

[1] Daniel Kreps, "Jimmy Carter: US Is an 'Oligarchy With Unlimited Political Bribery,'" *Rolling Stone* 31 July 2015: https://tinyurl.com/ya3gejwl

[2] Martin Gilens and Benjamin I. Page, "Testing Theories of American Politics: Elites, Interest Groups, and Average Citizens," *Perspectives on Politics* September 2014 (Vol. 12: No. 3), 577.

[3] Jeffrey A. Winters and Benjamin I. Page, "Oligarchy in the United States?," *Perspectives on Politics* December 2009 (Vol. 7: No. 4), 731, 744.

[4] Ibid., 731.

[5] Liisa L. North and Timothy D. Clark (eds.). *Dominant Elites in Latin America: From Neo-Liberalism to the 'Pink Tide'* (London: Palgrave Macmillan, 2018).

frequent media attention.[6] In US history, oligarchy has been referenced with regard to such nineteenth-century "robber barons" as John J. Astor, Cornelius Vanderbilt, John D. Rockefeller, Andrew Carnegie, John P. (JP) Morgan, and Andrew W. Mellon.[7] These industrialists and financiers have been both lauded and loathed. In his book *Oligarchy*, Winters selects cases ranging from ancient Athens and Rome to contemporary examples in Asia and North America, namely the United States.[8]

All the above interprets oligarchy as synonymous with plutocracy (from Greek *ploutokratía*, "rule of the wealthy"). Winters emphasizes this point: "oligarchs in all the cases studied are empowered by wealth."[9] Aristotle understood oligarchy this way, as power concentrated in the hands of the wealthiest few citizens.[10] While these pages will certainly demonstrate the power of extreme wealth in US politics and society through the leading role played by billionaires in both oligarchic factions, it will also examine the key participation of less wealthy political actors in each faction. The plutocrats occupy a commanding position but rely on the efforts of other individuals from the government and private organizations to attain their political objectives. In this study, the

---

[6] Z. Byron Wolf, "Russia's oligarchs are different from other billionaires," *CNN* 6 April 2018: https://www.cnn.com/2018/04/06/politics/oligarch-russia-billionaires-government-putin-sanctions/index.html

[7] Matthew Josephson. *The Robber Barons: The Great American Capitalists, 1861-1901* (New York: Harcourt, Brace & World, 1962).

[8] Jeffrey A. Winters. *Oligarchy* (New York: Cambridge University Press, 2011).

[9] Ibid., xvii.

[10] Stanford Encyclopedia of Philosophy. "Aristotle's Political Theory" (7 November 2017): https://plato.stanford.edu/entries/aristotle-politics

oligarchy is defined by wealth and connections to wealth being actively parlayed into political power. Therefore, a billionaire who is not a direct or indirect political actor will not be named as a plutocrat or an oligarch.

If one adopts a broader view of oligarchy, one of the most notable scholarly explorations of oligarchic power in the United States is C. Wright Mills' seminal *The Power Elite*. Mills argued that a "power elite" from a similar educational and social background of prominent families dominates high-level positions in the most important institutions.[11] The work of G. William Domhoff, another social scientist, built on Mills' book in a dissection of US power. In *Who Rules America?*, originally published in 1967 and now in its seventh edition, Domhoff contends that an economic-based class representing corporate interests rules the United States. For Domhoff, the United States is undoubtedly an oligarchy, or more specifically, a plutocracy.[12] Recently, social scientist Peter Phillips scrutinized the concentrated wealth and organized power of the global power elite, which this study investigates as an extension of the US power elite in chapter 2.[13]

Formal and informal factions are ubiquitous in the political world and their existence is not limited to any geographic area. Within political parties, political organizations of all types, ruling or revolutionary and insurgent groups of any substantial size, factions often form to pursue a particular agenda or specific policy and, in many cases, to advance

---

[11] C. Wright Mills. *The Power Elite* (New York: Oxford University Press, 1956).
[12] G. William Domhoff. *Who Rules America?: Power, Politics, and Social Change* (New York: McGraw-Hill, 2006).
[13] Peter Phillips. *Giants: The Global Power Elite* (New York: Seven Stories Press, 2018).

personal ambitions. Sub-factions or cliques can also form within larger factions due to ideological and other differences. Factionalism may result in intense intragroup conflict but paradoxically may also provide overall stability by reducing the number of individual conflicts that would otherwise arise in the absence of factions. A significant degree of secrecy allows factions to operate without public knowledge. If the level of secrecy is considerable, the very existence of one or more factions may remain unknown to the majority of the public. Such is the case with respect to the factions of the US oligarchy.

Probably rather obvious at this point, the factions of the US oligarchy are informal in character. Yet they are no less real for their lack of formal structure. The most influential think tanks, essentially the core of each faction, are themselves highly organized entities with official leadership positions. Moreover, the network analysis presented will demonstrate the integrated nature of each faction, revealing the existence of two distinct camps maintaining some limited affiliations with one another. They are not static and are subject to change, but their fundamental continuity is evident. It can also be asserted that the informal members of these factions very likely possess a keen awareness of their faction's chief powerbrokers.

Certain criteria will be applied to determine which networks qualify as oligarchic factions for the purposes of this analysis. A political network must be well established to receive consideration as a faction of the oligarchy. This network must consist of like-minded individuals and their collection of think tanks, foundations and other private organizations. Advocacy and planning of economic policies, particularly those with a domestic impact, need to be combined with close attention to foreign policy issues. Another critical requirement is network extension into the White House during the past decades principally through the election of the network's favored presidential candidate. An ongoing presence in government agencies and departments is also crucial. Considerable influence and representation in one of the main political parties must be observed. Finally, at least some mass media outlets, whether print publications or television networks, must correspond to a political network for it to receive the designation of a faction.

Taking into account all of the criteria enumerated above, only two political networks qualify as factions of the US oligarchy since World War II. They can reasonably be seen as "liberal" right and "conservative" right, and for the sake of brevity these terms will be the ones commonly used to refer to the two factions throughout this study. Both are located on the right side of the political spectrum because they primarily represent oligarchic interests, a reflection of the seating arrangements in the post-revolution French parliament from which the political terms "left" and "right" originate. In the second half of the twentieth century, the more liberal faction was often referred to as the Eastern Establishment, or simply "the establishment," as it incorporated West Coast persons as well. Other terms for this power elite which could be considered appropriate include center-right, corporate liberal, and corporate internationalist or globalist. Wall Street, the Ivy League, and the State Department are some of its traditional milieus.

Supporters of the more conservative faction and perhaps even many liberals themselves may refer to it as the political left but that would be incorrect as this faction does not serve the public interest either and its global objectives tend toward neo-totalitarianism. By comparison, the conservative power elite has a right-wing, reactionary, and more nationalistic orientation. Some elements of this faction tend toward neo-fascism. As these pages will demonstrate, these oligarchic factions do not reflect genuine liberalism or conservatism.

The one clique closest to satisfying the conditions but still falling short of faction status are the neoconservatives, usually abbreviated to neocons, who gained prominence as foreign policy advisors during the George W. Bush administration. They certainly boast several influential think tanks and have held high-level government positions. However, their overwhelming focus on foreign affairs is not matched with sufficient concern for economic and social policies. Nor do they dominate any major media outlet. Many have actually appeared willing to be of service to either ruling faction. While most neocons emerged from the conservative faction in the 1980s, some of the most visible among them are attached to the liberal faction. As such, the neocons are a difficult group to classify but do not constitute an independent faction. Lobbies, even particularly large and influential ones such as the Israel and Cuban-American, obviously do not qualify as factions of the oligarchy either.

Overall, the liberal faction has been in the ascendancy in the post-WWII oligarchy. A far greater number of presidential administrations have been associated with this power elite and it has dominated the mass media including nearly all of the major television networks and leading newspapers, although the conservative faction has made some significant media inroads since the "Reagan Revolution" in the 1980s. In terms of think tanks and foundations, both factions are extremely well represented. Policy-oriented organizations, foremost among them the Council on Foreign Relations (CFR), and grantmaking foundations like The Rockefeller Foundation are critical components of the liberal faction just as the Council for National Policy (CNP) and the Sarah Scaife Foundation, for example, serve the same function for its conservative counterpart.

The two major political parties, Democratic and Republican, now broadly fall under the direction of the liberal and conservative factions, respectively, but this was not always the case. Rockefeller Republicans once represented the liberal power elite in Congress while Southern conservatives had a home in the Democratic Party. Conservative takeover of the Republican Party began in earnest with Barry M. Goldwater's nomination for president in 1964.[14] This transformation forced the liberal faction of the oligarchy to recruit operatives in the Democratic Party and the party became more identified with the establishment. The liberal power elite forged a close relationship with leading Democrats and backed the Democratic presidential administrations of Carter, William J. (Bill) Clinton, and Barack H. Obama. It has enjoyed progressively less influence in the Republican Party during this period but there are still some Republicans who are liberal on social issues and supportive of multilateral free trade.

Given the size, strength, and global reach of the US military and intelligence apparatus, it is not surprising to

---

[14] Mary C. Brennan. *Turning Right in the Sixties: The Conservative Capture of the GOP* (Chapel Hill: The University of North Carolina Press, 1995), 81.

find within them the presence of the oligarchy and its factions. The Pentagon has remained subordinate to civilian authority and therefore has not challenged oligarchic control in the United States. Instead, military officers have been active in the politics of the conservative faction from the outset. The postwar development of the "military-industrial complex," made famous by President Dwight D. Eisenhower's warning in his farewell address, supplied tremendous impetus to the formation of this faction in the 1950s. Some high-ranking officers have been associated with the liberal power elite but in general they have played a more peripheral role in that faction. Rather than threatening oligarchic prerogatives, individual members of the armed forces and related industry have contributed to the durability of the US oligarchy.

The Central Intelligence Agency (CIA), for its part, was established in 1947 through the efforts of powerful members of the Eastern Establishment seeking to safeguard Wall Street interests in foreign countries. These individuals, led by Wall Street lawyer Allen W. Dulles acting on behalf of his clients, campaigned for the creation of a civilian government agency that could clandestinely act as an intelligence service to protect corporate interests abroad. The liberal faction managed the CIA at its highest level for decades, but officers affiliated with the conservative faction rose high in the ranks of the agency, particularly in the branch responsible for covert operations, the Directorate of Plans/Operations. A labyrinth agency which has featured both power struggles and necessary cooperation between the factions, the CIA has defended oligarchic privileges from its inception in its official capacity of preserving US "national security."

This analysis takes the years following World War II as its starting point for a couple of important reasons. The first is the widely accepted view that the United States became the world's preeminent superpower after the war notwithstanding the global challenge presented by the Soviet Union. This reality was only reinforced by US hegemony in the post-Cold War era and has persisted well into this century. Since World War II the nature of the US power structure has been relevant to the lives of not only Americans but people everywhere on the planet. Secondly, the factional split in the oligarchy, which began prior to the war, only became permanent in the 1950s when the conservative faction firmly took shape.

Two momentous issues, one domestic and the other international, caused a breakdown in the cohesion of the US oligarchy in the 1930s. President Franklin D. Roosevelt's New Deal response to the Great Depression unsurprisingly proved unpopular with many oligarchs but eventually received acceptance from the more farsighted of them in financial circles. Conservative oligarchs, on the other hand, continued to reject the New Deal outright and equated it with socialism and even communism. Meanwhile, disagreement over US involvement in World War II prior to the attack on Pearl Harbor exacerbated the division, with the fledgling conservative faction organizing opposition to US entry into the war while the Eastern Establishment advocated for an active war effort to assist Britain in its fight against Nazi Germany. As will be seen in the third chapter of this book, several plutocratic funders of the America First Committee (AFC), the largest pre-WWII "isolationist" organization, would later appear at the forefront of the oligarchy's new conservative faction.

The outline of *A Tale of Two Factions* will now be addressed. After examining the domestic network of the liberal power elite in the opening chapter, the following chapter will explore the faction's international network, built through exclusive discussion groups and conferences. Subsequent chapters will take up the conservative faction, also both domestically and internationally. In the fifth chapter, cases of foreign intervention by the US oligarchy will be considered, mainly in Latin America but also in Africa during the Cold War, each orchestrated by one of the factions. The final chapter will present factional conflict in the 1990s and its ongoing reality. In the conclusion, the potential for creating alternatives to the rule of the US oligarchy and its factions will be evaluated.

The decades-long work of scholar and former Canadian diplomat Peter Dale Scott on "deep politics" has exposed the serious limitations of more conventional approaches to the study of US politics. He defines deep politics as "all those arrangements, deliberate or not, that are usually repressed in public discourse rather than acknowledged."[15] Scott differentiates between a "deep state" and a "public state" in the United States, the latter consisting of public institutions more responsive to democratic demands. The less transparent deep state, in contrast, "is organized by the military and intelligence apparatus."[16] It has strong ties to the US "overworld," which essentially corresponds to the oligarchy outlined above, "that realm of wealthy or privileged society that, although not formally authorized or institutionalized, is the scene of successful influence of government by private power. It includes both (1) those

---

[15] Peter Dale Scott. *The Road to 9/11: Wealth, Empire, and the Future of America* (Berkeley: University of California Press, 2007), 267.
[16] Ibid., 268.

whose influence is through their wealth, administered personally or more typically through taxfree foundations and their sponsored projects, and (2) the first group's representatives."[17]

Studying deep politics offers a superior understanding of political developments, its analysis not limited to superficial and often misleading appearances. Of course, it would be naive to suggest that evaluations based on deep politics are always accurate and complete. Much remains unknown or barely understood. Assessments can certainly prove incorrect. Still, it permits a greater appreciation for the depth of political processes. In the context of the present study of the two oligarchic factions, deep politics provides a lens through which to view the apparent routine of daily politics.

---

[17] Ibid., 268.

CHAPTER 1
THE ESTABLISHMENT: THE POWER NETWORK OF THE LIBERAL FACTION

It is difficult to argue against the notion that the liberal faction of the US oligarchy has been dominant during the post-WWII period. Its domestic network of think tanks and foundations expanded following the war, which along with control of key institutions, furthered the entrenchment of its power at home. International connections flourished and were combined with the projection of US power overseas to ensure the worldwide reach of the liberal power elite. By the 1960s, its monopoly on power was being contested by the conservative faction but it persevered through setbacks as the latter became a genuine rival.

This chapter will discuss the liberal power network and its constituent parts. Its leading policy think tanks will be reviewed as well as its main foundations. Other facets of the faction will feature in the analysis, including its perennial representation in presidential administrations and associated major media. The liberal faction's international network will follow in the next chapter. The discussion integrates a faction of power in which some ideological differences exist.

THINK TANKS

The policymaking process in the United States originates in the nation's dominant think tanks, also known therefore as policy institutes. These organizations are the site of research, debate, and formulation of both policy agendas and specific policies. The most influential think tanks of the liberal faction will be reviewed here. While policy implementation occurs in government institutions in Washington, DC, a substantial amount of policy discussion and planning takes place elsewhere, such as at the New York-based Council on Foreign Relations (CFR).

Council on Foreign Relations

As its name suggests, the CFR focuses its attention on issues pertaining to US foreign policy and international relations, but these should not be viewed narrowly. They include the promotion of corporate-driven international economic relations in the form of multilateral free-trade agreements. These free trade and associated economic policies have fundamentally altered the structure of the domestic economy with a concomitant impact on US society. It will also be demonstrated that in addition to foreign policy-related appointments, CFR members have been routinely appointed to the top economic positions in the US government, revealing a direct relationship between CFR-linked personnel and economic policy.

The CFR has served as the principal think tank of the liberal power elite from the conclusion of World War II. This commanding position is due in no small part to the organizational structure of the Council. As a membership think tank, the CFR offers both individual and corporate membership categories. Individual members join through an application process. Government officials and corporate leaders account for a substantial share of this membership. The financial sector is particularly well represented at the Council including at the leadership level. Among the corporate members are many of the largest companies with global operations in banking, oil, pharmaceuticals, technology, and various other industries.[18]

Individual membership currently numbers approximately five thousand and includes US citizens from a range of business sectors and professional fields. Many have held government positions in recent administrations. Journalists and leaders in the non-governmental organization (NGO) sector are found among the membership as are academics from Ivy League and other universities.[19] These "intellectual" members are vital for fulfilling the CFR's mission as a think tank. However, their numbers are limited to ensure a balance in the sectoral backgrounds of the overall membership. Over the years the Council's membership has become significantly more diverse in terms of ethnicity, race, religion, sex, and age.[20]

In his second book on the CFR, *Wall Street's Think Tank*, Laurence H. Shoup relates a story from 1999 that encapsulates the Council's powerful membership and direct ties to government at the highest level. Then-chairman Peter G. Peterson is describing a special dinner at CFR headquarters on the Upper East Side of Manhattan, open to all members through videoconferencing:

> It was the kind of event only the Council on Foreign Relations seems able to stage. With our beloved Honorary Chairman David Rockefeller presiding,

---

[18] CFR. "About CFR: Membership":
https://www.cfr.org/membership
[19] CFR. "Membership: Individual Membership":
https://www.cfr.org/membership/individual-membership
[20] Laurence H. Shoup. *Wall Street's Think Tank: The Council on Foreign Relations and the Empire of Neoliberal Geopolitics, 1976-2014* (New York: Monthly Review Press, 2015), 58-59.

the following Secretaries of State, Council members all, glittered onto the video screen: George Shultz from San Francisco, James Baker from Houston, Warren Christopher from Los Angeles, Henry Kissinger and Cyrus Vance from New York, and Madeleine Albright from Washington. For good measure, President Clinton greeted us from Washington, Council Vice Chairman Hank Greenberg joined us from Hong Kong, and U.N. Secretary General Kofi Annan delivered the keynote address. All, as you would expect, did a splendid job of talking about new world challenges and opportunities and answering questions from our members. It demonstrated the quality discussions the Council, almost uniquely, can generate. It showed as well the technological possibilities now open to us for conversations among our members.[21]

With more than 130 members, the CFR's corporate program connects many of the largest transnational corporations to government officials and policymakers. Members are classified into three groups: Founders, President's Circle, and Affiliates. Founders is the smallest in number with 13 companies listed on the current roster while Affiliates accounts for the greatest number. Founders pay $100,000 per year for membership compared to $75,000 for President's Circle and $40,000 for Affiliates. The first category includes financial and corporate giants ExxonMobil, Goldman Sachs, Bank of America, JPMorgan Chase, Citi, Google, Facebook, and PepsiCo. Although these are all US-based corporations, corporate membership is open to foreign enterprises. Several

---

[21] Ibid., 55-56.

European, Asian, and Canadian companies are members in the other categories.[22]

In addition to hundreds of Council meetings every year throughout the United States and some locations abroad, corporate members are "offered briefings by in-house experts, a members-only website with CFR resources tailored to the private sector, and roundtables designed specifically for executives. The highlight of the program year is the annual Corporate Conference, which addresses such topics as competitiveness, geopolitical risk, and the global economic outlook."[23] These member benefits bolster the government-corporate nexus in the United States and reflect the plutocratic and oligarchic nature of policymaking in economic and foreign policy areas.

President Richard N. Haass, whose background is in government and academia, manages the CFR on a full-time basis and the Council is governed by a thirty-five-person board of directors, each serving a five-year term. Directors are either elected by the general membership after preselection by the nominating committee or they are appointed by the board itself.[24] Among the current directors are Timothy F. Geithner and Janet A. Napolitano, secretaries of the Treasury and homeland security, respectively, in the Barack H. Obama administration. Another board member, Ashton B. (Ash) Carter, was Obama's last defense secretary. They are joined on the board by Stephen J. Hadley, national security advisor to President George W. Bush, and Fareed R. Zakaria, the host of his own show on CNN. Laurence D. (Larry) Fink,

---

[22] CFR. "Membership: Corporate Program":
https://www.cfr.org/membership/corporate-membership
[23] Ibid.
[24] Shoup, 57.

chairman and CEO of BlackRock, the world's largest investment management firm, is also a director.[25]

Since 2017 the board has been headed by David M. Rubenstein, co-CEO of the Carlyle Group, a top private equity firm associated with former heads of state and past senior government officials, notably Bush and CFR members James A. Baker and Frank C. Carlucci. From 2007 to 2017, Carla A. Hills and Robert E. Rubin were the first co-chairs in CFR history. Hills, the Council's first chairwoman, was a chief negotiator of the North American Free Trade Agreement (NAFTA) as US trade representative for the George H.W. Bush administration and Rubin was secretary of the Treasury in the Bill Clinton administration. Members of the Global Board of Advisors include F. Javier Solana, the secretary general of the North Atlantic Treaty Organization (NATO) in the 1990s, and Paul G. Desmarais, the chairman of Power Corporation of Canada.[26]

Emeritus and honorary titles link the current CFR to some of its most prominent figures from the past decades. David Rockefeller was honorary chairman from 1985 until his death in 2017 at the age of 101. Peterson, chairman from 1985 to 2007 following Rockefeller's tenure, was chairman emeritus until his recent death, and ex-vice chairman Maurice R. Greenberg is now honorary vice chairman.[27] Peterson, once chairman and CEO of Lehman Brothers, departed the investment bank to co-found the private equity Blackstone Group while Greenberg served for many decades as chairman and CEO of American International

---

[25] CFR. "About CFR: Board of Directors":
https://www.cfr.org/board-directors
[26] CFR. "About CFR: Global Board of Advisors":
https://www.cfr.org/global-board-advisors
[27] CFR. *Annual Report (AR) 2016*, 38.

Group (AIG), one of the largest insurance and financial services companies and an investor in Blackstone under Greenberg's leadership. The aforementioned individuals attest to the modern CFR's continuity with the plutocratic dominance and oligarchic essence of its origins at the forefront of the Eastern Establishment.

Founded in 1921 by the merger of two existing groups, the CFR was established as a sister organization to the Royal Institute of International Affairs (Chatham House) in London. The early CFR was dominated by men connected to JP Morgan Jr., the leading banker of that era who had inherited the family business. Investment bankers Otto H. Kahn and Paul M. Warburg represented prestigious Wall Street firms Kuhn Loeb and M. M. Warburg, respectively, on the CFR's first board of directors. Other directors were drawn from prominent East Coast families. Until shortly after World War II, the head decision-maker of the CFR (first president, then chairman) was always linked to the Morgan family.[28]

In the early 1950s, a transition in the CFR leadership reflected the changing dynamics in the postwar liberal faction of the oligarchy. The Rockefeller family, whose vast wealth was derived from the unrivalled Standard Oil fortune of John D. Rockefeller, effectively secured control of the CFR as the family's financial operations expanded. This shift became obvious in 1953 when John J. McCloy assumed the chairmanship of the Council. McCloy, a Wall Street lawyer, had worked for the Rockefellers in his college days and also in 1953 began a seven-year term as chairman of the family's Chase National (soon Chase Manhattan) Bank. He served as chairman of the Ford

---

[28] Shoup, 13-15.

Foundation and prior to that was a trustee of The Rockefeller Foundation, two leading foundations of the liberal faction. In the late 1940s, McCloy was president of the World Bank, one of the international institutions conceived in CFR planning sessions and consultations with State Department officials during World War II which also produced plans for the International Monetary Fund (IMF) and the UN system.[29] McCloy was serving as assistant secretary of war when the United States entered World War II, and played a pivotal role in crucial decisions, including the internment of Japanese-Americans and the choice to not bomb the Auschwitz concentration camp.[30]

McCloy's already well-established relationship with President Dwight Eisenhower, a favorite of the oligarchy's liberal faction, afforded him direct access to the White House upon taking the helm at the CFR and Chase National. Eisenhower had chaired a CFR study group on aid to Europe from 1948 to 1951. In his biography of McCloy, author Kai Bird notes that "The businessmen to whom [Eisenhower] gravitated were invariably the kind of internationalist 'corporate liberals' who identified themselves as liberal Republicans. These men were not rock-ribbed conservatives; they did not intend to roll back Social Security, and they believed the federal government had a role to play in the 'maintenance of prosperity.' Politically speaking, there could not have been a better match between Eisenhower and McCloy."[31]

---

[29] G. William Domhoff. *Who Rules America?: Power, Politics, and Social Change* (New York: McGraw-Hill, 2006), 96-97.
[30] Kai Bird. *The Chairman: John J. McCloy and the Making of the American Establishment* (New York: Simon and Schuster, 1992), 13.
[31] Ibid., 430.

Eisenhower had considered McCloy for under secretary of state, but the latter was not interested in the position. According to McCloy, Eisenhower "indicated that there had been more to it than just the Under Secretaryship for State [. . .] [As] I understood the proposal, Mr. [John Foster] Dulles was still to be the general advisor on foreign affairs although no longer Secretary of State. If I was going to be Secretary of State I wanted to be responsible for foreign policy."[32] Nevertheless, McCloy did accept an appointment to the president's Commission on Foreign and Economic Policy.[33] He maintained ongoing contact with Eisenhower and acted as his unofficial advisor. The first year of the Eisenhower administration McCloy would also publicly champion the president's appropriations requests to Congress for the Mutual Security Program, a foreign aid program for US allies that benefited CFR members from the financial and corporate sectors by providing new investment opportunities in countries with US-supported governments.[34]

In the first half of 1953, McCloy met with the president regarding Senator Joseph R. (Joe) McCarthy's investigations into "communist subversion" in the United States. Both Eisenhower and McCloy were the target of McCarthy's allegations even though all three men were Republicans, an early example of conflict between the liberal and emerging conservative factions and the general irrelevance of party affiliation in this discord. McCarthy's chief counsel, Roy M. Cohn, who would later serve as attorney and mentor to future president Donald J. Trump,

---

[32] Nomi Prins. *All the Presidents' Bankers: The Hidden Alliances that Drive American Power* (New York: Nation Books, 2014), 209.
[33] Bird, 411.
[34] Prins, 210-211.

enjoyed access to confidential Federal Bureau of Investigation (FBI) files.[35] These were most likely used for McCarthy's attacks on McCloy for alleged communist sympathies, focused on McCloy's acceptance of communists in the US military during World War II.[36] Referring to McCloy and others opposed to his investigations, McCarthy claimed "The closer we get to the nerve center, the louder and louder will be the screams."[37] McCarthy's political career would soon be destroyed by his zealotry, however, and McCloy's political life would suffer no damage.

Early in 1954, the interlocking relationship between the CFR and government was evident at a Council dinner held to welcome McCloy as the new chairman. The guest of honor and main speaker was Secretary of State John Dulles, one of more than three hundred CFR members in attendance.[38] Also present was his brother, Allen Dulles, a member of the Council's board of directors since 1927 and CFR president in the late 1940s.[39] He would become one of the longest serving CFR directors, sitting on the board until his death in 1969. Allen Dulles had been appointed director of the Central Intelligence Agency (CIA) by Eisenhower the previous year and would remain in that position throughout his presidency. A close friend of McCloy, the two would later serve together on The President's Commission on the Assassination of President Kennedy (Warren Commission).

---

[35] Cleve R. Wootson Jr., "The president accused Obama of 'McCarthyism.' But Trump's mentor helped enforce it," *The Washington Post* 4 March 2017: https://tinyurl.com/y89whfl9
[36] Bird, 415-420.
[37] Ibid., 415.
[38] Ibid., 432.
[39] CFR. *AR 2016*, 37-38.

At this time disagreement arose over US nuclear policy toward the Soviet Union and the CFR was naturally a central venue for the debate. John Dulles announced at the Council that the US government would pursue a "massive retaliation" nuclear doctrine in response to any Soviet aggression.[40] At the CFR many found the secretary of state to be too rigid and regarded this policy as dangerous and unrealistic.[41] A study group was thus organized at the Council to address the issue. High-ranking military officials participated and shared classified information. Henry A. Kissinger, then a young Harvard professor, spent a year observing the group and his resulting book *Nuclear Weapons and Foreign Policy* advocated gradual escalation instead and the potential use of tactical nuclear weapons.[42]

Kissinger did not believe the limited use of nuclear weapons would escalate into a massive nuclear exchange. According to Kissinger, the United States had to demonstrate to the Soviet Union its willingness to wage both conventional wars and even limited nuclear ones. The book was a bestseller and sold seventeen thousand copies in its first year. Although he later reconsidered these views, Kissinger's time at the CFR marked the onset of his rise to power as a close associate of the Rockefellers. Through McCloy he was hired by Nelson A. Rockefeller, David's brother who was special assistant to Eisenhower on national security, to direct a study financed by the Rockefeller Brothers Fund. In McCloy's words, Kissinger "wanted to get close to the Rockefellers [and so] took up the offer as a trout takes to bait."[43]

---

[40] Shoup, 18.
[41] Bird, 461.
[42] Shoup, 18.
[43] Bird, 461-465.

Another major CFR study group in the mid-1950s reflected more generally on US-Soviet relations for over two years. Future John F. Kennedy administration officials Dean Rusk, McGeorge Bundy, and Walt W. Rostow participated in the discussions along with officials from the CIA, Department of State, and armed forces. As with all of the Council's study and discussion groups, the overriding purpose was to influence the direction of US policy. The Ford Foundation funded six full-time researchers for the project. The end product in this case was also a book, *Russia and America: Dangers and Prospects*, written by Henry L. Roberts of Columbia University.[44]

McCloy chaired the group and penned the book's foreward. In the aftermath of McCarthyism, he argued, "The American public has good reason to guard against subversion, but we must not shrink from our faith that free exchanges of ideas are our strength and that ultimately they will prevail."[45] In relation to nuclear policy, he urged "the most far-reaching proposals, including those for total disarmament."[46] McCloy also called for more exchanges in a variety of areas between Eastern and Western Europe. He recommended "constructive political and economic solutions" for African and Asian countries and the acceptance of their neutrality rather than the imposition of military alliances. It was a proposal for a different approach than the one pursued by John Dulles.[47]

Under McCloy's leadership the CFR maintained its oligarchic character. Individual membership in the 1950s

---

[44] Ibid., 460.
[45] Ibid., 446.
[46] Ibid., 446.
[47] Ibid., 446.

was numbered in the hundreds, divided into resident and nonresident members. The resident category was comprised of less than seven hundred men living in the New York City area and membership approval was an intensive process. A much smaller inner circle dominated the decision making. McCloy, David Rockefeller, and Allen Dulles occupied this realm along with several others including Hamilton Fish Armstrong, the editor of the CFR's still highly-influential *Foreign Affairs* publication. McCloy was responsible for creating the corporate membership section, thriving today as discussed earlier, partly to increase funding and supplement the sizeable grants from the Rockefeller and Ford foundations. Some members also voluntarily contributed funds beyond their annual dues.[48]

Foreign leaders, including heads of state and foreign ministers, recognized the organization as a center of power. Several spoke at the CFR in any given year. Fidel A. Castro, for example, addressed the Council in the early months of the Cuban Revolution following the overthrow of US-backed dictator Fulgencio Batista in January 1959. Unlike other guests, however, he was subjected to harsh questioning, particularly on his government's plans for the expropriation of private US assets. When asked how much aid his government was seeking, Castro insisted, "We don't want your money. We want your respect." He finally declared, "I can see that I am not among friends" before exiting.[49] The next year the Eisenhower administration would terminate diplomatic relations with Cuba and within

---

[48] Ibid., 457-458.
[49] Laurence H. Shoup and William Minter. *Imperial Brain Trust: The Council on Foreign Relations and United States Foreign Policy* (New York: Monthly Review Press, 1977), 42-43.

a short time Castro would officially proclaim himself, and the revolution, Marxist-Leninist.

The CFR's interlocking relationship with the US government would continue into the Kennedy administration even though Kennedy was not personally familiar with the Council and was initially greeted with skepticism by much of the liberal power elite. Arthur M. Schlesinger, special assistant to Kennedy, commented on this matter in his book on the Kennedy administration, entitled *A Thousand Days*: "In particular, he was little acquainted in the New York financial and legal community -- that arsenal of talent which had so long furnished a steady supply of always orthodox and often able people to Democratic as well as Republican administrations. This community was the heart of the American Establishment. Its household deities were Henry L. Stimson and Elihu Root; its present leaders, [former secretary of defense] Robert A. Lovett and John J. McCloy; its front organizations, the Rockefeller, Ford and Carnegie foundations and the Council on Foreign Relations; its organs, the *New York Times* and *Foreign Affairs*."[50]

Kennedy's lack of contacts was at least partially due to his Irish Catholic background, in contrast to the mainly Anglo-Saxon Protestant composition of the liberal faction of the oligarchy at the time. Despite this distance, he reached out to the Eastern Establishment soon after his election victory. He appointed sixty-three CFR members to State Department positions. Rusk and Bundy, participants in the US-Soviet study group, were respectively chosen for secretary of state and national security advisor. CFR

---

[50] Arthur M. Schlesinger. *A Thousand Days: John F. Kennedy in the White House* (Boston: Mariner Books, 2002), 128.

member Robert S. McNamara, the president of Ford Motor Company, became secretary of defense upon the recommendation of Lovett, who was Kennedy's first choice for the position. Allen Dulles continued as the CIA director as did fellow CFR member General Lyman L. Lemnitzer as the chairman of the Joint Chiefs of Staff. Lemnitzer would unsuccessfully propose Operation Northwoods in March 1962.[51] Future CFR vice chairman C. Douglas Dillon was selected for Treasury secretary. McCloy was tasked with creating a new arms control and nuclear disarmament agency. These appointments by the new outsider president reflected the permanent power and influence of the ruling liberal faction. As Bird states, "The new administration was to be a government of the Establishment."[52]

This power and influence were apparent during the Cuban Missile Crisis. McCloy in particular was centrally involved in the events of October 1962 as architect of the US Arms Control and Disarmament Agency (ACDA) and presidential advisor. He advocated strong military action at the outset of the crisis. After immediately returning from a trip to Europe on a US Air Force plane, he provided briefings to UN delegates on the unfolding situation. Eventually traveling to Washington, McCloy was one of a small number of insiders active in the administration's deliberations. His stance on the negotiations with Soviet officials softened somewhat, and unlike the hardliners of the ad hoc Executive Committee of the National Security Council set up to advise Kennedy, he supported the decision to secretly remove US nuclear missiles from Turkey in exchange for the Soviets withdrawing theirs from

---

[51] David Ruppe, "U.S. Military Wanted to Provoke War With Cuba," *ABC News* 1 May 2001:
http://abcnews.go.com/US/story?id=92662&page=1
[52] Bird, 499.

Cuba, thus leading to a resolution of the world-threatening crisis.[53]

According to social scientist Donald Gibson, "Kennedy and McCloy were in fact at odds with each other on most major issues," but McCloy's liaison with the administration extended beyond nuclear arms issues.[54] He was granted an allowance by Kennedy and his brother Robert, the attorney general, to legally represent all of the major oil corporations, known as the "Seven Sisters," in their dealings with the Organization of the Petroleum Exporting Countries (OPEC) cartel. It was deemed a matter of "national security" by McCloy and he was "the rare kind of man everyone assumed could watch out for the public's national-security interests while simultaneously serving his corporate clients."[55] McCloy scheduled confidential briefings between company CEOs and CIA and State Department officials where all parties combined efforts to collectively protect US corporate interests globally in the name of national security.[56]

When President Kennedy was assassinated in Dallas in November 1963, his successor, Lyndon B. Johnson, established the Warren Commission to produce a report on the assassination.[57] McCloy and Allen Dulles were appointed to the commission. Dulles had been forced to resign as the CIA director two years prior. Congressman,

---

[53] Ibid., 524-532.
[54] Donald Gibson. *The Kennedy Assassination Cover-up* (San Diego: Progressive Press, 2014), 237.
[55] Bird, 518.
[56] Ibid., 518.
[57] National Archives JFK Assassination Records. *Warren Commission Report*:
https://www.archives.gov/research/jfk/warren-commission-report

CFR member, and future president Gerald R. Ford along with another congressman and two senators served as the other commissioners. Although US Chief Justice Earl Warren was the chairman of the eponymous commission, McCloy and Dulles controlled it to such an extent that Gibson refers to it as "The McCloy-Dulles Commission."[58] The infamous single-bullet theory was promoted by McCloy, Dulles, and Ford despite the "strong doubts" of the other commissioners.[59] The *Warren Commission Report* "barely reflected the huge problems in this account and it did not reflect the opposition of three of the Commission's members; it was weighted heavily in favor of the Dulles-McCloy-Ford view."[60]

By the time Kennedy was assassinated, attention in Washington and at the CFR had begun to shift to developments in Southeast Asia, especially Vietnam. A 1963 book by Council member Russell H. Fifield, *Southeast Asia in United States Policy*, originated with one of the CFR's study groups. He concluded that the region was "of great strategic, economic and demographic significance" and "of special significance in the world balance."[61] Government officials, some of them Council members, attended CFR meetings in 1964-65 to justify an escalation of US involvement. Significantly, William Bundy, brother of McGeorge Bundy, was appointed assistant secretary of state for East Asian and Pacific affairs simultaneously with the commencement of his term as a CFR director in 1964.[62]

---

[58] Gibson, 89.
[59] Bird, 564-565.
[60] Gibson, 7.
[61] Russell H. Fifield. *Southeast Asia in United States Policy* (New York: Praeger for the Council on Foreign Relations, 1963), 4–5.
[62] Bird, 573-577.

President Johnson aggressively attempted to recruit McCloy for the ambassador posting in Vietnam. The CFR chairman, however, refused Johnson's demands of him. McCloy though would serve Johnson in an advisory capacity on Vietnam throughout his administration. Along with David Rockefeller and others, he joined the Committee for an Effective and Durable Peace in Asia in a public display of support for Johnson's escalation of the US war. After a short cessation of US bombing of North Vietnamese infrastructure, McCloy's opinion was that "it makes no sense now to let the highways and bridges be repaired and put in use again after we spent so much time bombing them."[63] He also believed "We've been too excited, too panicky--an indication of weakness to the enemy."[64] While McCloy allowed war detractors like political scientist Hans J. Morgenthau to present their views at the CFR, war backers like Kissinger were given ample opportunity to advocate for their position.

Vietnam was a topic of fierce debate at CFR events in late 1967 as some of the liberal power elite began to distance themselves from the US war in Southeast Asia. Briefings on the war were provided by individuals from an array of relevant fields. The war was claiming the lives of tens of thousands of US soldiers and Vietnamese civilians in the hundreds of thousands. For the liberal powerbrokers at the Council, the costliest aspect of the war was the resulting decline in US global standing and credibility. Overextension of US forces and neglect of US-European relations became the primary concerns at the CFR. By early 1968, most of the liberal faction of the oligarchy had turned against the US war in favor of de-escalation, preferring

---

[63] Ibid., 583.
[64] Ibid., 584.

"Vietnamization" as the South Vietnamese regime would be compelled to assume greater responsibility for combat operations. Johnson, feeling betrayed by the oligarchy's dominant faction, would soon announce he would not seek a second term as president.[65]

With the transition to Richard M. Nixon's presidency the liberal faction experienced the first reduction in its power under challenge from the rising conservative faction of the oligarchy. Nixon's election promised the conservative oligarchs regular access to the presidency for the first time. Backed by the conservative power elite, Nixon attempted to dismantle or overhaul Johnson's Great Society social programs. Nevertheless, the liberal faction continued to occupy an extensive presence in the executive branch and exercised considerable influence. Some of Nixon's policies, including the creation of the Environmental Protection Agency (EPA), were opposed by the conservative faction. Foremost in visibility among the CFR members in the Nixon administration was Kissinger, first as national security advisor and eventually as secretary of state. He would later serve a term on the Council's board of directors. A liberal faction hawk, Kissinger would be instrumental in the decision to bomb Cambodia from 1969 to 1973 as part of the US war strategy in Southeast Asia. From the outset of Nixon's tenure, Kissinger would be responsible for shaping the government's foreign policy more than any other individual.

The Nixon-Kissinger foreign policy of détente, in particular, was viewed as a profound betrayal by the conservative power elite. This reduction in Cold War tensions with the Soviet Union and China was at least

---

[65] Ibid., 599-603.

partially inspired by David Rockefeller's objective of expanding Chase Manhattan Bank's global operations. Rockefeller had been appointed chairman of the bank in 1969 and the following year succeeded McCloy as CFR chairman. The new policy of détente, in contrast with the containment policy followed by US foreign policymakers since World War II, permitted Chase Manhattan to become the first US bank to open an office in Moscow in 1973.[66]

Months later, in a visit arranged by Kissinger as part of rapprochement with China, Rockefeller reached an agreement with Chinese leaders in Beijing for Chase Manhattan to represent the Bank of China in the United States. Rockefeller was impressed with the Chinese Revolution: "The social experiment in China under Chairman Mao's leadership is one of the most important and successful in human history."[67] For the staunchly anti-communist conservative faction, which advocated confrontation rather than economic relations with the Soviet Union and China, this cooperation was regarded as an appeasement of the communist powers.

Other leading members of the liberal faction held cabinet-level positions in the Nixon administration.[68] George P. Shultz, a CFR director and secretary of state in the 1980s, served as Nixon's Treasury secretary from 1972 to 1974. Future CFR chairman Peterson was the secretary of commerce from 1972 until 1973, when he departed due to

---

[66] Scott, 38.
[67] David Rockefeller, "From a China Traveler," *The New York Times* 10 August 1973:
https://www.nytimes.com/1973/08/10/archives/from-a-china-traveler.html
[68] IPL. "POTUS: Presidents of the United States":
http://www.ipl.org/div/potus/rmnixon.html

conflict with right-wing officials in the administration.[69] Nixon appointed George H.W. Bush as United Nations ambassador in 1971. A CFR director in the late 1970s, the forty-first US president was born into a prominent East Coast family and had a close relationship with the Rockefellers, yet he was able to establish a personally beneficial association with conservative oligarchs as well after moving to Texas in order to profit from its lucrative oil industry. Nixon's CIA director, Johnson holdover Richard M. Helms, belonged to the Council.[70] Several other Council members, including McCloy, Rusk, Nelson and David Rockefeller, were given advisory positions in the administration. Upon Nixon's resignation resulting from the Watergate scandal, his vice president Gerald Ford assumed the presidency. Ford would select Nelson Rockefeller, former governor of New York State, as his replacement for vice president.

Jimmy Carter's administration from 1977 to 1981 signified the restored power of the liberal faction of the oligarchy, with CFR members named to all of the key positions. These Council members had joint membership in the Trilateral Commission, a group founded by David Rockefeller in 1973 to facilitate economic and political cooperation between North America, Western Europe, and an economically burgeoning Japan. Rockefeller delegated responsibility for organizing the commission to Zbigniew K. Brzezinski, a CFR director at the time.[71] Brzezinski, a Polish-born political scientist intensely antagonistic toward the Soviet Union, would become Carter's national security advisor a few years later. His decision to supply weapons to the

---

[69] Shoup, 37.
[70] Ibid., 169.
[71] Ibid., 135.

Mujahideen jihadist guerrillas fighting Soviet and Afghan military forces in Afghanistan became extremely controversial after Mujahideen leaders formed Al Qaeda in the late 1980s and focused their ire on the West.

CFR leaders and members effectively controlled the Carter administration. The first secretary of state, Cyrus R. Vance, had been Council vice chairman for three years and a director from 1968 to 1976. He would return to the board of directors for another lengthy period in the 1980s and serve another term as vice chairman. Secretary of the Treasury W. Michael Blumenthal also served as a director both prior to and following his position in the administration. Secretary of Defense Harold Brown would later serve as a director and eventually vice chairman. Carter's two UN ambassadors, Andrew J. Young and Donald F. McHenry, were also directors after leaving government office. Other CFR members included Edmund S. Muskie, Carter's second secretary of state, and G. William Miller, chairman of the Federal Reserve from 1978-79 and then Carter's second Treasury secretary. Vice President Walter F. Mondale was also a Council member. Carter has been a member since 1983.[72]

Carter's appointment of Paul A. Volcker to head the Federal Reserve in 1979 had far-reaching consequences for economic policy, marking the onset of what Shoup and other critics have labelled the "neoliberal" era. Volcker, a CFR director from 1975 to 1979 and again from 1988 to 1999, was once a special assistant to David Rockefeller at Chase Manhattan Bank. At the urging of Rockefeller and other Wall Street bankers, Carter selected Volcker for

---

[72] Ibid., 95.
CFR. *AR 2016*, 37-38.

Federal Reserve chairman "as the necessary choice to reassure the financial world."[73] Volcker introduced monetary policies associated with economists from the University of Chicago. He was credited with substantially curbing inflation through the raising of interest rates to high levels. These policies, however, caused a recession that severely impacted workers in several economic sectors.[74] Moreover, while defending social safety nets as "essential," Rockefeller became critical of "unaffordable safety nets."[75] Thus the liberal power elite, abandoning Keynesianism and principal elements of the social compromise that it had supported since the New Deal, adopted economic policies broadly compatible with the long championed policies of the conservative faction, soon to be nicknamed Reaganomics. The two factions' economic policy differences became a matter of degree, not kind.

Even though Ronald W. Reagan was the first president to unabashedly represent the conservative faction of the oligarchy, backed by The Heritage Foundation think tank, he was obliged to accept the enduring power of the liberal faction by offering it high-level posts in his administration. His choice for vice president, former CIA Director George Bush, was met with disapproval from conservative powerbrokers who preferred someone without Eastern Establishment credentials. Reagan's first secretary of state, Alexander M. Haig, chief of staff for Nixon and Ford, was a longtime CFR member as was his successor, George Shultz. John C. Whitehead, a CFR member and close Rockefeller associate, was appointed as Shultz's deputy in Reagan's second term to replace Kenneth W. Dam, a future CFR

---

[73] Shoup, 173.
[74] Ibid., 173.
[75] David Rockefeller. *Memoirs* (New York: Random House, 2002), 92.

director. Caspar W. Weinberger, like Shultz an executive with engineering giant Bechtel Corporation of San Francisco, became a CFR member while serving as Reagan's secretary of defense. Both secretaries of the Treasury, Donald T. Regan and James Baker, were Council members, as were UN Ambassador Jeane J. Kirkpatrick and CIA Director William J. (Bill) Casey.[76] Alan Greenspan was chosen for Federal Reserve chairman when he was a CFR director. Even John McCloy received an appointment to Reagan's foreign policy transition team.[77]

Certain aspects of the infamous Iran-Contra scandal can be attributed to a power struggle between the two oligarchic factions during the Reagan era. Exposure of Iran-Contra implicated much of the conservative faction in secret operations consisting of illegal arms sales to Iran with the profits financing the Contra insurgents in Nicaragua in violation of Congress' Boland Amendment. It also involved the release of US hostages by Iran-backed Hezbollah in Lebanon. Shultz and Weinberger opposed the operations, the latter's notes from a White House meeting stating, "I argued strongly that we have an embargo that makes arms sales to Iran illegal and President couldn't violate it [. . .] Shultz, Don Regan agreed."[78] Shultz's testimony at the Iran-Contra hearings related "the tale of how he, the nation's top diplomat [. . .] had been lied to, deceived, undercut, ignored and told what he described as cock-and-bull stories by some of his senior colleagues in the Reagan

---

[76] Shoup, 96.
[77] Bird, 655.
[78] Peter Kornbluh and Malcolm Byrne (eds.). *The Iran-Contra Scandal: The Declassified History* (New York: The New Press, 1993), 216.

Administration."[79] Due to his objections, Shultz was "criticized by right-wingers outside the Administration and a few inside it as insufficiently loyal to Mr. Reagan."[80]

Shortly thereafter, Bush won the presidential election and replaced Reagan in the White House. His presidency generally proved more appeasing to the liberal faction. Conservative influence remained to some extent, but the liberal power elite regained a greater degree of control in Washington. Bush's two secretaries of state, James Baker and Lawrence S. Eagleburger, were CFR members as was Secretary of the Treasury Nicholas F. Brady. His Secretary of Defense Richard B. (Dick) Cheney and National Security Advisor Brent Scowcroft had just served as directors at the Council. CIA Director Robert M. Gates belonged to the CFR and UN Ambassador Thomas R. Pickering would later become one of its directors.[81]

With the end of the Cold War, the processes of corporate-driven economic globalization moved to the forefront of the policy agenda. The Bush administration's negotiation of NAFTA, in particular, was pivotal in implementing the multilateral free-trade plans of liberal oligarchs. As Bush's trade representative, current CFR co-chair Carla Hills led negotiations for the pact with Canada and Mexico on behalf of the US government. NAFTA was then signed into law by President Clinton. From its inception, NAFTA was heavily criticized from both the left and right of the political spectrum. From the left, Shoup refers to NAFTA

---

[79] R. W. Apple Jr., "Iran-Contra Hearings; Of History and Honor: Shultz's Story," *The New York Times* 24 July 1987: http://www.nytimes.com/1987/07/24/world/iran-contra-hearings-of-history-and-honor-shultz-s-story.html
[80] Ibid.
[81] Shoup, 96-97.

as "a kind of socialism for the corporations and global competition for labor," and as "a key step in the global 'race to the bottom'" because "the neoliberal world order creates 'free market' competitive relationships between companies and countries resulting in cuts in wages, benefits, and conditions for workers in order to attract investment into a corporation or nation."[82] From the right, President Trump's demands for renegotiation of NAFTA reflected nationalist-oriented grievances with the existing agreement, namely its impact on the US economy.

David Rockefeller had long sought economic integration in the Western Hemisphere and was instrumental in the development and passage of NAFTA. He founded the Council of the Americas (COA) in 1965 as a corporate-interest group to "stimulate and support economic integration."[83] The COA membership "consists of leading international companies representing a broad spectrum of sectors."[84] The organization "played a key role in the passage of [NAFTA]."[85] Its main liaison in the Clinton administration was CFR member Thomas F. McLarty, chief of staff of the White House, who would later join Kissinger's consulting business to create a partner firm to Kissinger Associates. Rockefeller also sponsored NAFTA conferences and organized trips to Mexico for government and corporate officials in addition to hosting Mexican president Carlos Salinas at his family estate. Writing in the *Wall Street Journal* in October 1993 ahead of the congressional vote on NAFTA, Rockefeller asserted, "I truly

---

[82] Ibid., 176.
[83] Will Banyan, "The 'Proud Internationalist': The Globalist Vision of David Rockefeller" (March 2006), 29.
[84] COA. "About AS/COA": http://www.as-coa.org/about/about-ascoa
[85] Banyan, 29

don't think 'criminal' would be too strong a word to describe rejecting NAFTA."[86] This article was one more Rockefeller contribution to the success of the pro-NAFTA campaign.

For his NAFTA endeavors, Rockefeller was recognized at the highest level of government in both the United States and Mexico. He was awarded the Mexican Order of the Aztec Eagle in 1997, the highest honor Mexico bestows upon foreign citizens.[87] At a COA-sponsored conference in 1992, then President Bush acknowledged Rockefeller's role: "thank you for your really vital work in rallying the private sector and congressional support for the North American free trade agreement [. . .] David's personal involvement has been a major factor in the success we've enjoyed so far."[88] At a similar conference in 2000, President Clinton declared, "David Rockefeller, I want to thank you for taking the lead 35 years ago now in establishing the Council of the Americas. And I want to thank the Council for its support of our efforts, beginning with NAFTA [. . .] Let me say to all of you, especially to you, David [. . .] you had the vision to see the North and South in this increasingly small globe of ours could come together."[89] By 1994, Rockefeller, Honorary Chairman of both the CFR and COA at the time, had decisively led the

---

[86] Ibid., 33.
[87] Ibid., 35.
[88] George Bush, "Remarks to the Forum of the Americas" (23 April 1992):
https://www.presidency.ucsb.edu/documents/remarks-the-forum-the-americas
[89] Bill Clinton, "Remarks by President Bill Clinton at the 2000 Washington Conference on the Americas" (3 May 2000):
http://www.as-coa.org/articles/remarks-president-bill-clinton-2000-washington-conference-americas

liberal faction of the oligarchy in securing the implementation of its regional free-trade agenda.

Along with its endorsement of NAFTA, the Clinton administration designed economic policies to deepen domestic neoliberalism and accelerate economic globalization on behalf of the liberal faction. Current CFR co-chair Robert Rubin and CFR member Lawrence H. Summers, successive Treasury secretaries for Clinton, were the architects of the deregulatory Financial Services Modernization Act of 1999, which permitted the consolidation of commercial banks, investment banks, and insurance companies. It repealed part of the Glass–Steagall Act of 1933, adopted during the Great Depression to prevent a repeat of the financial crash of 1929. As a result of the 1999 legislation, financial speculation surged until the 2008 financial crisis. Internationally, the establishment of the World Trade Organization (WTO) in 1995 offered new opportunities for global financial liberalization. Timothy Geithner, later Treasury secretary in the Obama administration and currently a director at the CFR, negotiated a financial services agreement at the WTO in 1997 as a representative of the administration.[90]

President Clinton himself was one of the many CFR members in his administration. Warren Christopher was Council vice chairman before being appointed secretary of state. His successor, Madeleine K. Albright, would later serve a long term as a director and is currently the CFR's Director Emerita. Clinton's national security advisors, W. Anthony Lake and Samuel R. Berger, were both members. All three secretaries of defense, Les Aspin, William J. Perry, and William S. Cohen, were also CFR members, with

---

[90] Shoup, 177.

Aspin later becoming a director while Cohen was a director prior to his government appointment. Likewise, all three of Clinton's UN ambassadors, Albright, William B. Richardson, and Richard C. Holbrooke, were members, Holbrooke eventually serving a total of three non-consecutive terms as a director. Clinton's three CIA directors, R. James Woolsey, John M. Deutch, and George J. Tenet, were all members, and Deutch later became a director. Finally, James D. Wolfensohn, who Clinton appointed president of the World Bank, was yet another member of the Council.[91]

George W. Bush's administration during the turbulent first decade of the new century also had solid connections to the CFR. Vice President Dick Cheney, as mentioned above, had previously been a Council director. Both secretaries of state, Colin L. Powell and Condoleezza Rice, were members. Rice was a CFR international fellow in the 1980s and Powell would later become a director for a decade. Stephen J. Hadley, Bush's national security advisor, is currently a director. Secretary of the Treasury Henry M. Paulson was a member as was Secretary of Defense Robert Gates. Bush's first secretary of defense, Donald H. Rumsfeld, who was also Ford's secretary of defense, had been a Council member in the 1970s. Tenet continued as CIA director until 2004 and then was followed by Porter J. Goss and Michael V. Hayden, both also CFR members. Three of Bush's UN ambassadors, John D. Negroponte, John R. Bolton, and Zalmay M. Khalilzad, were members. His selections for World Bank president, Paul D. Wolfowitz

---

[91] Ibid., 97.
CFR. *AR 2016*, 2, 37-38.

and Robert B. Zoellick, were Council members and the latter was earlier a director.[92]

The CFR was in fact pivotal in the planning and decisions surrounding the controversial war executed by the Bush administration in Iraq. The think tank held thirty-nine private meetings on Iraq and the Middle East during the buildup to the war in 2002-2003. Assuming a leading role in these sessions were Rumsfeld, Wolfowitz, Deutch, and Senator Joseph I. Lieberman, also a CFR member. A few years into the war, in 2006, Congress and the White House established a bipartisan Iraq Study Group (ISG) to review US policies in Iraq and propose recommendations. As is common with US government task forces and ad hoc committees, most of the members of the ISG were also CFR members.[93] Many of the neoconservatives from the Project for the New American Century (PNAC), a think tank which lobbied intensively for the war, were members of the CFR as well. Of PNAC's twenty-five founding signatories, sixteen were Council members, including Cheney, Wolfowitz, and Khalilzad.[94] This clearly demonstrates a neoconservative association with the liberal faction, albeit an often conflicted one due to the neoconservative promotion of US unilateralism in foreign affairs clashing with the multilateralism favored by the liberal power elite.

Most CFR-connected powerbrokers, neoconservative or not, supported the war in Iraq. James M. Lindsay, a vice president and Director of Studies at the Council, seemed to summarize the CFR's overall views in a 2005 interview: "It

---

[92] Ibid., 98.
Ibid., 37-38.
[93] Shoup, 227.
[94] Ibid., 204.

was always hard to sustain the argument that if the United States withdrew from Vietnam there would be immense geopolitical consequences. As we look at Iraq, it's a very different issue. It's a country in one of the volatile parts of the world, which has a very precious resource that modern economies rely on, namely oil."[95] Lindsay co-authored a book covering the decision making on the war, *America Unbound: The Bush Revolution in Foreign Policy*, which revealed, without naming the CFR, that the vast majority of the individuals responsible for the decision to invade Iraq in 2003 were CFR members and several had been directors or fellows of the Council.[96] Fewer than half of these policymakers were neoconservatives, disproving the notion that the Iraq war can be attributed solely, or even mainly, to the neocons.[97]

The CFR's interlocking relationship with the US government was uninterrupted following Obama's defeat of CFR member John S. McCain in the 2008 presidential election. The new administration reflected a continuation of oligarchic control despite Obama's campaign emphasis on change. His first Treasury secretary, Geithner, currently sits on the CFR's board of directors. Like several other senior government officials, Geithner had previously worked at Kissinger Associates. His successor, Jacob J. Lew, was a CFR member as well. Robert Gates was initially retained as defense secretary and Charles T. (Chuck) Hagel and Ash Carter, two of Obama's later defense secretaries, were also members, as was CIA Director David H. Petraeus. Thomas E. Donilon, and Susan E. Rice, Obama's

---

95 Ibid., 201.
96 Ivo H. Daalder and James M. Lindsay. *America Unbound: The Bush Revolution in Foreign Policy* (Hoboken, NJ: John Wiley and Sons, Inc., 2005).
97 Shoup, 214.

national security advisors, have been very involved with the Council beyond their membership, with Donilon currently a distinguished fellow and Rice serving on a number of Council advisory committees in the past. She was also Obama's first UN ambassador. Former Federal Reserve Chair Janet L. Yellen, appointed by Obama, is a member, and Secretary of State John F. Kerry became a Council member in the early 1990s.[98]

Kerry's predecessor, Hillary Rodham Clinton, is not a CFR member but her husband, Bill, and daughter, Chelsea, are both members.[99] Nevertheless, Hillary Clinton's own association with the Council is significant. In a 2009 address at the CFR's Washington office, she revealingly remarked, "I am delighted to be here in these new headquarters. I have been often to, I guess, the mothership in New York City, but it's good to have an outpost of the Council right here down the street from the State Department. We get a lot of advice from the Council, so this will mean I won't have as far to go to be told what we should be doing and how we should think about the future."[100] Clinton also delivered her farewell speech as secretary of state to an audience at the CFR in Washington.[101]

In every administration one can find CFR members in cabinet positions not mentioned thus far. In the Obama

---

[98] Ibid., 98-99.
[99] CFR. *AR 2016*, 47.
[100] Freethinker2012. "Hillary Clinton admits the CFR gives the Orders" [Video] (22 July 2009): https://www.youtube.com/watch?time_continue=28&v=Ba9wxl 1Dmas
[101] Josh Rogin, "Clinton says farewell at CFR," *Foreign Policy* 31 January 2013: http://foreignpolicy.com/2013/01/31/clinton-says-farewell-at-cfr

administration, the secretaries of homeland security, energy, commerce, and health and human services were all Council members. John E. Bryson, commerce secretary, and Sylvia Mathews Burwell, secretary of health and human services, were both directors prior to their government appointments. Penny S. Pritzker, the administration's second secretary of commerce, was a director when Obama selected her.[102] On the other hand, Obama's first secretary of homeland security, Janet Napolitano, joined the CFR's board of directors after her time in government.[103] She was succeeded at the Department of Homeland Security by Council member Jeh C. Johnson.[104] These appointments of CFR members and directors to head government departments primarily responsible for domestic issues indicate the traditional power and influence of the Council in nearly all areas of policymaking. Clearly, it is not merely a foreign policy think tank.

However, in stark contrast to every president since Eisenhower, including Nixon and Reagan, President Trump has virtually no CFR representation in his administration as of 2017. Trump's secretaries of state, the Treasury, and defense, positions typically occupied by CFR members, are not Council members. In the cabinet, only Secretary of Transportation Elaine L. Chao is a CFR member, yet she is closely linked to the conservative power elite through The Heritage Foundation.[105] Perhaps Trump's apparent rejection of the CFR explains much of the persistent animosity the liberal power elite has expressed toward him. Whether the CFR's loss of power and

---

[102] Shoup, 99.
[103] CFR. *AR 2016*, 2.
[104] CFR. *AR 2016*, 54.
[105] Ibid., 47.

influence in government extends beyond the short term remains to be seen. Regardless, it certainly would be shortsighted to declare a shift in power in the US oligarchy. Administrations do not exceed eight years whereas the Council on Foreign Relations is deeply entrenched in the permanent US power structure.

The Brookings Institution

The origins of The Brookings Institution date to 1916, and it was established in 1927 in its present form as the first public-policy think tank at the national level in the United States. Based in Washington, Brookings states its mission is to "conduct in-depth research that leads to new ideas for solving problems facing society at the local, national and global level."[106] Brookings influences a range of domestic and foreign policies. Its research programs cover economics, the global economy, foreign policy, and national and local governance.[107] In one of its recent annual reports, it stated that it "strives for impact in at least three ways: designing policy recommendations, shaping critical debates and setting the longer-term policy agenda."[108] Unlike the CFR, Brookings is not a membership organization, but the two think tanks are closely associated through their leadership and political orientation. Author Sam Husseini captured this similarity with the CFR in the title of his article on the organization: "Brookings: The Establishment's Think Tank."[109]

---

[106] Brookings. "About Us": https://www.brookings.edu/about-us
[107] Brookings. "Research Programs, Centers, and Projects": https://www.brookings.edu/programs
[108] Brookings. *2011 Annual Report*, 1.
[109] Sam Husseini, "Brookings: The Establishment's Think Tank," *FAIR* 1 November 1998: http://fair.org/extra/brookings-the-establishments-think-tank

Brookings' leadership has extensive links with the CFR. Co-chairs Glenn H. Hutchins and Suzanne N. Johnson are both members.[110] Until 2018, the Brookings board of trustees was co-chaired by David Rubenstein and John L. Thornton.[111] Rubenstein is now the chairman of the CFR and Thornton a Council member. Rubenstein donated more than $2 million to Brookings from mid-2015 to mid-2016.[112] Nelson S. (Strobe) Talbott, deputy secretary of state in the Clinton administration, was Brookings' last president and served as a CFR director from 1988 to 1993.[113] Among the trustees and honorary trustees are many CFR members.[114] They include Kenneth Dam, Thomas Donilon, and Zoë E. Baird.[115] Dam was a CFR director for almost a decade prior to serving as deputy secretary of the Treasury from 2001 to 2003. Donilon is a CFR fellow and Baird was a Council director.[116] These leadership connections ensure ongoing contact between Brookings and the CFR.

Current CFR President Richard Haass has an important history with Brookings as well. He was a vice president and headed the think tank's foreign policy program in the 1990s prior to working at the Department of State as the director of policy planning. Haass has been president of the CFR since 2003.[117] In a speech at the Council in 2002, he commented on the working relationship between the two

---

[110] Brookings. "Board of Trustees":
https://www.brookings.edu/about-us/board-of-trustees
[111] Brookings. *2016 Annual Report (AR)*, 39.
[112] Ibid., 41.
[113] Ibid., 38.
[114] Shoup, 103.
[115] Brookings. *2016 AR*, 39.
[116] CFR. *AR 2016*, 37-38.
[117] Shoup, 48.

organizations and the primacy of the CFR: "The Council remains the blue chip think tank in the field. I can say this in all honesty because when I worked next door at a fellow--some might say rival--institution we often measured success by how many of our scholars appeared in the pages of *Foreign Affairs* or participated in Council study groups and task forces."[118]

In recent years, one of the strongest personal ties between the CFR and Brookings was John Whitehead. A prominent figure at Brookings, Whitehead held the title of chair emeritus at the time of his death in 2015.[119] He served as a trustee for more than twenty-five years and as chairman of the board in the 1990s.[120] For the period from mid-2015 to mid-2016, Whitehead posthumously donated more than $1 million to the think tank, a substantial sum for an individual benefactor.[121] He retired as co-chairman of Goldman Sachs after decades with the financial firm and then was appointed deputy secretary of state early in Reagan's second term. Whitehead was a CFR member for many decades and had a longtime association with fellow liberal oligarch David Rockefeller, particularly through their participation and leadership roles in various bodies. Whitehead became the founding chairman of the Lower Manhattan Development Corporation (LMDC), created in late 2001 to rebuild the World Trade Center site after 9/11.[122] Rockefeller was also involved with the LMDC, having previously served as the chairman of the Downtown-Lower Manhattan Association, during which

---

[118] Ibid., 103.
[119] Brookings. *2014 Annual Report*, 36.
[120] Brookings. *2015 Annual Report*, 32.
[121] Brookings. *2016 AR*, 41.
[122] LMDC. "About Us":
http://www.renewnyc.com/AboutUs/board.asp

time he was the "visionary and leading force behind the development of the original World Trade Center site."[123] In fact, the twin towers were nicknamed David and Nelson in honor of the Rockefeller brothers.[124]

Funding is crucial for any think tank, and as with the CFR, corporate money is critical to Brookings' operations and activities. Some corporate giants aid in the financing of both think tanks. For instance, JPMorgan Chase contributed more than $2 million to Brookings from July 2015 to June 2016. Other major corporate funders of Brookings during this period included Microsoft, Bank of America, and Google. In the $100,000 to $249,000 range, AIG, AT&T, Barrick Gold, BlackRock, Chevron, Citi, PepsiCo, Shell, and Toyota were all donors. Amounts under $100,000 were received from BP, ExxonMobil, and Goldman Sachs, among others.[125] Brookings had an annual budget of over $100 million in fiscal year 2016.[126] Similar to the CFR, on its website Brookings informs potential corporate contributors of donation benefits: "Brookings provides a number of ways for donors to get involved in the intellectual life of the Institution. These include exclusive invitations to private events and conference calls on pressing policy topics, private issue briefings from scholars, complimentary publications, and reserved seating at public events. Donors also can choose to receive periodic

---

[123] LMDC. "The Plan for Lower Manhattan":
http://www.renewnyc.com/memorial/competition.asp
[124] David W. Dunlap, "What David Rockefeller Wanted Built Got Built," *The New York Times* 26 March 2017:
https://www.nytimes.com/2017/03/26/nyregion/david-rockefeller-development-nyc.html
[125] Brookings. *2016 AR*, 41-42.
[126] Ibid., 44.

communications from the Institution that highlight recent research and impact."[127]

Funding the major think tanks is one of the means employed by corporations to influence public policymaking in Washington. As reported in *The New York Times*, "Thousands of pages of internal memos and confidential correspondence between Brookings and other donors [. . .] show that financial support often came with assurances from Brookings that it would provide 'donation benefits,' including setting up events featuring corporate executives with government officials."[128] US Senator Elizabeth A. Warren is not alone in her assessment that "This is about giant corporations who figured out that by spending, hey, a few tens of millions of dollars, if they can influence outcomes here in Washington, they can make billions of dollars."[129] These corporate funding arrangements for influential think tanks like the CFR and Brookings perpetuate plutocracy in the United States as the wealthiest one percent of the population directly owned half of the value of corporate stock according to a recent study.[130]

---

[127] Brookings. "Donor Guidelines":
https://www.brookings.edu/donor-guidelines
[128] Eric Lipton and Brooke Williams, "How Think Tanks Amplify Corporate America's Influence," *The New York Times* 7 August 2016: https://www.nytimes.com/2016/08/08/us/politics/think-tanks-research-and-corporate-lobbying.html
[129] Ibid.
[130] Edward N. Wolff, "Household Wealth Trends in the United States, 1962-2013: What Happened Over the Great Recession" (Cambridge, MA: National Bureau of Economic Research, December 2014), 56.

Center for Strategic and International Studies

Another think tank with CFR connections is the Center for Strategic and International Studies (CSIS) in Washington. CSIS was founded in 1962 as a national security and foreign policy think tank at Georgetown University. It claims to be "dedicated to providing strategic insights and policy solutions to help decision makers chart a course toward a better world."[131] Its origins and initial funding derived from the conservative faction, as CSIS "set themselves up in competition with such august bodies as the Council on Foreign Relations and the Trilateral Commission."[132] By the 1980s, however, CSIS received a combination of "right-wing and traditional conservative [liberal] funds, getting its $8.7 million budget from both [right-wing plutocrat] Richard Scaife and from the Rockefeller, Ford and Carnegie foundations."[133]

CSIS has moved even closer to the CFR and liberal power elite in recent decades and it has broadened its programs beyond traditional security issues.[134] Chairman Emeritus Sam Nunn and Chairman Thomas J. Pritzker are both CFR members, as is John J. Hamre, the president and CEO of CSIS. On the current board of trustees are familiar names from the CFR and past presidential administrations. Henry Kissinger, Maurice Greenberg, Carla Hills, William Cohen,

---

[131] CSIS. "About Us": https://www.csis.org/about-us
[132] Jerry W. Sanders. *Peddlers of Crisis: The Committee on the Present Danger and the Politics of Containment* (Boston: South End Press, 1983), 221.
[133] Thomas Bodenheimer and Robert Gould. *Rollback!: Right-wing Power in U.S. Foreign Policy* (Boston: South End Press, 1989), 184.
[134] CSIS. "Programs": https://www.csis.org/top-programs

and Brent Scowcroft are all trustees.[135] David Rubenstein recently served on the board and Zbigniew Brzezinski was a trustee until his death in 2017.[136] Liberal faction hawks Kissinger and Brzezinski had established their association with CSIS immediately following their exit from government, opening the door at CSIS to the liberal faction.[137] Nonetheless, some elements of conservative influence still remain in the organization and Trump was willing to select a longtime CSIS trustee, Rex Tillerson, for his secretary of state. In a statement on Tillerson's confirmation by the US Senate, CSIS President Hamre referred to him as a "sophisticated internationalist," presumably in an attempt to distance Tillerson from Trump's right-wing appointments.[138]

CSIS' largest corporate donors are from the weapons manufacturing and oil sectors. These include Lockheed Martin, Boeing, General Dynamics, and Northrop Grumman from the former, and ExxonMobil, Chevron, and Saudi Aramco from the latter. Bank of America is the sole financial company among the top donors, although Citigroup also donated over $100,000 along with Coca-Cola, Bechtel, and Raytheon, another military contractor. Many other corporations from various sectors contributed

---

[135] CSIS. "Board of Trustees": https://www.csis.org/about-us/board-trustees
[136] CSIS. "2016 Annual Report": https://www.csis.org/features/annual-report-2016-overview
[137] James Allen Smith. *Strategic Calling: The Center for Strategic and International Studies 1962-1992* (Washington DC: Center for Strategic and International Studies, 1993), 33.
[138] CSIS. "Statement From CSIS President and CEO on Tillerson Confirmation as Secretary of State": https://www.csis.org/news/statement-csis-president-and-ceo-tillerson-confirmation-secretary-state

smaller amounts.[139] Striking but unsurprising is the prominence of "military-industrial complex" companies in CSIS funding in comparison to the corporate contributors to the CFR and Brookings. These funding relationships reflect the national security focus of CSIS. Some of the same companies formed an integral component of the conservative faction in its early decades. Although transnational corporations primarily oriented toward the civilian economy have also benefited from Pentagon spending as military contractors, the liberal faction has been more reluctant to support substantial increases in military expenditure.[140] Both factions, however, agree on maintaining the largest military budget in the world without peer.[141]

Other Think Tanks

There are a number of other think tanks with ties to the CFR. The Aspen Institute and the Peterson Institute for International Economics (PIIE) "have extensive links with and are closely connected to the CFR, part of its inner circle."[142] Aspen has fifteen locations worldwide including Aspen, Colorado, but it is now headquartered in Washington. It describes itself as an "educational and policy studies organization" with a mission "to foster leadership based on enduring values and to provide a

---

[139] CSIS. "Corporation and Trade Association Donors":
https://www.csis.org/support-csis/our-donors/corporation-and-trade-association-donors
[140] Bodenheimer and Gould, 171-172.
[141] World Atlas. "Military Spending By Country":
https://www.worldatlas.com/articles/countries-with-the-biggest-military-expenditure.html
[142] Shoup, 102.

nonpartisan venue for dealing with critical issues."[143] CFR member Walter S. Isaacson is the president and CEO. Condoleezza Rice is one of many CFR members sitting on its board of trustees.[144]

PIIE, as its name suggests, concerns itself with international economic policy and it too is based in Washington. President Adam S. Posen is a CFR member. Michael A. Peterson is the chairman of the board of directors of the think tank named for his late father, former CFR chairman Peter Peterson. Other current directors include Maurice Greenberg, Lawrence Summers, and Robert Zoellick, as well as Richard E. Salomon, a longtime CFR director. Lynn Forester de Rothschild, a CFR member who married into the oligarchic Rothschild family of Western Europe, is also a PIIE director. Carla Hills, Alan Greenspan, and George Shultz are all honorary directors, and David Rockefeller had served as a director.[145] The Washington-based Atlantic Council and Carnegie Endowment for International Peace (CEIP), and New York-based Human Rights Watch (HRW) are three other organizations with strong CFR connections in their leadership ranks.[146]

FOUNDATIONS

In this section, the most important grantmaking foundations of the liberal faction of the oligarchy will be

---

[143] Aspen. "What We Do": https://www.aspeninstitute.org/what-we-do

[144] Aspen. "Board of Trustees": https://www.aspeninstitute.org/team/board-of-trustees

[145] PIIE. "Board of Directors": https://piie.com/about/board-directors

[146] Shoup, 106-107.

discussed. These tax-exempt foundations have binding connections to the above think tanks through funding relationships and their leadership. The think tanks have long received the financial support of these foundations and prior to vast corporate funding relied heavily on their grants. As will be apparent, the think tanks and foundations are integrated into the same power network.

Ford Foundation

Headquartered in New York City since the 1950s, for most of the post-WWII period the Ford Foundation was widely regarded as the leading foundation in the United States and the world. It was established in 1936 by the pioneering automobile manufacturer Henry Ford and his son, Edsel, through an initial donation of $25,000, but it was not until after the deaths of its founders in the 1940s that the Ford Foundation assumed the major grantmaking role it has continued to the present. Edsel's son, Henry Ford II, as the foundation's president, together with the board of trustees adopted the recommendations of the Gaither Study Committee in 1949 to transform the foundation into "an international philanthropy dedicated to the advancement of human welfare."[147] Ironically, Henry Ford II would later repudiate the Ford Foundation: "I think the Foundation's been a fiasco from my point of view from day one. And it got out of control and it got in the control of a lot of

---

[147] Ford Foundation. "About Us: Our origins": http://www.fordfoundation.org/about-us/our-origins

liberals."[148] His perspective represents the common right-wing objection to the liberal faction's foundations.[149]

Shortly after the Ford Foundation's relocation from Michigan to New York, John McCloy took up the position of chairman in 1958 while simultaneously chairing the CFR and Chase Manhattan. Beginning in the early 1960s, he became embroiled in conflict with foundation president Henry T. Heald over leadership of the organization. McCloy eventually demanded a direct relationship between the trustees and program directors.[150] In a fundamental area of discord, the two disagreed over the type of grant recipients they each favored. McCloy believed Heald "was a little too prone to confine the benefactions of the Ford Foundation to conventional university academic areas." McCloy "never hesitated to push his own agenda, urging funding for such projects as [. . .] the Council on Foreign Relations, and various 'Atlanticist' projects such as conference grants for things like the Bilderberg Group gatherings." Furthermore, he regularly met with the White House National Security Council (NSC) to inquire about any projects the NSC would like funded. In the words of one foundation officer, "McCloy chose to be the first among equals and regarded all the other [board] members around as potentates and he was simply the first baron among barons."[151]

---

[148] Larissa MacFarquhar, "What Money Can Buy," *The New Yorker* 4 January 2016: https://www.newyorker.com/magazine/2016/01/04/what-money-can-buy-profiles-larissa-macfarquhar
[149] Mark Dowie. *American Foundations: An Investigative History* (Cambridge, MA: The MIT Press, 2001), 12.
[150] Bird, 519-520.
[151] Ibid., 519.

While serving on the board of trustees prior to becoming chairman, McCloy forged a working relationship between the Ford Foundation and the CIA. In general, the relationship was "close, enduring, and smooth."[152] Allen Dulles and other CIA officials "repeatedly approached the Foundation to fund Agency projects and provide access to Foundation officials or fellows abroad for use in intelligence-gathering."[153] McCloy later said that Dulles was "always coming to me to ask me to get the Ford Foundation to help behind the Iron Curtain."[154] Within a short time the agency and foundation struck an agreement according to which McCloy and the current president and chairman of the foundation would review the CIA's proposed projects, and if this three-man committee approved of these projects, it would then present them to the board of trustees without acknowledging their CIA origins. A number of CIA projects were approved under this arrangement, and foundation fellows based overseas were recruited by the agency although Dulles promised to only contact them after their foundation grants had expired.[155] McCloy's ties to the CIA and push for control at the Ford Foundation were facets of what one foundation officer described as "his role of running around the world and being the God. He watched everything from that point of view."[156]

---

[152] Inderjeet Parmar. *Foundations of the American Century: The Ford, Carnegie, and Rockefeller Foundations in the Rise of American Power* (New York: Columbia University Press, 2012), 119.
[153] Bird, 426.
[154] Ibid., 427.
[155] Ibid., 427-429.
[156] Ibid., 520.

Since McCloy forced Heald out of the foundation presidency and replaced him with his CFR colleague McGeorge Bundy, every president of the Ford Foundation has been linked to the CFR.[157] Former presidents Franklin A. Thomas (1979-1996), Susan V. Berresford (1996-2007), and Luis A. Ubiñas (2008-2013) are all CFR members.[158] With Bundy (1966-1979) at the helm, the foundation supported civil and women's rights, launched microfinance, and funded the creation of the Public Broadcasting Service (PBS). Franklin oversaw projects on urban poverty, anti-apartheid activism, and new programs in Russia and China. Berresford presided over work on HIV/AIDS, higher education in Africa, and the arts. Under Ubiñas' tenure, the foundation implemented projects on climate change, "market-based approaches" to combating poverty, and global democracy promotion. Darren Walker, the current president and also a CFR member, previously worked as an investment banker and was a vice president at The Rockefeller Foundation.[159]

The Ford Foundation has an endowment of $12 billion, and its grantmaking is global in scope. In 2016, US grantees received more than $392 million and the total for grantees from the rest of the world was just over $143 million.[160] Among the more than twelve hundred grantees of the foundation, the CFR, Brookings, and Aspen think tanks were recipients of $100,000, $900,000, and $4.5 million, respectively. Human Rights Watch was given two grants totaling $1.4 million. The Clinton Foundation,

---

[157] Ibid., 520.
[158] CFR. *AR 2016*, 45-66.
[159] Ford Foundation. "About Us: Our origins."
[160] Ford Foundation. "Grants Database":
https://www.fordfoundation.org/work/our-grants/grants-database/grants-all

established by Bill Clinton, also received a grant in the amount of $500,000. Some issue areas covered by grants are "Natural Resources and Climate Change," "Future of Work(ers)," and "Gender, Racial and Ethnic Justice."[161] The Movement for Black Lives, which includes Black Lives Matter, obtained a multi-year commitment of $100 million.[162] As is the case for other foundations of the liberal faction, the program and issue areas of the Ford Foundation feature many socially progressive initiatives but, as to be expected, they avoid challenging the fundamental wealth and power interests of the oligarchy.

The Rockefeller Foundation

Closely associated with the Ford Foundation, The Rockefeller Foundation is an even older grantmaking institution. Founded in New York City in 1913 by Standard Oil magnate John D. Rockefeller, his son, John D. Rockefeller Jr., and business advisor Frederick T. Gates, the foundation concentrated its funding on the education and medical fields in its first decades of existence. This money was used for medical training in the United States and foreign countries on virtually every continent.[163] Subsidizing of scientific research included funding for eugenics studies in Nazi Germany. The Kaiser Wilhelm Institute of Anthropology, Human Heredity, and Eugenics in Berlin was financially supported by The Rockefeller Foundation until 1939, even after the foundation was

---

161 Ibid.
162 Brook Kelly-Green and Luna Yasui, "Why black lives matter to philanthropy," *Ford Foundation* 19 July 2016: https://www.fordfoundation.org/ideas/equals-change-blog/posts/why-black-lives-matter-to-philanthropy
163 The Rockefeller Foundation. "About Us: Our History": https://www.rockefellerfoundation.org/about-us/our-history

aware that the institute's research was being used to justify Nazi racial laws.[164] However, the foundation did assist in relocating scientists and scholars escaping the Third Reich. After World War II, The Rockefeller Foundation expanded or inaugurated programs in medicine, public health, psychiatry, science, education, agriculture, arts, and culture.[165]

Leading members of the post-WWII liberal power elite have served on The Rockefeller Foundation's board of trustees. Besides McCloy, other trustees have been John Dulles, Douglas Dillon, Robert Lovett, Dean Rusk, Paul Volcker, James Wolfensohn, and Winthrop W. Aldrich, chairman of Chase National before McCloy. Dulles was the foundation's chair for two years and was then succeeded by John D. Rockefeller III in the same year Rusk became the president.[166] One of David Rockefeller's daughters, Peggy Dulany, was a trustee from 1989 to 1994, and one of his sons, David Rockefeller Jr., served as chair of the board from 2010 until 2016, continuing the Rockefeller family leadership of the foundation into another generation. They are both CFR members as well and Dulany was a director at the Council for eight years.[167] The foundation currently is governed by a thirteen-person board of trustees including several foreign citizens who are thus ineligible for CFR

---

[164] Gretchen E. Schafft. *From Racism to Genocide: Anthropology in the Third Reich* (Chicago: University of Illinois Press, 2004), 47-56, 251.
[165] The Rockefeller Foundation. "About Us: Our History."
[166] Ibid.
[167] CFR. *AR 2016*, 38-61.

membership.[168] Chair Richard D. Parsons and President Rajiv J. Shah are both CFR members.[169]

With respect to its grantmaking, The Rockefeller Foundation claims "to promote the well-being of humanity throughout the world" through partnerships between the private, public, and nonprofit sectors. Like the Ford Foundation, The Rockefeller Foundation routinely provides grants to the CFR, Brookings, and Aspen. The CFR was allocated $270,000 for 2016-2017, Brookings was the recipient of a $1 million grant beginning in 2016, and Aspen received half a dozen grants totaling $1.9 million starting in 2015.[170] "Commitments" covered by the foundation's funding are "End Energy Poverty," "Achieve Health for All," "Nourish the World," "Expand Equity and Economic Opportunity," and "Seize Upon Emerging Frontiers."[171] Many of these topic areas overlap with the issues addressed by Ford Foundation grants.

The two foundations collaborated in sponsoring the so-called Green Revolution in Latin America and Asia. It consisted of the transfer of modern agricultural technology to the "Third World" in order to increase food production and eliminate hunger. Its origins date to the 1930s, but it was following World War II that the enormous fifty-year undertaking, which largely was the creation of The Rockefeller Foundation, gained momentum and eventually

---

[168] The Rockefeller Foundation. "About Us: Board of Trustees":
https://www.rockefellerfoundation.org/about-us/board-of-trustees
[169] CFR. "Membership: Membership Roster":
https://www.cfr.org/membership/roster
[170] The Rockefeller Foundation. "About Us: Our Grants":
https://www.rockefellerfoundation.org/grants
[171] The Rockefeller Foundation. "Our Commitments":
https://www.rockefellerfoundation.org/our-work

attracted the cooperation of the Ford Foundation. There was a geopolitical motive to the project, with the foundations believing that it would assure some social stability, "still regarded by Cold War strategists, politicians, and foundation trustees as the antidote to insurgency." An internal memorandum from the Ford Foundation from the 1950s is revealing in this regard: "If our aid to [undeveloped countries] is lacking or wasteful, the Communists will do the job on their own, to the irreparable loss of the West and the United States." According to historian Keith Griffin, "technical progress was regarded as an alternative to land reform," a politically-charged issue in the Global South.[172] More recently, The Rockefeller Foundation partnered with the Bill and Melinda Gates Foundation to form the Alliance for a Green Revolution in Africa (AGRA).[173]

Overall, the Green Revolution did achieve significant success in substantially expanding crop production, benefiting the urban population, but it had deleterious social and environmental impacts. Environmentally, a massive amount of topsoil was lost due to industrial agriculture and the chemicals used contaminated groundwater, also causing adverse health effects. The social harm was considerable as well. Smaller farmers usually could not compete with large landowners since they could not readily afford the new technologies and either accumulated unpayable debt or lost their livelihoods.[174] In the opinion of investigative journalist Mark Dowie, the Green Revolution "illuminates so many of philanthropy's best and worst aspects." It is a case study of

---

[172] Dowie, 112-114.
[173] AGRA. "Our Partners": https://agra.org/our-partners
[174] Dowie, 118.

a "long-term philanthropic effort to solve a complex, seemingly intractable problem without addressing the fundamental reasons for its existence."[175] The fundamental problem for liberal foundation leaders, as Dowie suggests, is that economic justice is required for improving conditions in the Global South but "economic justice [. . .] suggest[s] socialism" and therefore they cannot advocate for it.[176]

In 2010, The Rockefeller Foundation published a report entitled "Scenarios for the Future of Technology and International Development." One of the scenarios envisioned was "Lock Step," described as "A world of tighter top-down government control and more authoritarian leadership" arising from the response to a global pandemic. According to the scenario, one that is strikingly similar to the COVID-19 lockdown, "China's government was not the only one that took extreme measures to protect its citizens from risk and exposure. During the pandemic, national leaders around the world flexed their authority and imposed airtight rules and restrictions, from the mandatory wearing of face masks to body-temperature checks at the entries to communal spaces like train stations and supermarkets. Even after the pandemic faded, this more authoritarian control and oversight of citizens and their activities stuck and even intensified."[177]

---

[175] Ibid., 105.
[176] Ibid., 117.
[177] The Rockefeller Foundation. "Scenarios for the Future of Technology and International Development" (May 2010), 19: https://archive.org/details/pdfy-tNG7MjZUicS-wiJb

Open Society Foundations

According to the Open Society Foundations (OSF), billionaire financier George Soros launched the OSF in 1979 "to build a more open world."[178] The New York-based foundation funds human rights and civil society groups worldwide for "change in the way we think about others, and in the ways we work together."[179] OSF works on every continent in the areas of "equality and antidiscrimination," human rights movements and institutions," "justice reform and the rule of law," "information and digital rights," among many others.[180] The vast majority of grantees are organizations that the OSF seeks out and approaches.[181] Human Rights Watch was the recipient of an unprecedented $100 million grant from OSF in 2010.[182]

OSF founder and chair of its main global board, Soros is one of the most prominent figures of the liberal power elite. A CFR member, Soros was a director of the Council from 1995 to 2004.[183] Born to a Jewish family in Hungary where he survived the Nazi occupation, Soros began his financial career in London and then moved to New York City in the 1950s. In 1969, he established Soros Fund

---

[178] OSF. "Who We Are: Our History":
https://www.opensocietyfoundations.org/who-we-are/our-history
[179] OSF. "What We Do":
https://www.opensocietyfoundations.org/what-we-do
[180] Ibid.
[181] OSF. "Grants, Scholarships, and Fellowships":
https://www.opensocietyfoundations.org/grants
[182] HRW. "George Soros to Give $100 million to Human Rights Watch," *HRW* 7 September 2010:
https://www.hrw.org/news/2010/09/07/george-soros-give-100-million-human-rights-watch
[183] CFR. *AR 2016*, 38.

Management, an investment management firm which became one of the most profitable hedge funds. The firm is one of the CFR's corporate members.[184] Soros is famous for making \$1.5 billion in a single month in 1992 by speculating against the British pound and other European currencies.[185] He is a despised by right-wing groups for OSF's contributions to many liberal causes on issues ranging from immigration to LGBT rights. *The Washington Times*, the chief newspaper of the conservative power elite, regularly publishes articles on OSF funding as well as anti-Soros commentary.[186] Soros also has financed political campaigns, donating more than \$10.5 million to Hillary Clinton's presidential run.[187] In a 1995 interview, he boasted of his access to the Clinton administration: "We actually work together as a team."[188]

---

[184] CFR. "Corporate Members":
https://www.cfr.org/membership/corporate-members
[185] Steve Schaefer, "Forbes Flashback: How George Soros Broke The British Pound And Why Hedge Funds Probably Can't Crack The Euro," *Forbes* 7 July 2015:
http://www.forbes.com/sites/steveschaefer/2015/07/07/forbes-flashback-george-soros-british-pound-euro-ecb
[186] Kelly Riddell, "Beware the George Soros zombies," *The Washington Times* 14 July 2016:
http://www.washingtontimes.com/news/2016/jul/14/beware-the-george-soros-zombies
[187] Center for Responsive Politics. "Top Contributors, federal election data for Hillary Clinton, 2016 cycle":
https://www.opensecrets.org/pres16/contributors?id=N0000000
19
[188] Rowan Scarborough, "Hillary Clinton embraces George Soros' 'radical' vision of open-border world," *The Washington Times* 20 October 2016:
https://www.washingtontimes.com/news/2016/oct/20/hillary-clinton-embraces-george-soros-radical-visi

Lately, Soros' funding has included candidates in district attorney elections in California and other states.[189]

There are, of course, other grantmaking foundations associated with the liberal faction of the oligarchy besides the ones already discussed. Along with the Ford Foundation and The Rockefeller Foundation, the Carnegie Corporation of New York has been one of the "big three" throughout the twentieth century.[190] Established in 1911 by steel tycoon Andrew Carnegie "to promote the advancement and diffusion of knowledge and understanding," it is in fact the oldest of the three.[191] The foundation manages programs on education, democracy, higher education in Africa, and international peace and security.[192] The CFR, Brookings, CSIS, Aspen, and HRW are all annual grantees, with the CFR receiving $2.5 million in 2016 and the others obtaining substantial sums. The Atlantic Council is a yearly recipient as well and was allocated $600,000 in 2016.[193] The Corporation's current chair of the board of trustees, Thomas H. Kean, was appointed chairman of the National Commission on Terrorist Attacks Upon the United States (9/11

---

[189] Paige St. John and Abbie Vansickle," Here's why George Soros, liberal groups are spending big to help decide who's your next D.A.," *Los Angeles Times* 23 May 2018: http://www.latimes.com/local/california/la-me-prosecutor-campaign-20180523-story.html

[190] Robert Arnove and Nadine Pinede, "Revisiting the 'Big Three' Foundations," *Critical Sociology* May 2007 (Vol. 33: No. 3), 389.

[191] Carnegie Corporation. "About: Our History": https://www.carnegie.org/about/our-history

[192] Carnegie Corporation. "Our Approach": https://www.carnegie.org/programs

[193] Carnegie Corporation. "Grants: Grants Database": https://www.carnegie.org/grants/grants-database

Commission) by President Bush and he is also a CFR member.[194]

While taking into account their many worthwhile efforts, ultimately, as political scientist Rob Reich maintains, "foundations are, virtually by definition, the voice of plutocracy." For Reich, "The modern foundation is an institutional oddity in a democracy," owing to its lack of accountability to the general public. Its "considerable private assets give it considerable public power. And with growing wealth and income inequality, their apparent tension with democratic principles only intensifies."[195] From a leftist perspective, social scientist Robert F. Arnove offers his longstanding criticisms of the liberal faction's foundations: "They represent relatively unregulated and unaccountable concentrations of power and wealth which buy talent, promote causes, and, in effect, establish an agenda of what merits society's attention. They serve as 'cooling-out' agencies, delaying and preventing more radical, structural change."[196] In this capacity, they are an important component of the liberal power network.

MEDIA

Throughout the world major media plays a central role in shaping public discourse and the media in the United States is no exception to this universal reality. In fact,

---

[194] Carnegie Corporation. "Trustees and Staff":
https://www.carnegie.org/about/trustees-and-staff
CFR. *AR 2016*, 54.
[195] Rob Reich, "What Are Foundations For," *Boston Review* 1
March 2013: http://bostonreview.net/forum/foundations-
philanthropy-democracy
[196] Robert F. Arnove (ed.). *Philanthropy and Cultural
Imperialism: The Foundations at Home and Abroad* (Boston:
G.K. Hall, 1980), 1.

unlike other national media whose influence is geographically limited, US media enjoys tremendous global influence and establishes the general framework for coverage of international affairs. Within the United States, its vast resources and its ubiquitousness allow the mass media to effectively set the agenda for society while simultaneously adapting to new developments and reflecting social change. A multitude of studies have demonstrated the media's powerful role in political, economic, social, and cultural domains, and academic programs in media studies have proliferated in recent times. Edward S. Herman and A. Noam Chomsky explored the media's role in their seminal work, *Manufacturing Consent*, the book's title adopted from the "manufacture of consent," coined by famed journalist Walter Lippmann who was a CFR director in the 1930s.[197] Considering this immense influence, the major media linked to the liberal power elite serves as an indispensable part of the faction's oligarchic network.

In "Ruling Class Journalists," an exceedingly rare and remarkably candid article appearing in *The Washington Post* in 1993, former senior editor and columnist Richard Harwood addressed the media's extensive connections to the CFR. Harwood contended that Council members "are the nearest thing we have to a ruling establishment in the United States," and CFR-affiliated "journalists are part of that establishment whether they like it or not, sharing most of its values and world views." He elaborated: "The membership of these journalists in the council, however they may think of themselves, is an acknowledgment of

---

[197] Edward S. Herman and Noam Chomsky. *Manufacturing Consent: The Political Economy of the Mass Media* (New York: Pantheon Books, 1988).
CFR. *AR 2016*, 37.

their active and important role in public affairs and of their ascension into the American ruling class." Harwood enumerated the Clinton administration officials with membership in the CFR, and then named the media figures:

> In the past 15 years, council directors have included Hedley Donovan of Time Inc., Elizabeth Drew of the New Yorker, Philip Geyelin of The Washington Post, Karen Elliott House of the Wall Street Journal and Strobe Talbott of Time magazine, who is now President Clinton's ambassador at large in the Slavic world. The editorial page editor, deputy editorial page editor, executive editor, managing editor, foreign editor, national affairs editor, business and financial editor and various writers as well as Katharine Graham, the paper's principal owner, represent The Washington Post in the council's membership. The executive editor, managing editor and foreign editor of the New York Times are members, along with executives of such other large newspapers as the Wall Street Journal and Los Angeles Times, the weekly newsmagazines, network television executives and celebrities -- Dan Rather, Tom Brokaw and Jim Lehrer, for example -- and various columnists, among them Charles Krauthammer, William Buckley, George Will and Jim Hoagland.[198]

Although influential *Time* and *Life* publisher Henry R. Luce and other media owners were early CFR members,

---

[198] Richard Harwood, "Ruling Class Journalists," *The Washington Post* 30 October 1993, A21: https://tinyurl.com/ydh2haz2

journalists only began joining the CFR in earnest in the 1960s, then steadily increased in number thereafter. Leslie H. Gelb and James F. Hoge are two recent CFR leaders with a media background. Gelb, president emeritus of the CFR, was a reporter and columnist for *The New York Times* until the 1990s when he became the Council's president. Hoge, a CFR director in the 1980s and the editor of the Council's *Foreign Affairs* from 1992 to 2010, was editor-in-chief of *Chicago Sun-Times* and publisher of *New York Daily News*.[199] He also served as chair of HRW's board of directors after leaving *Foreign Affairs*.[200] Currently, many journalists and media executives are Council members. A few were already mentioned by Harwood but are still members today.

With their media affiliations provided in parentheses, the following individuals are CFR members: Tom Brokaw (NBC), Fareed Zakaria (CNN), Thomas L. Friedman (The New York Times), Charles Krauthammer (The Washington Post/Fox), Lesley R. Stahl (CBS), Barbara Walters (ABC), Bob L. Schieffer (CBS), Diane Sawyer (ABC), Brian D. Williams (NBC), Dan Rather (CBS), George R. Stephanopoulos (ABC), Katherine A. (Katie) Couric (ABC/CBS/NBC/CNN), Jacob P. (Jake) Tapper (CNN), Jim C. Lehrer (PBS), Charles P. (Charlie) Rose (CBS/PBS), Judy C. Woodruff (PBS/CNN/NBC), Andrea Mitchell (NBC), Mika E. Brzezinski (MSNBC), Joe Scarborough (MSNBC), David R. Gergen (CNN), Paula A. Zahn (CNN/ABC/CBS/Fox) Judith Miller (The New York Times/Fox), Margaret E. (Peggy) Noonan (Wall Street Journal/NBC), Jeffrey R. Toobin (CNN/The New Yorker),

---

[199] Ibid.
CFR. *AR 2016*, 39.
[200] HRW. "Board of Directors":
https://www.hrw.org/about/people/board-directors

Michael R. Bloomberg (Bloomberg), Mortimer B. Zuckerman (US News & World Report), Reena Ninan (CBS), and Margaret M. Brennan (CBS). Brokaw and Zakaria were both Council directors for a decade and Sawyer briefly served on the board. Jeffrey L. Bewkes, chairman and CEO of CNN parent company Time Warner, was a CFR director from 2002 to 2006.[201] This list is not exhaustive but includes many of the best-known media persons.[202]

Given the CFR-media interlocking relationship, the hostility between President Trump and a majority of the mass media should not be surprising. The war of words pitting Trump against CFR members Scarborough and Mika Brzezinski, daughter of Zbigniew Brzezinski, was a glaring illustration of this predictable animosity. As the list in the preceding paragraph demonstrates, most of the major media is integrated into the liberal power elite. Conservative Fox News Channel, on the other hand, is not well represented at the CFR. The few CFR members with past or present Fox News affiliations also appear in other media. Krauthammer, for example, is a commentator for Fox News but he has written a column for *The Washington Post* since the 1980s. None of Fox News' "big names" are CFR members, nor will one find columnists from *The Washington Times* at the CFR. Conservative faction media will be discussed in chapter 3.

---

[201] CFR. *AR 2016*, 38-67.
[202] Swiss Policy Research. "The CFR and the Media": https://cfrmedia.com

Alternative Media

Operating outside of, and in opposition to, the major or mainstream media, alternative media offers dissenting views and opinions not typically found in the mass media. Since it reaches a smaller audience than the mass media, alternative media has less influence in society. Yet a growing number of people rely on alternative media sources for their news and commentary. Alternative media to the left of the major media questions the motivations behind US foreign policy decisions and exposes the consequences of these decisions for affected populations, particularly the ramifications of US wars and other interventions in the Global South. In regard to economic matters, left alternative media features critical analysis and reporting on corporations and the economic system. Similar assessments are rarely seen in the mass media.

Much of the alternative media, especially web-based media, is self-funded or financed by donations from readers and viewers, but some of the larger alternative media on the left receives grants from the liberal faction's foundations. A journal article from 2007 explored the foundation funding of left media and questioned its impact on this media's purported independence. The results of author Bob Feldman's investigations indicated that funding from the Ford Foundation and other foundations helped to sustain several alternative media outlets in the 1990s and early 2000s.[203] More recently, the Ford Foundation grants database includes a $325,000 grant in 2016 to the Foundation for National Progress, publisher of

---

[203] Bob Feldman, "Report from the Field: Left Media and Left Think Tanks -- Foundation-Managed Protest?," *Critical Sociology* May 2007 (Vol. 33: No. 3), 431-438.

progressive *Mother Jones* magazine.[204] Another telling example is the Center for Media and Democracy (CMD). It describes itself as a "nationally-recognized watchdog that leads in-depth, award-winning investigations into the corruption that undermines our democracy, environment, and economic prosperity." An invaluable resource for information on the conservative faction's funding relationships, the CMD only documents the funding record of conservative power brokers and is subsidized by the leading foundations of the liberal power elite. The CMD's work has appeared in *The New York Times*, *The Washington Post*, CNN, MSNBC, NBC, CBS, PBS, and Bloomberg.[205]

One can reasonably speculate about the implications of such funding. Political scientist Joan Roelofs argues that "the dependence of the 'Left' press on elite subsidies can result in mellowing and avoiding topics embarrassing to the funders."[206] Feldman quotes another critic of foundation financing of alternative media: "The big establishment foundations are likely to seek out 'alternative' media that is more bark than bite, which they can rely on to ignore and dismiss sensitive topics [. . .] as 'irrational distractions' or 'conspiracy theory.'"[207] Why would the liberal foundations want to fund the left?," Feldman asks. Echoing the accusation of other critics of the liberal power elite's foundation funding, he answers, "Since their creation, an important goal has been to channel all protest and dissent into activities that do not threaten the

---

[204] Ford Foundation. "Our Grants: Grants Database."
[205] CMD. "About Us: What We Do": http://prwatch.org/cmd
[206] Joan Roelofs. *Foundations and Public Policy: The Mask of Pluralism* (Albany, NY: SUNY Press, 2003), 58.
[207] Feldman, 444.

wealth and power of the large corporations, or their access to the resources and markets of the world."[208]

The Nation, the country's oldest and most widely read progressive magazine, has been one of the alternative media recipients of foundation money. Reflecting on the positions taken by the magazine and its publisher Katrina vanden Heuvel, herself a CFR member, Shoup opines: "this, in turn, indicates one of the functions of this supposed 'flagship of the left' with its connections to the CFR, is to guide rank and file working people into support for the Democratic Party's 'left' wing which is, in reality, no left at all."[209] If these critics are correct, some of the most influential alternative media may actually be mitigating opposition to the liberal faction of the oligarchy and insulating it from potential threats to its power.

CONCLUSION

This chapter has examined the integrated network of the liberal power elite and evaluated its three main components. It has demonstrated that through domestic think tanks, foundations, and media, the liberal faction has been the hegemonic faction of the oligarchy in US politics and society since World War II. With the leadership and membership of the Council on Foreign Relations at the forefront, the liberal power elite has been synonymous with "the establishment." This power and influence extend overseas in alliance with its international network, which follows in the next chapter.

---

[208] Ibid., 429.
[209] Laurence Shoup. "WSTT Extras: Additional Media and the CFR": http://laurenceshoup.com/?page_id=134

CHAPTER 2
ASSOCIATES ABROAD: THE INTERNATIONAL NETWORK OF THE LIBERAL FACTION

Considering the internationalist or later globalist outlook of the liberal faction, the extension of its power network beyond the United States in the post-WWII era seems rather inevitable. The initial impetus for the building of this transnational network, however, originated in Western Europe in the 1950s. European oligarchs and political leaders were responsible for the creation of the Bilderberg Group, a secretive US-European policy discussion forum that organized private meetings for invitees from Europe and North America. By the early 1970s, Japan's economic development convinced David Rockefeller and other US oligarchs of the necessity of integrating leaders from a new region into the global power elite, thus forming the Trilateral Commission. Both the Bilderberg and Trilateral conferences have been held annually since their inception.

BILDERBERG GROUP

The creation of Bilderberg was a reflection of Atlanticist cooperation in the wake of World War II. Establishment of the North Atlantic Treaty Organization (NATO) and the US Marshall Plan for postwar reconstruction in Western Europe in the late 1940s were the products of this partnership. Bilderberg was a logical development in the evolution of the Atlantic relationship which, despite NATO and the Marshall Plan, was suffering from disharmony. In this case, Europeans assumed the organizational lead. Not only was the transatlantic relationship bolstered by Bilderberg, but the CFR-centered liberal power elite in the United States benefited from foreign support in consolidating its postwar domestic power and influence.

CFR members and leaders have dominated the US section of Bilderberg from the outset. A steering committee, and at times an advisory committee, have been responsible for selecting the invitees and setting the agenda for each meeting. Bilderberg has also recognized certain individuals with the title of honorary secretary-general. Over fifty US citizens have served in these leadership positions, and nearly all of them have been members of the CFR including fifteen Council directors.[210] Joseph E. Johnson, president of the Carnegie Endowment for International Peace and a CFR director from 1950 to 1974, and William Bundy were among the honorary secretaries general. David Rockefeller, Henry Kissinger, Richard Holbrooke, and Kenneth Dam, all mentioned in the previous chapter, as well as former CFR president Winston Lord, were members of the Bilderberg steering committee in the past as were individuals from the corporate sector. Rockefeller was also the sole person in the Member Advisory Group until his death. Henry J. Heinz II, John Whitehead, James Wolfensohn, Lawrence Summers, Paul Wolfowitz, George J. Mitchell, Nicholas Brady, and Thomas Donilon have been other prominent Council members on the steering committee at various times.[211] Robert Zoellick presently

---

[210] Shoup, 135.
[211] Bilderberg. "Background: Former Steering Committee Members": http://www.bilderbergmeetings.org/former-steering-committee-members.html

sits on the committee with Eric E. Schmidt, ex-CEO of Google, and six other Council members.[212]

Some of the European leaders of Bilderberg have been from families with noble ancestry while others have backgrounds in business and politics. Prince Bernhard of the Netherlands was the founder of Bilderberg. Edmond Adolphe de Rothschild of France represented the legendary banking family on the steering committee. Two brothers from the Italian Agnelli family, the owners of the automobile manufacturing giant FIAT founded by their grandfather, served on the committee. Giovanni (Gianni) Agnelli was FIAT's principal shareholder and became a close associate of Rockefeller and Kissinger through Bilderberg. He sat on Chase Manhattan's international advisory committee for three decades. Henri de Castries, former chairman and CEO of French insurance conglomerate AXA, is the current chairman of the committee. All seven chairmen to date have been Europeans.[213] Newspaper mogul Conrad M. Black and George W. Bush speechwriter David J. Frum have been two of the six steering committee members from Canada in Bilderberg history.[214] Participants in the yearly conferences from Western Europe and North America have similar backgrounds to the CFR membership. Notably, there has always been strong representation from the financial and corporate sectors and from governments of the past, present, and future.

---

[212] Bilderberg. "Background: Steering Committee":
http://www.bilderbergmeetings.org/steering-committee.html
[213] Bilderberg. "Background: Steering Committee."
[214] Bilderberg. "Background: Former Steering Committee Members."

The idea for Bilderberg was reportedly conceived by Polish political advisor Józef H. Retinger, although in his eulogy of David Rockefeller, Kissinger credits the latter with having "encouraged a discussion group, which later was developed into what is now known as the Bilderberg Group."[215] In an essay, Retinger wrote about a "growing distrust of America which was making itself manifest in Western Europe and which was paralleled by a similar distrust of Western Europe in America." He shared his idea with Prince Bernhard, ex-Belgian prime minister Paul G. van Zeeland, and Paul Rijkens, the Dutch chairman of Unilever. "To these meetings we would invite influential and reliable people [. . .] whose personal contact with men at the summit of political activity could help to smooth over these difficulties," Retinger stated. Discounting the involvement of the public, "it was of far greater consequence to us to have mutual understanding and goodwill among men occupying the highest positions in the life of each country."[216] He justified the secrecy by insisting "such conversations had to be conducted privately, unofficially, and confidentially" so that "participants are never afraid that anything they say will be used against them." Moreover, "everybody who attends our meetings does so in his private capacity [. . .] and thus he is not responsible to his supporters for anything he may say."[217]

Retinger traveled to the United States in 1952 to seek the participation of CFR members. CIA Director Walter Bedell Smith placed him in contact with Charles Douglas (CD)

---

[215] Henry A. Kissinger, "Henry Kissinger: My friend David Rockefeller, a man who served the world," *The Washington Post* 30 March 2017: https://tinyurl.com/y74hkhpl
[216] Józef H. Retinger, "The Bilderberg Group" (August 1956), 3-4: https://publicintelligence.net/bilderberg-group-retinger
[217] Ibid., 5.

Jackson, who would soon be appointed Eisenhower's special assistant for psychological warfare. Jackson then organized the US section of Bilderberg.[218] It is fair to describe it as "little more than an extension of the Council on Foreign Relations."[219] The first Bilderberg meeting finally occurred in 1954 in Oosterbeek, Netherlands at the Hotel De Bilderberg, hence the name of the group. Prince Bernhard was chairman and Retinger the secretary-general of the conference. Attendees numbered seventy-five in total. Rapporteurs for the meeting included CFR members David Rockefeller, George W. Ball, and Paul H. Nitze. Rockefeller was also already a Council director, having commenced his thirty-six-year board membership in 1949. The European contingent hailed from the Netherlands, Belgium, the United Kingdom, France, Italy, Germany, Norway, Sweden, and Denmark. Political and corporate leaders predominated as they have at every subsequent Bilderberg conclave.[220]

According to the confidential conference report and a press statement, the agenda for the meeting consisted of four subjects. They were listed in the following order: "A. The attitude towards communism and the Soviet Union. B. The attitude towards dependent areas and people overseas. C. The attitude towards economic policies and problems. D. The attitude towards European integration and the European Defense Community."[221] The results were

---

[218] Kai Bird. *The Chairman: John J. McCloy and the Making of the American Establishment* (New York: Simon and Schuster, 1992), 472.
[219] Ibid., 472.
[220] Public Intelligence. "Bilderberg Meetings 1954 Conference Report Oosterbeek, Netherlands," 3-5: https://publicintelligence.net/bilderberg-conference-1954
[221] Ibid., 10.

apparently more than satisfactory: "As a result of the discussion, it developed that the extent of agreement among the members was far greater than had been foreseen, and even where there was a divergence of attitude the reasons for differing views were fully and frankly discussed, and are now better understood."[222] The success of this meeting ensured its regular occurrence in Bilderberg's formative years.

Two meetings were convened in 1955 and another two in 1957 before organizers settled on an annual conclave beginning in 1958. Communism and economic issues were again discussed by the participants, and the agendas reflected continued interest in European integration and the future of NATO.[223] The United States hosted Bilderberg and Kissinger participated for the first time in February 1957, the onset of his lifelong association with Bilderberg. St. Simons Island in Georgia was the chosen location. Italy played host later in the year and then the United Kingdom in September 1958. John McCloy made his first appearance at the 1958 Bilderberg conference, having naturally been invited but unable to attend the previous gatherings.[224] Prince Bernhard remained chairman while Retinger and Johnson served as honorary secretaries for Europe and the United States, respectively. Attendance was still limited to seventy-five.[225] According to the conference report, "many participants expressed their

---

[222] Ibid., 10.
[223] Public Intelligence. "Bilderberg Primary Source Material Academic Archive": https://publicintelligence.net/bilderberg-archive
[224] Bird, 471.
[225] Public Intelligence. "Bilderberg Meetings 1958 Conference Report Buxton, United Kingdom," 3: https://publicintelligence.net/bilderberg-conference-1958

belief that the setting up of the European Economic Community and eventually of the Free Trade Area would considerably improve our position in our dealings with the underdeveloped countries [. . .] our competitive position as regards the Soviet bloc would improve and the underlying principles of European integration were likely to prove attractive to the uncommitted nations."[226]

Bilderberg meetings in the 1960s addressed the political and economic developments and issues of the time. In the early part of the decade, discussion topics included nuclear weapons, the United Nations, the European common market, East-West international trade, and the West's relations with developing countries. Canada hosted Bilderberg for the first time in 1961 and among the sixteen Canadian attendees was Lester B. Pearson. He would return to Bilderberg as the nation's prime minister in 1964 and was joined by future US president Gerald Ford who also participated in this conference in Williamsburg, Virginia.[227] Later in the decade, as the US war in Vietnam escalated, the "imminent threat of a collapse of the South-Vietnamese regime led to a shift of American priorities from the European to the Asian and Pacific theatre," in the words of one presenter at the 1968 conclave.[228] In regards to relations with the Soviet Union, "the prospects of détente did not appear very encouraging."[229] Outgoing Canadian Prime Minister Pearson was present at this meeting in Canada together with the new prime minister,

---

[226] Ibid., 29.
[227] Public Intelligence. "Bilderberg Primary Source Material Academic Archive."
[228] Public Intelligence. "Bilderberg Meetings 1968 Conference Report Mont Tremblant, Canada," 17: https://publicintelligence.net/bilderberg-conference-1968
[229] Ibid., 23.

Pierre E. Trudeau, who had only been in office for less than a week.[230]

Social changes resulting from the civil rights and antiwar movements in the United States and the West generally were an ongoing area of concern for the Bilderberg leadership. "Elements of instability in Western Society" and the "Future Function of the University in our Society" were the first items on the agendas for the 1969 and 1970 meetings, respectively. One of the working papers for the 1970 convention stated, "Young people's dissatisfaction with society has led to problems which are not merely complex but explosive. In these circumstances it was inevitable that the University, while trying to deal with its internal priorities, should find the new social concerns of its students almost impossible to resolve, the more so since the students were not content to have the University function as a neutral forum."[231] The subsequent meeting in 1971, held at a Vermont inn built by members of the Rockefeller family, deliberated "The Contribution of Business in Dealing with Current Problems of Social Instability." The US author of a working paper introduced the subject of social instability in the United States with reference to "problems relating to the Vietnam war, poverty, the plight of the blacks and other minorities, crime in the streets, drug abuse, college unrest, 'consumerism', the women's liberation movement, and

---

[230] Ibid., 7.
[231] Public Intelligence. "Bilderberg Meetings 1970 Conference Report Bad Ragaz, Switzerland," 15: https://publicintelligence.net/bilderberg-conference-1970

environmental pollution." The implication was that "business had to defend itself on several fronts at once."[232]

The 1970s witnessed important developments for Bilderberg. The group itself was not immune to some of these "elements of instability." Women, for instance, were finally invited to Bilderberg in 1972. Princess Beatrix of the Netherlands, daughter of Prince Bernhard and future Queen of the Netherlands, was one of a few women to attend. Queen Sofía of Spain has also attended in more recent years.[233] The 1972 gathering also saw the first appearance of Zbigniew Brzezinski at Bilderberg in the same year he became a CFR director.[234] Not unrelated, the concept for the Trilateral Commission was introduced at this conference. After the presentation of a working paper by an "American author," an unidentified "fellow American participant [. . .] recommended bringing together a group of some 30 to 50 'wise men' from the leading industrial nations of the non-Communist world: Europe, North America and Japan. These citizens would represent a broad spectrum of the private sector."[235] The Trilateral Commission will be explored in the second section of this chapter. European energy policy, the Arab-Israeli conflict, inflation, and prospects for the transatlantic community

---

[232] Public Intelligence. "Bilderberg Meetings 1971 Conference Report Woodstock, United States," 13: https://publicintelligence.net/bilderberg-conference-1971
[233] Public Intelligence. "2011 Bilderberg Meeting Participant List": https://publicintelligence.net/2011-bilderberg-meeting-participant-list
[234] Public Intelligence. "Bilderberg Meetings 1972 Conference Report Knokke-Heist, Belgium," 5-9: https://publicintelligence.net/bilderberg-conference-1972
[235] Ibid., 55-56.

and NATO were topics covered over the next few years at Bilderberg.[236]

In another development, the top leadership of Bilderberg changed in the latter half of the decade. The 1976 conclave was cancelled altogether due to a corruption scandal involving Prince Bernhard in which he accepted more than $1 million in bribery payments from Lockheed to secure Dutch contracts for the company. He was not criminally charged but his admission of guilt was revealed upon his death in 2004.[237] He resigned from his twenty-two-year chairmanship of Bilderberg and was replaced by Alec Home of the Hirsel, former prime minister of the United Kingdom. Lord Home presided over the 1977 meeting that debated "Third World" demands for a New International Economic Order (NIEO). A working paper prepared by a US participant contended that Western countries were the target "in part because the communist countries cannot so easily be held hostage to [Global South countries] in terms of needed materials or vulnerable foreign investment."[238] One attendee seemed to capture the general sentiment on North-South dialogue: "for the present we could hope at least to forestall a coalition of the Soviet Union, OPEC and the LDCs [less developed countries], and to work at separating the moderates of the Third World from the

---

[236] Public Intelligence. "Bilderberg Primary Source Material Academic Archive."

[237] Anthony Browne, "From beyond the grave, Prince finally admits taking $1m bribe," *The Times* 4 December 2004: https://www.thetimes.co.uk/article/from-beyond-the-grave-prince-finally-admits-taking-dollar1m-bribe-mp8kp7nbfsf

[238] Public Intelligence. "Bilderberg Meetings 1977 Conference Report Torquay, United Kingdom," 64: https://publicintelligence.net/bilderberg-conference-1977

radicals."[239] The 1978 and 1979 agendas included international trade and Western security.[240]

Throughout the 1980s Bilderberg devoted overwhelming attention to the Soviet Union and the Communist bloc in the final decade of the Cold War. The first item on the agenda for the 1983 convention was "East-West Relations: Containment, Detente or Confrontation." Awareness of the USSR's significant economic decline did not translate into widespread belief among the participants that the Communist bloc in Eastern Europe was on the verge of collapse. Rather, "it was unlikely that major systemic change would take place" and the West had to be prepared for confrontation.[241] The ascension of Mikhail S. Gorbachev to USSR leader was not expected to produce dramatic changes because of the entrenched Soviet bureaucracy.[242] The Reagan administration's missile defense system known as the Strategic Defense Initiative (SDI), or "Star Wars," was part of the discussion in 1985.[243] Attendees at the 1984 gathering, however, argued against viewing Central America and other conflict areas in purely East-West terms.[244] The 1986 and 1987 conclaves deliberated Gorbachev's leadership and Western strategy toward the

---

[239] Ibid., 76.
[240] Public Intelligence. "Bilderberg Primary Source Material Academic Archive."
[241] Public Intelligence. "Bilderberg Meetings 1983 Conference Report Château Montebello, Canada," 26: https://publicintelligence.net/bilderberg-conference-1983
[242] Public Intelligence. "Bilderberg Meetings 1985 Conference Report Rye Brook, United States," 42-44: https://publicintelligence.net/bilderberg-conference-1985
[243] Ibid., 47-51.
[244] Public Intelligence. "Bilderberg Meetings 1984 Conference Report Saltsjöbaden, Sweden," 74-78: https://publicintelligence.net/bilderberg-conference-1984

USSR. Charles, Prince of Wales participated in 1986.[245] During these years Paul Volcker, Walter Mondale, Jeane Kirkpatrick, Brent Scowcroft, and neoconservative guru Richard N. Perle all attended Bilderberg, and Volcker, Scowcroft, and Perle became regular participants.[246]

In the late 1980s and early 1990s, "glasnost" and other rapid developments maintained a focus on the USSR, but economic issues also received considerable treatment. Such agenda topics as "Domestic Developments in Eastern Europe" and "The New Soviet (Dis)Union" were combined with "What Can Be Done With the World Economy" and "Economic Relations With Eastern Europe."[247] The 1990 conference addressed the future of NATO in light of the fading of Cold War hostilities.[248] While one British attendee believed "NATO had to evolve into something different" other participants cautioned against the perception of Russian powerlessness, as "they had rapidly recovered from periods of weakness in the past."[249] Maurice Greenberg, George Soros, and Lesley Stahl were some of the familiar names participating in these conferences. The implications of the USSR's dissolution were revisited in 1991 at a meeting attended by then obscure Arkansas Governor Bill Clinton as well as *The*

---

[245] Public Intelligence. "Bilderberg Meetings 1986 Conference Report Gleneagles, United Kingdom," 8: https://publicintelligence.net/bilderberg-conference-1986
[246] Public Intelligence. "Bilderberg Primary Source Material Academic Archive."
[247] Ibid.
[248] Public Intelligence. "Bilderberg Meetings 1990 Conference Report Glen Cove, United States," 57-63: https://publicintelligence.net/bilderberg-conference-1990
[249] Ibid., 61.

Washington Post chair Katharine Graham and current CFR President Richard Haass.[250]

For the next few years economic concerns continued to feature alongside the prospects for Eastern Europe. 1993 attendees included Anthony C. (Tony) Blair, future UK prime minister, at the time the shadow home secretary.[251] "What Is NATO Supposed To Do," a 1995 Bilderberg panel moderated by Kissinger, was organized to determine "to what extent the participants agreed on enlargement of NATO, with the debate centering on the method of selecting new members, which countries should be selected and in what order and, finally, how quickly this should happen."[252] The panelists concluded "that the future of NATO will be solid and secure only with strong leadership in its member governments, particularly the United States."[253] Another session with Wolfensohn as a panelist debated "Our Agendas for the WTO and World Bank."[254] There was media representation from ABC's Peter Jennings and Thomas Friedman of *The New York Times*, while David Gergen, today a CNN analyst, participated in his second Bilderberg meeting after serving in the Clinton administration.[255]

---

[250] Public Intelligence. "Bilderberg Meetings 1991 Conference Report Baden-Baden, Germany," 7-13:
https://publicintelligence.net/bilderberg-conference-1991
[251] Public Intelligence. "Bilderberg Meetings 1993 Conference Report Vouliagmeni, Greece," 3:
https://publicintelligence.net/bilderberg-conference-1993
[252] Public Intelligence. "Bilderberg Meetings 1995 Conference Report Burgenstock, Switzerland," 13:
https://publicintelligence.net/bilderberg-conference-1995
[253] Ibid., 18.
[254] Ibid., 12.
[255] Ibid., 5-6

By the mid-1990s, the number of participants had climbed to 118 from twenty-two countries and Bilderberg was being presided over by its fifth chairman, Peter A.R. Carrington of the United Kingdom, the chairman of Christie's auction house and ex-secretary general of NATO.[256] The European Union, NATO's future, the Asian financial crisis, emerging markets, the Atlantic relationship, Kosovo, migration, US domestic politics, and global economic institutions were all discussion topics in the second half of the decade.[257] Media figures George Stephanopoulos and James Hoge attended in 1997 and 1998, respectively. High-ranking government officials both past and future, John Deutch and Colin Powell, were also among the attendees during those years in addition to steering committee members already named at the beginning of this section. Hoge, Deutch, and Powell have all been CFR directors as noted in chapter 1. As always, the corporate sector was also well represented.[258]

New individuals joined the perennial attendees at Bilderberg meetings early in the new century. Philip D. Zelikow, a Council member who was the executive director of the belated 9/11 Commission, attended Bilderberg as had the commission's chair, Thomas Kean, and its vice chair, Lee H. Hamilton. Kean was appointed to head the commission after Kissinger resigned the position rather than disclose the names of his firm's clients. In his resignation letter, Kissinger wrote: "To liquidate Kissinger

---

[256] Ibid., 2.
[257] Bilderberg. "Meetings":
http://www.bilderbergmeetings.org/conferences/1990.html
[258] Public Intelligence. "1997 Bilderberg Meeting Participant List": https://publicintelligence.net/1997-bilderberg-meeting-participant-list
Public Intelligence. "1998 Bilderberg Meeting Participant List": https://publicintelligence.net/1998-bilderberg-meeting-participant-list

Associates cannot be accomplished without significantly delaying the beginning of the joint commission's work."[259] Hamilton was a replacement for George Mitchell, who did not want to break ties with his law firm.[260] The commission's final publication, *The 9/11 Commission Report*, has been heavily criticized by a wide range of researchers and experts.[261]

Some of the Bilderberg attendees this century have already been noted as members of the steering committee. Others include the late Martin S. Feldstein, director emeritus of the CFR, who participated in multiple conventions.[262] Carla Hills, Alan Greenspan, Timothy Geithner, Fareed Zakaria, Charlie Rose, and current CFR fellow Max Boot made appearances, as did George Shultz and Condoleezza Rice in 2008.[263] John Thornton, the chair of Brookings since retiring as the president of Goldman Sachs in 2003, attended several conclaves. Billionaire financier Henry R. Kravis, a former CFR director, and wife Marie-Josée, also a Council member, became annual attendees, and the latter

---

[259] Cable News Network, "Kissinger resigns as head of 9/11 commission," *CNN* 13 December 2002: http://www.cnn.com/2002/ALLPOLITICS/12/13/kissinger.resigns

[260] Ibid.

[261] National Commission on Terrorist Attacks Upon the United States (9/11 Commission). *The 9/11 Commission Report*: https://www.9-11commission.gov/report

David Ray Griffin. *The 9/11 Commission Report: Omissions and Distortions* (Northampton, MA: Olive Branch Press, 2005). Architects and Engineers for 9/11 Truth: http://www.ae911truth.org

Patriots Question 9/11: http://patriotsquestion911.com

[262] CFR. *AR 2016*, 2.

[263] Public Intelligence. "Official List of Participants for the 2008 Bilderberg Meeting": https://publicintelligence.net/official-list-of-participants-for-the-2008-bilderberg-meeting

presently sits on the steering committee.[264] Angela D. Merkel participated mere months before assuming the chancellorship of Germany in 2005.[265] Obviously the "global war on terrorism" was a principal topic on the agenda during these years, but the rise of China, the Iraq war, climate change, and the global economic crisis were other subjects addressed during the decade.[266] Unfortunately, the unavailability of conference reports for this period does not allow for a complete picture.

Bilderberg remains a forum principally for the liberal power elite of the United States and its international allies. Recent Bilderberg gatherings have typically discussed a minimum of a dozen separate issues. Weapons of mass destruction, technology, the Middle East, Africa, the global economy, Russia and Ukraine, China, nationalism and populism, demographic changes, and cyber security are only some of the topics listed on the agendas since 2010.[267]

At the 2017 meeting in Chantilly, Virginia, the Trump administration was scrutinized alongside globalization, nuclear proliferation, and transatlantic relations.[268] David Petraeus was one of many CFR members present, including its incoming chairman David Rubenstein and outgoing co-chair Robert Rubin, the latter a regular

---

[264] CFR. *AR 2016*, 38, 55.
[265] Public Intelligence. "Bilderberg Participant Lists":
https://publicintelligence.net/category/documents/bilderberg/bilderberg-participant-lists
[266] Bilderberg. "Meetings":
http://www.bilderbergmeetings.org/conferences/2000.html
[267] Bilderberg. "Meetings":
http://www.bilderbergmeetings.org/conferences/2010.html
[268] Bilderberg. "65th Bilderberg Meeting":
https://www.bilderbergmeetings.org/meetings/meeting-2017/press-release-2017

attendee, as well as 94-year-old Kissinger.[269] Senator Lindsey Graham participated, as have other US senators in the past, namely Council members John Kerry, Christopher J. Dodd, Chuck Hagel, Thomas A. Daschle, John D. (Jay) Rockefeller IV, and Dianne G. Feinstein while still mayor of San Francisco.[270] Trump's commerce secretary, Wilbur Ross, a former Brookings trustee and financier, attended in 2017. He is one of the administration's few links to the liberal power elite, although Jared C. Kushner, Trump's son-in-law, participated in the 2019 meeting in Switzerland.[271] China, Russia, Brexit, and artificial intelligence (AI) featured on that agenda.[272]

The precise nature and function of Bilderberg has long been a contentious issue. The headline of an article in UK newspaper *The Independent* ahead of the 2016 conclave poses the question: "What actually happens at the world's most secretive gathering of global elites?"[273] Another UK newspaper, *The Telegraph*, refers to Bilderberg as "No

---

[269] Bilderberg. "Participants 2017":
https://www.bilderbergmeetings.org/meetings/meeting-2017/participants-2017
[270] Public Intelligence. "Bilderberg Participant Lists."
 CFR. *AR 2016*, 48-52. "Membership: Membership Roster":
https://www.cfr.org/membership/roster
[271] Bilderberg. "List of Participants 2019":
https://www.bilderbergmeetings.org/meetings/meeting-2019/participants-2019
[272] Bilderberg. "67th Bilderberg Meeting":
https://www.bilderbergmeetings.org/meetings/meeting-2019/press-release-2019
[273] Adam Lusher, "Bilderberg group meeting: What actually happens at the world's most secretive gathering of global elites, and who is attending?," *The Independent* 7 June 2016:
https://tinyurl.com/jg8epnq

conspiracy, just the most influential group in the world."[274] The title of a 2012 article from *The Washington Post* summarizes the debate thusly: "Is Bilderberg a conference on world affairs or a powerful global cabal? Depends on who you ask."[275] Several anti-Bilderberg protesters propounding various views are quoted in the short piece, representing different segments of the political spectrum. Right-wing opposition to Bilderberg has been based on an interpretation of the group as planning the implementation of "global socialism," an apparent contradiction given the dominant private sector representation at Bilderberg.[276]

Other observers offer a different analysis. In *Bilderberg People*, after reviewing their anonymous interviews of Bilderberg attendees, the three academic authors opine, "the suggestion that Bilderberg was, and is, helping to facilitate the development of a new world order, is considered, in an extremely qualified manner, the closest depiction of actual outcomes."[277] Denis W. Healy, a British member of the steering committee for thirty years, once stated, "We make a point of getting along younger politicians who are obviously rising, to bring them together with financiers and industrialists who offer them wise words. It increases the chance of having a sensible global

---

[274] Matthew Holehouse, "Bilderberg Group? No conspiracy, just the most influential group in the world," *The Telegraph* 6 June 2013: https://tinyurl.com/kaamkew

[275] Annie Gowen, "Is Bilderberg a conference on world affairs or a powerful global cabal? Depends on who you ask.," *The Washington Post* 1 June 2012: https://tinyurl.com/ybly68jd

[276] Shoup, 133.

[277] Ian N. Richardson, Andrew P. Kakabadse, and Nada K. Kakabadse. *Bilderberg People: Elite Power and Consensus in World Affairs* (London: Routledge, 2011), 30.

policy."[278] Whether or not Bilderberg has been primarily responsible for the direction of public policy in the West and the promotion of political careers, it has certainly been highly influential because of its intimate connection to the center of power in the United States through the liberal faction of the country's oligarchy.

TRILATERAL COMMISSION

Bilderberg also inspired the formation of the Trilateral Commission in the early 1970s. In certain key aspects, including the backgrounds of its membership, the Commission has represented a geographical extension of Bilderberg to Asia. Unlike Bilderberg but similar to the CFR, however, the Commission has organized study groups and has published reports since its inception. Annual conventions for the entire Trilateral membership are supplemented by yearly meetings in changing locations for each of the Commission's three regional groups, which are North America, Europe, and Asia Pacific. The North American Group is based in Washington, the European Group in Paris, and the Asia Pacific Group in Tokyo. The Commission characterizes itself as "a non-governmental, policy-oriented forum that brings together leaders in their individual capacity from the worlds of business, government, academia, press and media, as well as civil society." Furthermore, "The Commission offers a global platform for open dialogue, reaching out to those with different views and engaging with decision makers from around the world with the aim of finding solutions to the

---

[278] Adam Lusher, "Bilderberg: it's not a conspiracy of the global superelite. It's 'a summer school for the influential,'" *The Independent* 8 June 2016: www.independent.co.uk/news/world/bilderberg-group-meeting-global-elite-summer-school-a7071096.html

great geopolitical, economic and social challenges of our time."[279]

Trilateral leadership is geographically divided. Each of the three regions have a chairman, two deputy chairmen, and a director. Joseph S. Nye was the chairman of the North American Group for a decade. A political scientist and international relations specialist, Nye was a CFR director from 2004 to 2013.[280] He was replaced as chairman in 2018 by Meghan O'Sullivan, a current CFR director and also an international relations professor. NAFTA negotiator Herminio Blanco Mendoza is the Mexican deputy chairman. North American director Richard H. Fontaine is a CFR member. Paul Volcker was honorary North American chairman and David Rockefeller held that title as well as the title of founder at the time of their deaths.[281] The North American chairman prior to Nye was Thomas S. Foley, speaker of the US House of Representatives from 1989 to 1994 while also a CFR director during those years.[282] Jean-Claude Trichet, former president of the European Central Bank (ECB), is the chairman of the European Group. The last European chairman, Mario Monti, resigned the post to become the prime minister of Italy in 2011.[283] All chairmen of the Asia Pacific Group have been from Japanese power elite

---

[279] Trilateral. "About the Trilateral Commission":
http://trilateral.org/page/3/about-trilateral
[280] CFR. *AR 2016*, 38.
[281] Trilateral. "Leadership: North American Group":
http://trilateral.org/page/10/north-american-group
[282] CFR. *AR 2016*, 37.
[283] Trilateral. "Leadership: European Group":
http://trilateral.org/page/9/european-group

circles.[284] There is also a single executive committee comprised of more than fifty members.[285]

Membership in the Commission is by invitation only and now numbers 415 in total. The European Group has a limit of 170 members and they are from dozens of countries representing all regions of Europe, but there are no Russian members. The Asia Pacific Group, which expanded beyond Japan in 2000, has over 100 members from East Asia, Southeast Asia, India, Australia, and New Zealand.[286] In the words of the Commission, "Its members share a firm belief in the values of rule of law, democratic government, human rights, freedom of speech and free enterprise that underpin human progress. Members are also committed to supporting a rules-based international system, closer cooperation across borders and respect for the diversity of approaches to policy issues."[287]

The North American Group currently consists of 120 members, eighty-seven of them from the United States, twenty from Canada, and thirteen from Mexico. As of 2011, sixty-eight of the Trilateral members from the United States were also CFR members, many of them past or current Council directors.[288] Recent Trilateral members include the aforementioned Madeleine Albright, Michael Bloomberg, Harold Brown, Ash Carter, John Deutch, Thomas Donilon, Martin Feldstein, Larry Fink, David

---

[284] Trilateral. "Leadership: Asia Pacific Group":
http://trilateral.org/page/11/asia-pacific-group
[285] Trilateral. "Executive Committee":
http://trilateral.org/page/12/executive-committee
[286] Trilateral. "Membership":
http://trilateral.org/page/7/membership
[287] Trilateral. "About the Trilateral Commission."
[288] Shoup, 137.

Gergen, Richard Haass, John Hamre, Carla Hills, Karen Elliott House, Henry Kissinger, Winston Lord, Thomas McLarty, Andrea Mitchell, John Negroponte, Thomas Pickering, David Petraeus, Adam Posen, David Rubenstein, Eric Schmidt, Anne-Marie Slaughter, Lawrence Summers, Strobe Talbott, Robert Zoellick, and Mortimer Zuckerman. Paula J. Dobriansky and Kenneth M. Duberstein are current Trilateral members who were CFR directors at one time, and Judith A. (Jami) Miscik and R. Nicholas Burns are both Council directors and Commission members at the present time.[289]

Due to the relatively small size of the Commission, membership has circulated on a regular basis to permit participation from a greater number of individuals. Over the course of the Commission's history, many other powerbrokers named in chapter 1 and the first section of this chapter, but not mentioned in the preceding paragraph, have been Trilateral members. These include George H.W. Bush and Bill Clinton prior to their presidencies. Peter Peterson, George Ball, William Cohen, Caspar Weinberger, Jay Rockefeller, and James Hoge were early members.[290] John Whitehead, Maurice Greenberg, Alan Greenspan, Robert McNamara, Alexander Haig, and Frank Carlucci became members in the 1980s.[291] George Shultz and Dick Cheney joined in the 1990s in addition to Paul Wolfowitz, Leslie Gelb, Lee Hamilton, William Perry,

---

[289] Trilateral. "Membership."
CFR. *AR 2016*, 2.
[290] Internet Archive. "Trilateral Commission Membership List 1973": https://tinyurl.com/y7hvb6rc
Internet Archive. "Trilateral Commission Membership List 1978."
[291] Internet Archive. "Trilateral Commission Membership List 1985": https://tinyurl.com/yd43xrwx

Dianne Feinstein, Marie-Josée Kravis, Susan Berresford, and Paul A. Allaire, a former CFR director and ex-member of the Bilderberg steering committee. Financier and convicted sex offender Jeffrey E. Epstein was also a member during this decade.[292] More recently, George Soros, Condoleezza Rice, Timothy Geithner, George Tenet, Susan Rice, Philip Zelikow, Sylvia Burwell, Zoë Baird, Charlie Rose, Fareed Zakaria, Richard Perle, and Walter Isaacson have all been Commission members.[293]

As with the CFR and Bilderberg, the US financial and corporate sectors have been heavily represented in the Commission. By the mid-1980s, approximately two-thirds of the largest public corporations in the world had been represented through membership and some of them had been essential to its funding. Executives from global banking, insurance, oil, automobile, and pharmaceutical companies have been members, with individuals sometimes representing their corporations more than themselves personally.[294] For example, the investment banking and management firm Goldman Sachs has been continuously represented, currently in all three regional groups. In the North American Group, E. Gerald Corrigan, managing director at Goldman Sachs and a CFR director in the 1990s, is a member, and Zoellick is chairman of the

____

[292] Internet Archive. "Trilateral Commission Membership List 1995": https://tinyurl.com/ych62fbg
 Internet Archive. "Trilateral Commission Membership List 1998": https://tinyurl.com/ya7djjhq
[293] Public Intelligence. "Trilateral Commission Complete Membership List May 2010":
https://publicintelligence.net/trilateral-commission-complete-membership-list-may-2010
[294] Dino Knudsen. *The Trilateral Commission and Global Governance: Informal Elite Diplomacy, 1972-1982* (London: Routledge, 2016), 95-96.

firm's international advisors.[295] Overall, there was "an overrepresentation of the business and banking sectors" from the outset.[296]

Zbigniew Brzezinski furnished the intellectual foundation for the Commission in *Between Two Ages*, published in 1970. He argued that from "an American standpoint, the more important and promising changes in the years to come will have to involve Western Europe and Japan [. . .] Western Europe and Japan offer greater possibilities for initiatives designed to weave a new fabric of international relations, and because, like America, they are in the forefront of scientific and technological innovation, they represent the most vital regions of the globe."[297] The presentation of these ideas at the 1972 Bilderberg meeting and David Rockefeller's endorsement initiated the process leading to the creation of the Commission. Political scientist Stephen Gill notes that the "wider context was a pervasive view within the Western and Japanese foreign policy establishments that the international system was entering a period of crisis or transition."[298]

Upon confirming interest from Western Europe and Japan, Rockefeller scheduled a meeting at his family estate in Pocantico Hills, New York in July 1972 for their representatives and those of the United States. Besides Rockefeller and Brzezinski, other Americans in attendance included McGeorge Bundy, then CFR director George S.

---

[295] CFR. *AR 2016*, 38.
[296] Knudsen, 95.
[297] Zbigniew K. Brzezinski. *Between Two Ages: America's Role in the Technetronic Era* (New York: The Viking Press, 1970), 111.
[298] Stephen Gill. *American Hegemony and the Trilateral Commission* (Cambridge, UK: Cambridge University Press, 1990), 132-133.

Franklin, and Bayless A. Manning, the CFR president at the time. Among the Japanese invitees were Kiichi Miyazawa, former minister of foreign affairs, and Tadashi Yamamoto, then president of the Japan Center for International Exchange, a think tank that is the current home of the Commission's Asia Pacific Group. The European contingent hailed from Germany, Britain, Italy, France, and the Netherlands.[299] Dutch attendee Max Kohnstamm, a former member of the Bilderberg steering committee, would become the founding European chairman.[300] Former Asian Development Bank president Takeshi Watanabe became the first Japanese chairman and Gerard C. Smith, ex-director of the US Arms Control and Disarmament Agency and a CFR member, was selected as the founding North American chairman. Brzezinski was appointed the Director of the Commission.[301]

Achieving a funding balance between the three regions proved challenging. The chief donor to the Commission in the United States was the Ford Foundation.[302] As noted, Ford Foundation president Bundy attended the initial meeting in Pocantico Hills and was consulted during the planning stages.[303] Securing funding in Western Europe and Japan was difficult due to suspicions about US hegemony. "Eighteen months after its inception, the [Commission] was still 'largely American-financed'

---

[299] Holly Sklar, "Founding the Trilateral Commission: Chronology 1970-1977," in Holly Sklar (ed.). *Trilateralism: The Trilateral Commission and Elite Planning for World Management* (Boston: South End Press, 1980), 78-79.
[300] Bilderberg. "Background: Former Steering Committee Members."
[301] Sklar, 79.
[302] Knudsen, 80.
[303] Ibid., 81.

Brzezinski wrote to Rockefeller."[304] Eventually it was accepted that funding would be proportional to the Gross Domestic Product (GDP) of each geographical area. Rockefeller suggested European funding should be obtained from bankers and industrialists as well as from Prince Bernhard. Agnelli of FIAT offered $50,000 per year. Rockefeller, accompanied by his brother Nelson and Agnelli, spent a night at the castle of Edmond Adolphe de Rothschild in Switzerland and received a financial commitment from him for the European Group. In Japan, partially through pressure from Rockefeller, financing was finally secured from the Japan Federation of Economic Organizations, known as Keidanren, and the Japanese government.[305]

Coordinating public policies in the three geographical areas was the driving motivation behind the establishment of the Commission. Rockefeller believed that "a successful attempt to induce the governments of the three democratic, industrialized regions concerned to pursue common or parallel policies in the face of powerful disintegrative trends would amply justify the effort entailed in forming such a commission."[306] One of the fundamental purposes of the Commission was to "sell the ideas developed to the public and governments of the various nations." In an interview in the 1980s, Brzezinski claimed credit for the Commission's name, stating that the intention was to invent "as official sounding a name as possible - so as to underline the fact that it had a political purpose ... to shape policy by influence."[307] Brzezinski and fellow Trilateral organizer Henry D. Owen wrote that

---

304 Ibid., 77.
305 Ibid., 78-79.
306 Ibid., 42.
307 Ibid., 42.

Commission members would be "chosen primarily for the influence that they can bring to bear upon their respective governments and societies."[308] Particularly valuable were "men and women who already are in a position, or are soon likely to be in a position from which they can significantly affect national policy."[309] Although not in control of the US government in 1972, leading Trilateral members would soon be afforded the opportunity to determine policy.

Following numerous consultations and meetings during the subsequent twelve months, the Commission was officially launched in July 1973. The founding session of the executive committee took place in Tokyo in October of that year, with the three regional chairmen attending with Brzezinski, Rockefeller, and dozens of other representatives from each region.[310] One of the CFR members present was Marina von Neumann Whitman, a future executive at General Motors who would be active in the Council as a director and at Bilderberg as a member of the steering committee.[311] The first plenary conference was not held until May 1975. 113 members attended this meeting in Kyoto, Japan and addressed such topics as "The Trilateral Community: Key Problems and Prospects" and "Global Redistribution of Power." The 1973 oil crisis precipitated by OPEC's embargo and the Global South's proposed NIEO were subjects of discussion. A concerted effort to develop Japanese-Western European relations was also initiated.[312]

---

[308] Ibid., 90.
[309] Ibid., 90.
[310] Sklar, 79-80.
[311] CFR. *AR 2016*, 37.
Bilderberg. "Background: Former Steering Committee Members."
[312] Sklar, 80.

The Commission was afforded substantial media coverage. Brzezinski and Franklin met with the editor-in-chief of *Time* and president of CBS in the lead-up to the official launch, both of whom would eventually become Trilateral members. They also approached other important media figures in an "informal but confidential" manner. In its first year, Trilateral activities were reported in *The New York Times*, *The Washington Post*, *Newsweek*, and major newspapers in Europe and Japan. To increase its visibility in the media, the Commission invited presidents and editors from *The Wall Street Journal*, *The New York Times*, and ABC News to a private luncheon in 1975. Brzezinski penned op-eds for newspapers, his comments were quoted in the press, and he made television appearances. The US press list for the Commission included seventy daily newspapers, twenty magazines, and fourteen news services. These endeavors proved worthwhile. In 1975, the Ford Foundation deemed the Commission a success if judged by media coverage.[313]

Relations with the US Congress were also considered crucial and serious efforts were undertaken to ensure its support for the nascent Commission. Smith consulted numerous senators and representatives in the planning stages and elicited positive responses. Brzezinski arranged informal lunches and formal meetings with congressional leaders to promote the Trilateral agenda. Members of Congress were contacted by mail and in person, and dinners were also organized to meet and influence them. In addition, seminars for congressional staff were held, and the foreign committees of the Senate and House of Representatives were regularly informed of Trilateral

---

[313] Knudsen, 184-185.

meetings and reports. To formalize the relationship, members of Congress were invited to join, and from the beginning there has been significant congressional representation in the Commission.[314]

Since its founding, Trilateral publications have included Task Force Reports and Trialogues. The first ones were published in 1973. Trialogues have primarily covered the Commission's various meetings whereas the Task Force Reports are the product of a team of authors from the three regions collaborating over the course of a year, presenting a draft for discussion at the annual plenary conference, and then publishing the report as part of the Triangle Papers series.[315] Therefore, the "reports are *to* the Trilateral Commission, not *of* the Commission."[316] Policy recommendations are prescribed in the reports. Topics for the papers are selected by the Trilateral chairmen, deputy chairmen, and directors with an advisory role for the executive committee, and authors are then invited from the Commission membership and elsewhere.[317] Consequently, the choice of issues to be analyzed reflects the priorities of the Trilateral leadership more accurately than the reports themselves.

Task Force Reports through the years and decades indicate the principal concerns of the time for the US liberal power elite and their international partners from the

---

[314] Ibid., 142-143.
[315] Trilateral. "Trialogues/Annual Meeting Reports and Special Publications": http://trilateral.org/page/14/trialogues
[316] Trilateral. "Trialogues/Annual Meeting Reports and Special Publications: Triangle Papers/Task Force Reports and Project Work": http://trilateral.org/file.showdirectory&list=Triangle-Papers
[317] Ibid.

industrialized countries. Early reports focused on world trade, energy and relations with OPEC, North-South economic relations, as well as prospects for international cooperation more generally. Owen, then director of foreign policy studies at Brookings and a CFR member, co-authored his first Commission report in 1974.[318] The most controversial Trilateral report was Task Force Report (TFR) 8, "The Crisis of Democracy," co-authored by political scientist and CFR member Samuel P. Huntington in 1975. Huntington's segment of the paper evaluated democracy in the United States, more specifically, the "excess of democracy" resulting from the "democratic surge" of the 1960s that he contended had undermined the authority of government institutions. "The Democratic Challenge to Authority" and "Decline in Public Confidence and Trust" were two sections of Huntington's contribution to the report. In his conclusion, he advocated reduced popular participation to restore a "democratic balance."[319] Many critics have interpreted his writing as a clear admission of the elitist and anti-democratic position of the US oligarchy.

In the latter half of the 1970s, leading Commission members from the United States were in a position to implement their policy plans as officials of the Carter administration. President Carter himself was, in fact, a member of the Commission. A group of prominent Atlantans affiliated with the CFR responded to a request from George Franklin by recommending Carter, governor of Georgia, for Trilateral membership in 1973. He attended all of the regional meetings and the first plenary

---

[318] Trilateral. "TFR 2: The Crisis of International Cooperation": http://trilateral.org/file/2
[319] Trilateral. "TFR 8: The Crisis of Democracy": http://trilateral.org/file/8

conference in Japan.[320] Although he acknowledged the popularity of his candidacy "whenever we'd project ourselves as the underdog fighting the establishment," in reality "Carter was an 'insider' who campaigned as an outsider.'"[321] Brzezinski wrote major campaign speeches and Huntington served as an advisor.[322]

Once elected, Carter appointed many Trilateral and CFR members to his administration, as mentioned in the first chapter. Brzezinski, Volcker, Walter Mondale, Cyrus Vance, Harold Brown, and Michael Blumenthal were Trilateral members given top posts. Among the other Commission members in the administration were Richard Holbrooke, Warren Christopher, and Paul C. Warnke. All of these individuals have also been directors of the CFR. C. Fred Bergsten, a Brookings fellow at the time, an attendee of the Pocantico Hills meeting, CFR member, and later the founding director of the Peterson Institute for International Economics, was appointed assistant secretary of the Treasury for international affairs. Gerard Smith resigned the North American chairmanship of the Commission to join the administration just as the others had to resign their membership in the Commission before serving in government, as per Trilateral rules. He was replaced as chairman by David Rockefeller.[323]

---

320 Laurence H. Shoup, "Jimmy Carter and the Trilateralists: Presidential Roots," in Holly Sklar (ed.). *Trilateralism: The Trilateral Commission and Elite Planning for World Management* (Boston: South End Press, 1980), 202.
321 Ibid., 204.
322 Ibid., 203.
323 Internet Archive. "Trilateral Commission Membership List 1978": https://tinyurl.com/ycvzz6m4

Policy implementation of the Trilateral vision, however, faced serious obstacles. The interests of the three regions differed on several key issues. Firstly, Japan and Europe were even more dependent on imported oil from the Middle East than the United States and adjusted their foreign policies accordingly. Secondly, US pursuit of détente with the Soviet Union, which continued under Carter, distracted from efforts to coordinate policy on a Trilateral basis. Carter's own international human rights policy was also undertaken unilaterally.[324] Yet his presidency is referred to as the "Trilateral administration" because of the interlocking relationship between the Commission and administration only years after the Commission's launch. A synopsis from an archived version of the US Department of State website suggests the liberal faction's markedly diminished influence once Carter exited the White House: "During the 1980s, the Trilateral Commission continued to meet, although it did not enjoy close ties to the Reagan Administration."[325] In fact, the Reagan campaign had attacked the Commission as part of its attempt to discredit Carter and candidate George Bush during the primaries. Still, eleven former Commission members, including Bush as vice president, held positions in the Reagan administration.[326]

In the years of Carter's campaign and presidency, East-West relations, international institutions, international financial stability, and food production in Asia were some of the themes discussed in Task Force Reports. During the 1980s, North-South trade, East-West trade, the Middle

---

[324] US Department of State. "Trilateral Diplomacy: the United States, Western Europe and Japan":
https://2001-2009.state.gov/r/pa/ho/time/qfp/103525.htm
[325] Ibid.
[326] Knudsen, 140-141.

East, arms control, "Third World" debt and development, science and technology, the rise of East Asia, international financial integration, and of course changing East-West relations toward the end of the decade were report topics. Smith, McNamara, Brzezinski, Bergsten, Feldstein, Holbrooke, and Kissinger all co-authored papers. Reports in the 1990s examined post-Cold War global cooperation, political and economic reform in Latin America, environmental degradation, multilateral peacekeeping, international migration, post-communist Russia, China's economic rise, energy security, globalization's impact on labor, management of the international system, and the future of Trilateral relations. The reports posited recommendations for Trilateral cooperation regarding these issues.[327]

In the new century, a vast range of topics have been covered in the reports. "The New Central Asia: In Search of Stability" was the title of the 2000 report. Brzezinski, who continued his membership in the Commission, emphasized the centrality of this region for US hegemony in his 1997 book *The Grand Chessboard*, although he submitted that forging a consensus on foreign policy in the United States would be difficult "except in the circumstances of a truly massive and widely perceived direct external threat."[328] Ultimately, he believed that "global politics are bound to become increasingly uncongenial to the concentration of hegemonic power in the hands of a single state. Hence, America is not only the first, as well as the only, truly

---

[327] Trilateral. "Trialogues/Annual Meeting Reports and Special Publications: Triangle Papers/Task Force Reports and Project Work."
[328] Zbigniew Brzezinski. *The Grand Chessboard: American Primacy and Its Geostrategic Imperatives* (New York: Basic Books, 1997), 211.

global superpower, but it is also likely to be the very last."[329] Besides international terrorism and multilateral cooperation in the post-9/11 "war on terror," global institutions, nuclear proliferation and disarmament, energy security and climate change, Iran, and the global economic crisis featured as the subjects of papers in the first decade. Relations with Russia were scrutinized twice, in 2006 and with input from a Russian contributor in 2014, and energy security and climate change were revisited in 2016. The last available report was on global health. Brown, Deutch, Nye, Talbott, Dobriansky, and Slaughter were among the contributing authors of the various reports.[330]

From its founding to the present day, the Commission has undoubtedly succeeded in reinforcing and expanding the international network of the liberal faction of the US oligarchy. Clearly, European historian Dino Knudsen is accurate in his assessment that from its inception "the Commission was an exclusive enterprise, even with regards to the elites represented."[331] Invitation for membership in the North American Group has been restricted to the liberal power elite. The Commission's regional and plenary conferences, including the presentation of draft reports, have provided a forum for oligarchic networking and policy planning. This faction's perpetual power and influence since World War II ensure that the Trilateral Commission is not a talking shop, but as its founders intended, a private venue for shaping public policy.

------

[329] Ibid., 209.
[330] Trilateral. "Trialogues/Annual Meeting Reports and Special Publications: Triangle Papers/Task Force Reports and Project Work."
[331] Knudsen, 97.

WORLD ECONOMIC FORUM

There are other important international meetings attended by persons from the US liberal power elite. The World Economic Forum (WEF), also known as Davos because the Swiss town hosts the annual meeting, is a gathering of "the foremost political, business and other leaders of society to shape global, regional and industry agendas."[332] Founded in 1971 by German engineer and economist Klaus M. Schwab, the WEF refers to itself as the International Organization for Public-Private Cooperation and states that it "carefully blends and balances the best of many kinds of organizations, from both the public and private sectors, international organizations and academic institutions."[333] In addition to the yearly meeting in Davos, regional meetings are held on several continents.

Terms commonly in use at the WEF are "'Public private partnerships,' 'social entrepreneurship,' 'mutual responsibility,' 'communitarian spirit,' 'global corporate citizenship,' and 'organic community'" as elements of a "stakeholder" philosophy that believes corporations are responsible to the broader society.[334] However, a "large number of WEF member corporations or their top leaders have often been involved in illegal and unethical activities, such as mortgage fraud, fixing LIBOR rates, insider stock trading, bribery, municipal bond fraud, and environmental crimes."[335]

---

[332] WEF. "Our Mission: The World Economic Forum":
https://www.weforum.org/about/world-economic-forum
[333] Ibid.
[334] Shoup, 140.
[335] Ibid., 140.

Many of the corporations represented in Davos are corporate members of the CFR. Dozens of individual Council members have participated in the WEF since it was established, including past Council directors Kissinger, Holbrooke, Zoellick, Soros, Cheney, Powell, Feldstein, and Zakaria.[336] CFR chairman David Rubenstein is currently on the WEF board of trustees, as are Council director Larry Fink and Albert A. (Al) Gore, Clinton's vice president.[337]

In October 2019, in partnership with the Bill and Melinda Gates Foundation and Johns Hopkins Center for Health Security, the WEF participated in Event 201 in New York City. It featured a high-level pandemic exercise and "illustrated areas where public/private partnerships will be necessary during the response."[338] Months later, COVID-19 precipitated a "lockdown" on a global scale. The WEF subsequently released an all-encompassing plan for the world referred to as "The Great Reset."[339]

The Washington-based Group of Thirty (G30) is yet another international group with substantial involvement from the liberal power elite. Founded in 1978 at the impetus of The Rockefeller Foundation, which supplied the original funding, the G30 is "a private, nonprofit, international body composed of very senior representatives of the private and public sectors and academia. It aims to deepen understanding of international economic and financial issues, and to explore the international

---

[336] Ibid., 141-142.
[337] WEF. "Leadership and Governance":
https://www.weforum.org/about/leadership-and-governance
[338] Center for Health Security. "Event 201: A Global Pandemic Exercise": https://www.centerforhealthsecurity.org/event201
[339] WEF. "The Great Reset": https://www.weforum.org/great-reset

repercussions of decisions taken in the public and private sectors."[340] About one third of the twenty-eight current members are from the United States, five of whom are CFR members, including Geithner and Summers. Some of the others, including the non-American members, have ties to the Council in some capacity.[341] The G30 has strong connections not only to the CFR but also the Trilateral Commission. Volcker, honorary North American chairman of the Commission, was chairman emeritus of the G30 until his death, and Trichet, current chairman of the Commission's European Group, is the G30's honorary chairman. Janet Yellen is a senior G30 member and Corrigan and von Neumann Whitman are among the emeritus members.[342]

CONCLUSION

Through the Bilderberg Group, Trilateral Commission, and World Economic Forum, as well as other conferences and groups, the liberal power elite has extended its network internationally. These partnerships have fortified its domestic power and influence, and at the same time they have assured its global reach, contributing significantly to the hegemony of the liberal faction of the oligarchy since World War II. In his 2002 autobiography, *Memoirs*, David Rockefeller declared, "Some even believe we [the Rockefellers] are part of a secret cabal working against the best interests of the United States, characterizing my

---

[340] Shoup, 142.
G30. "About the Group of Thirty": http://group30.org/about
[341] G30. "Current Members": http://group30.org/members
[342] G30. "Senior Members":
http://group30.org/members/senior
G30. "Emeritus Members":
http://group30.org/members/emeritus

family and me as 'internationalists' and of conspiring with others around the world to build a more integrated global political and economic structure -- one world, if you will. If that is the charge, I stand guilty, and I am proud of it."[343]

---

[343] David Rockefeller. *Memoirs* (New York: Random House, 2002), 405.

CHAPTER 3
RIVAL FOR POWER: THE RISE OF THE CONSERVATIVE FACTION

While the liberal power elite dominated US politics in the postwar period, its position was eventually challenged by a power elite of the "radical right" that emerged in the 1950s. Initially based predominantly in the Midwest and the Sunbelt (South and West) of the United States, it arose from the economic power of these two regions, the sources of which were the thriving manufacturing industry in the former and the burgeoning oil and military industries in the latter. These economic sectors produced a competing ideology and politics in conflict with the Wall Street-centered liberal faction. In Texas, Haroldson Lafayette (HL) Hunt, Clint Murchison, Sid Richardson, and other oil tycoons financed conservative political candidates and media in Dallas and beyond.[344] There, as in the rest of the Sunbelt, "attitudes have historically manifested as deep-seated hostilities toward established power, especially power perceived as centralized in the East Coast, particularly in New York City and Washington, D.C."[345]

Within a relatively short time span, the conservative or right-wing faction contended for power at the national level, positioning itself to contest presidential as well as congressional elections, formulate and implement policy,

---

[344] Sean P. Cunningham. *American Politics in the Postwar Sunbelt: Conservative Growth in a Battleground Region* (New York: Cambridge University Press, 2014), 49.
[345] Ibid., 19.

and shift US society politically rightward. In this chapter, the role of the conservative faction's major think tanks, foundations, and media will be analyzed through the decades, highlighted by the presidential administration of Ronald Reagan. Subsequent internal developments within the faction will be discussed, as will the election victory and early presidency of Donald Trump, whose administration has been at the service of the conservative power elite to an unprecedented degree.

THINK TANKS

Although the conservative faction is a complex collection of think tanks and sponsoring foundations of varying ideology, and perhaps not as cohesive as the liberal faction, at its core it has always promoted laissez-faire capitalism coupled with militarism in national security and foreign policy, accompanied by social conservatism inspired by "Judeo-Christian" traditional values. Zealous anti-communism was a unifying feature throughout the Cold War, replaced in the new century by anti-Islamism to a great extent, but a very broadly defined socialism remains a collective enemy. A grassroots conservative movement has certainly existed since the 1950s, yet it only became a political force under the sponsorship and management of the conservative power elite.

American Security Council

The origins of the American Security Council (ASC) predate World War II and can be traced to the America First Committee (AFC), launched in 1940 to advocate against US entry into the war. The Chicago-based AFC was comprised of hundreds of local chapters and a membership of approximately 800,000, representing views from across most of the political spectrum but united in opposition to US participation in the war.[346] Despite measures introduced by the national leadership, fascist sympathies and anti-semitism were prevalent in many of the local groups. When famous aviator Charles A. Lindbergh, an AFC national committee member, delivered a speech expressing sympathy with Jewish persecution in Europe but denouncing Jews who supported US involvement in the war, accusations of anti-semitism against both Lindbergh and the AFC were widespread and intense. Newspapers condemned the speech and a White House spokesperson compared it to statements from the Nazi regime a few days earlier.[347] It was enormously damaging to the AFC's "isolationist" campaign, but a few months later the Japanese military attack on Pearl Harbor would lead to the disbanding of the AFC in any case. The phrase "America First" would be revived as one of Trump's top campaign slogans in 2016.[348]

Among the leading national committee members of the AFC were General Robert E. Wood and William H. Regnery. They were also major benefactors and provided the initial financing. Originally supportive of Roosevelt's New Deal, they soon opposed its direction and later financially contributed to right-wing business groups.[349] Regnery, president of a textile manufacturing company, was the AFC's largest funder. Wood served as the

---

[346] Wayne S. Cole. *America First: The Battle against Intervention, 1940-41* (Madison: University of Wisconsin Press, 1953), 30.
[347] Ibid., 144-154.
[348] Brian Bennett, "'America First,' a phrase with a loaded anti-Semitic and isolationist history," *Los Angeles Times* 20 January 2017: http://www.latimes.com/politics/la-na-pol-trump-america-first-20170120-story.html
[349] Cole, 72-73.

organization's chairman. He was chairman of the Sears, Roebuck and Company department store chain and a director of the National Association of Manufacturers (NAM), and he also contributed a substantial amount to the AFC.[350] These two men would be instrumental in laying the foundation for the conservative faction after the war. Wood, assisted by Regnery, established the ASC and Regnery's son, Henry, launched the main conservative book publishing company in the United States in 1947.[351] Profoundly anti-communist, they and their associates aided Senator McCarthy's campaign to eradicate alleged communist subversion in the early 1950s.[352]

Wood, a key backer of General Douglas MacArthur's presidential bids in 1948 and 1952, founded the ASC in 1954 by purchasing the largest private library on communism in the Midwestern United States. John M. Fisher, a Federal Bureau of Investigation (FBI) agent who was hired by Wood as a security consultant for Sears, was given the responsibility of heading the operation to recruit donations from Chicago-headquartered companies to acquire the library. Twenty-five company heads agreed to contribute, including Paul Galvin of telecommunications corporation Motorola and Hughston McBain of department store chain Marshall Field and Company.

---

[350] Ibid., 32.
[351] Robert M. Thomas, "Henry Regnery, 84, Ground-Breaking Conservative Publisher," *The New York Times* 23 June 1996: http://www.nytimes.com/1996/06/23/us/henry-regnery-84-ground-breaking-conservative-publisher.html
[352] Russ Bellant. *Old Nazis, the New Right, and the Republican Party* (Boston: South End Press, 1991), 31-33.

Fisher was appointed chairman and CEO, positions he would retain throughout the organization's existence.[353]

The Council operated as a private intelligence outfit, a facilitator of military-industrial relations, and a public indoctrination organization. One of its missions was "to expose American leftists and deprive them of their livelihoods."[354] Companies paid fees to access library records on potential employees. Files on more than one million purportedly "subversive" Americans were compiled by 1958. The ASC publicly boasted of its superiority to the FBI, which could not legally share its files with businesses. The Council also co-sponsored National Military-Industrial Conferences from 1955 to 1961, annual events arranged for Pentagon and other national security officials to meet business executives. US Steel, United Fruit, Honeywell, and Standard Oil were some of the companies represented.[355] Interestingly, Eisenhower warned of the political encroachment of the "military-industrial complex" in his presidential farewell address in January 1961, likely referring to the ASC and its conferences. Former ASC field director W. Cleon Skousen hosted an anti-communist television series and the ASC produced radio programs reaching thirty-five million people in the United States and Europe.[356]

---

[353] John M. Fisher, "History Milestones: American Security Council and American Security Council Foundation," 1 November 2005, 1-3: http://ascfusa.org/history-of-milestones
[354] Sara Diamond. *Roads to Dominion: Right-Wing Movements and Political Power in the United States* (New York: The Guildford Press, 1995), 47.
[355] Ibid., 46-47.
[356] Ibid., 49-50.

At the 1958 conference, the Institute for American Strategy (IAS) was created to disseminate anti-communist ideology through publications and national security seminars for military officers. That year the White House National Security Council (NSC) had issued a directive allowing the "use of military personnel and facilities to arouse the public to the menace of the cold war."[357] Frank R. Barnett, research director for the Richardson (now Smith Richardson) Foundation, which funded the IAS, became the program director. He recommended "diverse forms of coercion and violence including strikes and riots, economic sanctions, subsidies for guerrilla or proxy warfare and, when necessary, kidnapping or assassination of enemy elites" as foreign policy methods.[358] Fisher took the helm as the chairman and CEO of the Institute in 1962 and Air Force Major General Edward G. Lansdale, a covert operations specialist, became the administrative director in the mid-1960s.[359] The IAS eventually changed its name to the American Security Council Foundation (ASCF), but it has never been a grantmaking foundation.

As the "personification of the military-industrial complex," the ASC lobbied for intervention in Vietnam.[360] Major military contractors were among the companies financing the ASC and the ASCF in the 1960s and 1970s: "Industrial members include[d] General Electric, Lockheed, Motorola, [Sears subsidiary] Allstate Insurance, Standard Oil of California, General Dynamics (San Diego), Reynolds

---

[357] Ibid., 48.
[358] Bellant, 37.
[359] Ibid., 37-38.
[360] Ibid., 30.
Peter Dale Scott. *The Road to 9/11: Wealth, Empire, and the Future of America* (Berkeley: University of California Press, 2007), 19.

Metals, Quaker Oats, Honeywell, U.S. Steel, Kraft Foods, Stewart-Warner, Schick, Illinois Central Railroad, and, of course, Sears, Roebuck. The publishing industry [was] represented by the *Detroit News*, the *St. Louis Globe-Democrat*, the *Oakland Tribune*, and the Henry Regnery book house in Chicago."[361] In essence, the "ASC united old-wealth oil and military corporations with new-wealth businesses in the South and the West, some of which incorporated investments from organized crime."[362] The ASC and its corporate backers were crucial in Nixon's political rise.[363] His successful electoral campaign in 1968 had accentuated his "antiestablishment 'outsider' conservatism."[364] In 1970, the ASC set their sights on defeating those candidates in the congressional elections who opposed Nixon's policies in Vietnam and Cambodia.[365]

The ASC's most extensive project, however, was launched under its auspices in 1978 as the Coalition for Peace Through Strength (CPTS). Hundreds of Congress members, high-ranking military officers, and businesspersons joined the CPTS, as did many right-wing groups, some of them fascist and racist.[366] The Strategic Arms Limitation Talks (SALT) II was the main target of the Coalition's activities. In addition, the CPTS seized on the opportunity to focus attention on Central America's Marxist insurrections and to discredit the anti-nuclear

---

[361] William W. Turner. *Power on the Right* (Berkeley, CA: Ramparts Press, 1971), 202.
[362] Scott, 18.
[363] Ibid., 39.
[364] Kevin Phillips. *Wealth and Democracy: A Political History of the American Rich* (New York: Broadway Books, 2002), 314.
[365] Bellant, 39.
[366] Russ Bellant. *The Coors Connection: How Coors Family Philanthropy Undermines Democratic Pluralism* (Boston: South End Press, 1991), 49.

movement.[367] The centerpiece of the CPTS campaign was the production of the film *The SALT Syndrome* by the ASCF. It featured interviews with anti-SALT II military officials and was broadcast on television hundreds of times. While the Soviet invasion of Afghanistan played a pivotal role in the Senate's refusal to ratify the SALT II treaty, the film's influence was widely perceived as partially responsible as well. The CPTS and ASC would also contribute to Reagan's presidential victory and the Republican Party's Senate takeover in 1980.[368] "Peace Through Strength" would be adopted as a foreign policy slogan by Reagan and Republican platforms in subsequent elections. Trump's first national security advisor, Lieutenant General Michael T. Flynn, announced in January 2017 that Trump's "foreign policy will emphasize 'peace through strength.'"[369]

Reagan maintained an ongoing relationship with the ASC and ASCF. In September 1983, he wrote to Fisher, the chairman of both organizations: "I am glad to hear that you are launching an In Defense Of America project to counter the massive Soviet propaganda and disinformation on issues like Central America and the nuclear weapons freeze [. . .] As the educational secretariat of the Coalition for Peace Through Strength, with 231 Members of Congress from both parties and 139 national organizations, you are uniquely qualified to reach the broad base of American people [. . .] My administration will cooperate fully with you in this project [. . .] I strongly support your project

---

[367] Diamond, 137.
[368] Bellant. *Old Nazis*, 39.
[369] Karen DeYoung, "Trump's national security adviser says foreign policy will emphasize 'peace through strength,'" *The Washington Post* 10 January 2017: https://tinyurl.com/y7k5htej

and want to be kept up to date."[370] Administration officials participated in ASCF strategy board meetings and the ASCF staged a media offensive during the 1984 election campaign. After Reagan was re-elected, he hosted a White House reception to thank the four hundred most important CPTS leaders as selected by Fisher.[371] Colorado beer magnate Joseph (Joe) Coors, a prominent member of Reagan's unofficial "kitchen cabinet," sat on the ASCF board throughout the 1980s.[372]

A number of notable military officers and CIA officials were affiliated with the ASC and ASCF in a formal capacity. General Richard G. Stilwell and Lieutenant General Daniel O. Graham, and Admirals Thomas H. Moorer and John S. McCain, father of Senator McCain, served on the ASC board of directors. Graham and Moorer were also co-chairs of the CPTS.[373] CIA officials included James Jesus Angleton, the legendary chief of CIA counterintelligence from 1954 to 1974. Angleton served on the ASC's National Strategy Committee and was associate editor of the ASC's *Journal of International Relations*.[374] On the ASCF strategy board in the early 1980s were Ray S. Cline, an ex-deputy director of the CIA, Major General John K. Singlaub, a covert operations specialist, and Edwin J. (Ed) Feulner, president of The Heritage Foundation think tank.[375] Cline, co-chair of the board, was an executive director of CSIS at a time when the think tank was closely

---

[370] Fisher, 56-57.
[371] Ibid., 57-58.
[372] Bellant. *The Coors Connection*, 48-49.
[373] David Teacher. *Rogue Agents: The Cercle and the 6I in the Private Cold War 1951-1991* (December 2015), 226, 273.
[374] Ibid., 228.
[375] Bellant. *The Coors Connection*, 49.

aligned with the conservative faction.[376] Post-Cold War, the ASC and ASCF significantly declined in influence and in 1997 the ASC was merged into the ASCF.[377] Its current nine-person board of directors is a combination of civilians and retired military officers.[378]

American Enterprise Institute

Founded in 1938, the American Enterprise Institute (AEI), operated as the only major conservative think tank in Washington for several decades. Its name reflects a focus on the promotion of "free enterprise." Nevertheless, a belief in "American strength and global leadership" also informs its work. According to the AEI, its "scholars pursue innovative, independent work across a wide array of subjects. From economics, education, health care, and poverty to foreign and defense studies, public opinion, politics, society, and culture, our experts drive the competition of ideas."[379] Officials from the Nixon, Ford, Reagan, and both Bush administrations have staffed the Institute.[380] Neoconservatives have been associated with the AEI since the 1970s, led by Irving Kristol, a longtime AEI fellow and the "godfather" of neoconservatism. Dick Cheney currently sits on the board of trustees. Two men from leading conservative faction families are also on the

---

[376] Tim Weiner, "Ray S. Cline, Chief C.I.A. Analyst, Is Dead at 77," *The New York Times* 16 March 1996:
http://www.nytimes.com/1996/03/16/us/ray-s-cline-chief-cia-analyst-is-dead-at-77.html
[377] Fisher, 38.
[378] ASCF. "Board of Directors": http://ascfusa.org/board-of-directors
[379] AEI. "About": http://www.aei.org/about
[380] John B. Judis. *The Paradox of American Democracy: Elites, Special Interests, and the Betrayal of Public Trust* (New York: Routledge, 2001), 124-125.

board, Peter H. Coors and Richard M. (Dick) DeVos.[381] Coors, vice chairman of the Molson Coors beer company, is the son of Joe Coors. DeVos is the former CEO of family company Amway and the husband of Elisabeth D. (Betsy) DeVos, the secretary of education in the Trump administration. He took his wife's place on the board after she was appointed by Trump.[382]

Opposition to the New Deal motivated the AEI in its early years. Academics were hired to draft reports "indistinguishable from those of the NAM."[383] Under its president William J. Baroody in the 1960s and particularly in the 1970s, the Institute was transformed by corporate and foundation funding. A watershed moment in the history of the conservative power elite occurred in 1971 when Lewis F. Powell, just prior to his appointment to the Supreme Court by Nixon, wrote a confidential memorandum lamenting "the assault on the enterprise system" and urged an aggressive response by the US Chamber of Commerce and business generally. The memo was widely distributed and galvanized the corporate community and right-wing plutocrats.[384] By 1980, the AEI's annual budget had multiplied to nearly $10 million, exceeding that of Brookings. Several hundred corporations and private grantmaking foundations financed the think tank. The latter benefactors included the Smith Richardson Foundation, the John M. Olin Foundation, and especially the Sarah Scaife Foundation of Pittsburgh, which was under the control of billionaire Richard Mellon Scaife, an

---

[381] AEI. "Board of Trustees": http://www.aei.org/about/board-of-trustees
[382] AEI. *2016 Annual Report,* 32.
[383] Judis, 123.
[384] Ibid., 116-117.

heir to the Mellon banking and oil fortune.[385] At the time he funded CSIS as well, and the Sarah Scaife Foundation is still one of CSIS' top donors after his death despite the virtual capture of this think tank by the liberal faction, as discussed in the first chapter.

Like the AEI, Scaife, whose politics were farther to the right than the rest of the Mellon family of his generation, actively supported Arizona senator Barry Goldwater's presidential run in 1964. Goldwater had defeated Nelson Rockefeller to win the Republican nomination, which marked the onset of the party's rightward shift.[386] Baroody and his AEI team acted as advisors to Goldwater and may have violated the Institute's tax-exempt status in doing so.[387] Scaife, meanwhile, financially contributed to the campaign and flew the senator on his family airplane. He reacted to Goldwater's heavy loss to Johnson in the general election by waging "the war of ideas" in the words of one of his associates, who continued, "you had [. . .] the Brookings Institution, the New York Times and Washington Post and all these other people on the left [sic] - and nobody on the right."[388] Nixon had promoted a "project of building *our* establishment in press, business, education, etc" according to his Chief of Staff Harry

---

[385] Ibid., 124.

[386] Mary C. Brennan. *Turning Right in the Sixties: The Conservative Capture of the GOP* (Chapel Hill: The University of North Carolina Press, 1995), 81.

[387] Jason Stahl. *Right Moves: The Conservative Think Tank in American Political Culture* (Chapel Hill : The University of North Carolina Press, 2016), 1.

[388] Robert G. Kaiser and Ira Chinoy, "Scaife: Funding Father of the Right," *The Washington Post* 2 May 1999, A1: http://www.washingtonpost.com/wp-srv/politics/special/clinton/stories/scaifemain050299.htm

Robbins (HR) Haldeman.[389] Although Scaife donated $1 million to Nixon's reelection campaign in 1972, after the Watergate scandal he distanced himself from political candidates and concentrated on influencing politics through right-wing think tanks.[390] Scaife thus emerged as one of the foremost champions of the Powell Memorandum, and a primary beneficiary of his financial largesse was The Heritage Foundation.

The Heritage Foundation

Despite its name, The Heritage Foundation is a think tank rather than a grantmaking foundation. It has been located in Washington since its establishment in 1973. Heritage is widely considered the most influential think tank of the conservative power elite and its supporting conservative movement base. Heritage states its mission "is to formulate and promote conservative public policies based on the principles of free enterprise, limited government, individual freedom, traditional American values, and a strong national defense."[391] On its board of trustees are Ed Feulner, longtime Heritage president, Edwin Meese, attorney general and counselor to the president in the Reagan administration, and Rebekah Mercer, "the most powerful woman in GOP [Republican Party] politics."[392]

---

[389] Scott, 30.

[390] Robert D. McFadden, "Richard Mellon Scaife, Influential U.S. Conservative, Dies at 82," *The New York Times* 4 July 2014: https://www.nytimes.com/2014/07/05/us/richard-mellon-scaife-influential-us-conservative-dies-at-82.html

[391] Heritage. "About Heritage: Mission": http://www.heritage.org/about-heritage/mission

[392] Kenneth P. Vogel and Ben Schreckinger, "The most powerful woman in GOP politics," *Politico* 7 September 2016: https://www.politico.com/story/2016/09/donald-trump-rebekah-mercer-227799

Mercer is the daughter of billionaire hedge fund manager and major Trump campaign donor Robert L. (Bob) Mercer, who funds "alt-right" Breitbart News. She is also a trustee of the Manhattan Institute (MI), another conservative faction think tank financed by the largest right-wing grantmaking foundations.[393]

Heritage's programs cover a vast array of issues areas and topics. Some "Top Issues" listed are "election integrity," "immigration" and "progressivism."[394] Foundation staff undertake research on both domestic and international topics, ranging from energy and infrastructure to national security and economic policy. In the realm of culture, the issue areas of interest to Heritage are gender, religion, marriage, family, and abortion. Its main audiences are members of Congress and their staff, executive branch policymakers, the media, academia, and other think tanks.[395] Membership in Heritage is open to the public and the Foundation boasts 500,000 individual paying members.[396]

Heritage was the brainchild of Feulner and Paul M. Weyrich, congressional staffers at the time who were frustrated with AEI's cautious approach to influencing policy because they "wanted to affect the legislative process

---

[393] MI. "About: Board of Trustees": https://www.manhattan-institute.org/board-of-trustees
Conservative Transparency. "Manhattan Institute for Policy Research": http://conservativetransparency.org/org/manhattan-institute-for-policy-research
[394] Heritage. "Explore Issues: Top Issues": http://www.heritage.org
[395] Heritage. "About Heritage: Staff": http://www.heritage.org/about-heritage/staff/leadership
[396] Heritage. "About Heritage: Membership": http://www.heritage.org/about-heritage/membership

promptly and directly."[397] In a joint venture with Adolph Coors Company, Joe Coors offered $250,000 in 1971-1972 to the Analysis and Research Association (ARA), the forerunner of Heritage, and pledged another $300,000 for a building to accommodate it. Failing to attract other donors, the ARA ceased operations and Heritage was founded as a new vehicle for the conservative faction of the oligarchy. Weyrich became the first president and Feulner and Coors served on the board.[398] Scaife soon joined in financing the Foundation, outpacing Coors' contributions, causing Heritage personnel to joke that "Coors gives six-packs; Scaife gives cases."[399] Scaife money accounted for forty-two percent of the think tank's 1976 budget.[400] From 1975 to 1998, the Sarah Scaife Foundation donated more than $23 million to Heritage.[401] Scaife became a member of the Foundation's board of trustees in 1985 and was the vice chairman for over twenty years. He was the recipient of Heritage's highest award in 2011.[402]

According to prolific conservative author and Heritage distinguished fellow Lee Edwards, the think tank struggled to establish itself in Washington in its first years. Seeking

---

[397] Lee Edwards, "The Power of Ideas: The Heritage Foundation at 25 Years," *The New York Times* 1997:
http://www.nytimes.com/books/first/e/edwards-ideas.html
[398] Ibid.
[399] Jane Mayer. *Dark Money: The Hidden History of the Billionaires Behind the Rise of the Radical Right* (New York: Anchor Books, 2017), 96.
[400] Kaiser and Chinoy.
[401] Conservative Transparency. "Sarah Scaife Foundation":
http://conservativetransparency.org/donor/sarah-scaife-foundation
[402] Ed Feulner, "FEULNER: Remembering Richard Scaife, a man of ideas," *The Washington Times* 7 July 2014:
http://www.washingtontimes.com/news/2014/jul/7/feulner-richard-scaife-a-man-of-ideas

to counter "the initiatives of the liberal-socialist 'think tanks'" in Heritage's words, the Foundation "was seen by most of the Washington establishment as part of the emerging New Right and was relegated to the fringe of politics and policy."[403] A small staff was overwhelmed by the vast number of issues it was tackling. A distinct change occurred when Feulner assumed the position of president in 1977. He professionalized the think tank and the profile of the Foundation increased steadily. Heritage became more focused, restricting its research and advocacy agenda to economic and foreign policy and national security matters. Social issues were not added to the Heritage program until the 1990s.[404]

Reagan's rise to the presidency coincided with Heritage's rise as an influential think tank in Washington. His election victory in 1980 heralded the genuine arrival of the conservative faction as a power elite. Heritage did not waste any time advising the new administration by providing policy prescriptions. Foundation analysts prepared *Mandate for Leadership,* a three-thousand-page publication detailing policy proposals. Reagan was so impressed with the ideas put forth by Heritage that he presented members of his cabinet with copies of the publication at their inaugural meeting. Feulner claimed that of the 1,270 policy recommendations, sixty-one percent were implemented in Reagan's first year in office.[405]

Reaganomics, a set of economic policies featuring tax cuts, reduction in most government spending, and deregulation,

---

[403] Edwards.
[404] Ibid.
[405] Mayer, 110.

but which allowed for protectionist measures and a sizeable increase in military spending, reflected the Foundation's mission. In addition, *Mandate for Leadership* authors served in the administration. Among them were the devoutly religious James G. Watt as the anti-environmentalist secretary of the interior and William J. (Bill) Bennett as the secretary of education.[406] Still, Heritage was not afraid to criticize Reagan for some of his appointments which did not meet their conservative expectations.[407] Reagan acknowledged Heritage's pivotal role in policymaking during the 1980s: "..it's not the money or numbers of people or size of the offices that measure Heritage's impact. Your frequent publications, timely research, policy papers, seminars and conferences account for your enormous influence on Capitol Hill and--believe me I know--at the White House."[408]

As with the ASC, Reagan's relationship with Heritage was a fixture in his administration's foreign policy as well. The Reagan Doctrine of supplying material assistance and training to counter-revolutionary forces in the Global South, building on Brzezinski's strategy of arming the Mujahideen in Afghanistan, rejected the strategies of containment and détente. The objective of this "rollback" strategy was to remove communist and other "anti-American" governments from power rather than merely containing them or seeking improved relations. Finally

---

[406] John J. Miller, "The Heritage Mandate," *National Review* 20 January 2005:
http://www.nationalreview.com/article/213426/heritage-mandate-john-j-miller
[407] Phil Gailey, "Heritage Foundation Disappointed by Reagan," *The New York Times* 22 November 1981:
http://www.nytimes.com/1981/11/22/us/heritage-foundation-disappointed-by-reagan.html
[408] Heritage. "About Heritage: Membership."

implementing the conservatives' long-held rollback aspirations, Reagan's rollback was developed by Heritage policy planners: "it was the Heritage Foundation that translated theory into concrete policy. Heritage targeted nine nations for rollback: Afghanistan, Angola, Cambodia, Ethiopia, Iran, Laos, Libya, Nicaragua, and Vietnam."[409]

Heritage's continuous conflict with the liberal faction-dominated State Department in the 1980s intensified early in Reagan's second term. Heritage leaders claimed to represent the president's views and accused State Department officials of undermining Reagan's policies. A transcript from a Heritage forum in mid-1985 was published as "The State Department vs. Ronald Reagan." Later in the year, Heritage demanded more appointments to the Department in order to fulfill the president's agenda but were refused these positions. A subsequent Heritage publication in January 1986 was entitled "Rhetoric vs. Reality: How the State Department Betrays the Reagan Vision." John Whitehead, the deputy secretary of state, responded by writing to Heritage trustees suggesting they resign from the Foundation board to protest Heritage's approach. Feulner was not impressed with the letter: "Unfortunately, the Whitehead letter was filled with innuendo and insults instead of specific responses to our criticisms."[410] The conservative faction row with the Department of State was never resolved and was soon on display in George Shultz's testimony at the Iran-Contra hearings.

---

[409] Thomas Bodenheimer and Robert Gould. *Rollback!: Right-wing Power in U.S. Foreign Policy* (Boston: South End Press, 1989), 82.
[410] Sidney Blumenthal, "A Schism Between Heritage and State," *The Washington Post* 11 March 1986:
https://tinyurl.com/y7werbcw

Following the Reagan era and particularly once Clinton took office, Heritage lost its sway in the executive branch but remained influential in Congress, as demonstrated by the *Contract with America*. This document was written by Newt L. Gingrich and Richard K. (Dick) Armey to serve as the detailed platform for the Republican Party in the 1994 congressional elections. It was unique in presenting a specific plan pertaining to various items of legislation. Gingrich and Armey borrowed many of their ideas from Heritage policy analysts. They adopted policy recommendations from *Issues '94*, a Heritage handbook. The alleged institutional failings of a malfunctioning Congress discussed in a 1993 Heritage study, published by Regnery Publishing with a distribution of 2.3 million copies, also were addressed in the document.[411] After the so-called Republican Revolution in which Republicans won a majority of seats in the House of Representatives for the first time since 1952, Speaker-elect Gingrich delivered his first post-election speech at a Heritage event and was introduced by Scaife.[412] New legislation passed so rapidly the next year that an article in *The New York Times* commented: "Perhaps not since the start of the New Deal, to which many of the programs now under attack can trace their origins, has Congress moved with such speed on so many fronts."[413]

Congress continued to be the branch of government most influenced by Heritage publications and activities until

---

[411] Jeffrey Gayner, "The Contract with America: Implementing New Ideas in the U.S.," 12 October 1995:
http://www.heritage.org/political-process/report/the-contract-america-implementing-new-ideas-the-us
[412] Feulner.
[413] Gayner.

Trump's election in 2016. While Heritage opposed the Obama administration on many fronts, the Trump administration has restored Heritage's influence in the executive branch to a level not seen since the Reagan Revolution. Trump's platform contained policy proposals from the Foundation's *Blueprint for Reform*, the latest incarnation of the *Mandate for Leadership*. The day after the election an article in the *Washington Examiner* suggested that the "Heritage Foundation might be the biggest winner of 2016."[414] Numerous Heritage staffers participated in the president's transition team. Feulner served as Trump's chief domestic policy advisor before and after the election, joined in the transition by other Heritage leaders, notably Edwin Meese and Becky N. Dunlop, a former senior official in the Reagan administration and Heritage's Ronald Reagan Distinguished Fellow. CNN referred to Heritage as "Donald Trump's think tank," noting that "No other Washington institution has that kind of footprint in the transition."[415] Vice President-elect Michael R. (Mike) Pence was the keynote speaker at the same annual Heritage President's Club meeting that Gingrich had addressed.[416]

Trump's inaugural year in the White House included significant contributions from Heritage. Approximately seventy of its former employees worked in the transition

---

[414] Philip Wegmann, "Heritage Foundation takes risk and wins big with Trump," *Washington Examiner* 10 November 2016: http://www.washingtonexaminer.com/heritage-foundation-takes-risk-and-wins-big-with-trump/article/2607078
[415] Tal Kopan, "Meet Donald Trump's think tank," *CNN* 7 December 2016: http://www.cnn.com/2016/12/06/politics/donald-trump-heritage-foundation-transition/index.html
[416] Ibid.

team or in the administration.[417] "Feulner's first law is people are policy" and Heritage's Project to Restore America recommended many of Trump's cabinet members, among them Betsy DeVos, Jefferson B. (Jeff) Sessions, J. Richard (Rick) Perry, and E. Scott Pruitt.[418] According to the think tank, the president adopted about two-thirds of its policy prescriptions in 2017, exceeding Reagan's record.[419] He incorporated many recommendations from Heritage's "Blueprint for Balance" into his 2018 budget. The Foundation's role in the budget plan was known to some civil society groups. One of them staged a protest outside Heritage headquarters, with a demonstrator declaring, "Trump is a puppet of The Heritage Foundation."[420] Heritage's *The Daily Signal* news service reported that the protesting group's sister organization had received a minimum of $1.3 million from George Soros' OSF.[421] Trump's selection for the Supreme Court, Neil M. Gorsuch, was a favorite of Heritage's legal analysts and sister organization The Federalist Society, an influential collection of conservative legal scholars and professionals

---

[417] Heritage. "Trump Administration Embraces Heritage Foundation Policy Recommendations" (23 January 2018): https://tinyurl.com/y7osfcq7

[418] Jonathan Mahler, "How One Conservative Think Tank Is Stocking Trump's Government," *The New York Times Magazine* 20 June 2018: https://www.nytimes.com/2018/06/20/magazine/trump-government-heritage-foundation-think-tank.html

[419] Philip Wegmann, "Heritage: Donald Trump has achieved more than Ronald Reagan in first year," *Washington Examiner* 23 January 2018: https://tinyurl.com/y7ycpan9

[420] Melissa Quinn, "Demonstrators Descend on Heritage Foundation to Protest Trump Budget," *The Daily Signal* 25 April 2017: http://dailysignal.com/2017/04/25/demonstrators-descend-on-heritage-foundation-to-protest-trump-budget

[421] Ibid.

funded by Scaife foundations, the Mercer family, and the Koch brothers.[422]

Heritage has furnished Trump and his administration with almost exclusively positive coverage in their commentaries on a vast array of issues and developments, ignoring some controversial ones, and has asked the public to "Join the fight to drain the swamp." The think tank states, "We are ramping up our efforts to get them [Trump and Republican congressmen] conservative policy solutions that will shrink the size of government, reform the tax code, dismantle Obamacare, and secure our borders."[423] In October 2017, Trump delivered an address on immigration, trade, and tax reform at Heritage President's Club meeting, becoming the fourth US president to speak at a Foundation event after Reagan and both of the Bushes. He praised Heritage by saying that for "nearly a half a century, you have been titans in the fight to defend, promote, and preserve our great American heritage."[424] When Feulner became the Foundation's interim president in May 2017 due to the departure of James W. (Jim) DeMint, he announced to staff: "We were Ronald Reagan's favorite think tank. And today we are, and will continue to be, Donald Trump's favorite think tank."[425]

---

[422] Eric Lipton and Jeremy W. Peters, "In Gorsuch, Conservative Activist Sees Test Case for Reshaping the Judiciary," *The New York Times* 18 March 2017:
https://www.nytimes.com/2017/03/18/us/politics/neil-gorsuch-supreme-court-conservatives.html
[423] Heritage. "Join the fight to drain the swamp":
http://www.heritage.org
[424] Heritage. "The Best of the 2017 President's Club Meeting":
http://www.heritage.org/impact/the-best-the-2017-presidents-club-meeting
[425] Philip Wegmann, "After Jim DeMint's exit, interim president Ed Feulner says Heritage 'will continue to be Donald Trump's

Council for National Policy

A secretive organization, the Council for National Policy (CNP) was founded in 1981 to function as "the conservative version of the Council on Foreign Relations" and to act "as a counterweight against liberal domination of the American agenda."[426] The Washington-based CNP is an umbrella think tank for the conservative power elite. Usually meeting three times a year, from the outset it has been closely tied to Heritage through its exclusive membership numbering in the hundreds. In its own words, the CNP "brings together the country's most influential conservative leaders in business, government, politics, religion, and academia to hear and learn from policy experts on a wide range of issues."[427] "Limited Government," "Traditional Values," and "Strong National Defense" constitute its core beliefs.[428] Unlike the CFR, the CNP does not release its membership list to the public, but a leaked copy of its directory from 2014 has disclosed a substantial amount of information about the CNP's organization, leadership, and current and past members.[429]

In 2014, CNP leadership included an executive committee and a board of governors. Stuart W. Epperson, chairman of the Christian conservative Salem Media Group, was the

---

favorite think tank," *Washington Examiner* 4 May 2017: https://tinyurl.com/ya2k5m66

[426] Marc J. Ambinder, "Inside the Council for National Policy," *ABC News* 2 May 2002: http://abcnews.go.com/Politics/story?id=121170&page=1

[427] CNP. "About Us": http://cfnp.org/about-us

[428] CNP. "Home": http://cfnp.org

[429] CNP. "Membership Directory 2014": https://www.splcenter.org/sites/default/files/cnp_redacted_final.pdf

president, and Tony Perkins, president of the Christian right Family Research Council (FRC), was the vice president. Perkins became the CNP president in 2015.[430] Other members of the executive committee were Kellyanne E. Conway, counselor to the president in the Trump administration, John K. (Ken) Blackwell, former Ohio secretary of state, and the now deceased anti-feminist conservative icon Phyllis M. Schlafly, who was eulogized by Trump at the Saint Louis Cathedral in 2016.[431] Political direct mail pioneer Richard A. Viguerie is listed as the senior executive committee member. Former presidents include Timothy F. (Tim) LaHaye, Nelson Bunker Hunt, Marion G. (Pat) Robertson, Richard M. DeVos, and the aforementioned Edwin Meese and Becky Dunlop.[432]

LaHaye, the Council's founding president, was an evangelical minister and author. Hunt, billionaire oil executive and son of HL Hunt, financed the Western Goals Foundation in the 1980s, a right-wing private network organized by John Singlaub, conservative Democratic Congressman Lawrence P. (Larry) McDonald from Georgia, and British journalist John Rees for the purpose of gathering intelligence on left-wing "subversives." On the board of Western Goals were congressmen, retired military officers, and Roy Cohn, Senator McCarthy's chief counsel

---

[430] Tim Alberta, "Why Trump Is Growing on Social-Conservative Leaders," *National Review* 23 October 2015:
http://www.nationalreview.com/article/425960/why-trump-growing-social-conservative-leaders-tim-alberta
[431] Eugene Scott, "In eulogizing Schlafly, Trump sees spiritual ally," *CNN* 10 September 2016:
http://www.cnn.com/2016/09/10/politics/donald-trump-phyllis-schlafly-funeral/index.html
[432] CNP. "Membership Directory 2014," 2-3.

and Trump's lawyer in the 1970s.[433] Many of these men, like Hunt himself, were also associated with the far-right John Birch Society (JBS). Robertson is a popular televangelist, founder of the Christian Broadcasting Network (CBN). DeVos, the father of Dick DeVos, is the co-founder of Amway, a multi-level marketing company. He has been one of Heritage's largest benefactors, donating more than $13 million to the think tank through the Richard and Helen DeVos Foundation.[434] One of Reagan's largest campaign donors, DeVos subsequently became the finance chair of the Republican National Committee (RNC).[435] He was the only CNP president to serve two terms, the first from 1986 to 1988 and the second from 1990 to 1993.[436]

Among the CNP's members in 2014 were Stephen K. (Steve) Bannon, senior counselor to the president in the Trump administration from January to August 2017 and the executive chairman of Breitbart News, and M. Stevenson (Steve) Forbes, the publisher of *Forbes* business magazine. 2012 Republican presidential candidate Richard J. (Rick) Santorum and Wayne R. LaPierre, the long-serving executive vice president and CEO of the National Rifle Association of America (NRA), are listed as members. Other individuals in the membership directory are Feulner,

---

[433] Scott Anderson and Jon Lee Anderson. *Inside the League: The Shocking Exposé of How Terrorists, Nazis, and Latin American Death Squads Have Infiltrated the World Anti-Communist League* (New York: Dodd, Mead and Company, 1986), 155-156.
[434] Conservative Transparency. "Top Supporters of The Heritage Foundation":
http://conservativetransparency.org/top/?recipient=29126&yr=&yr1=1980&yr2=2017&submit=
[435] Mayer, 285.
[436] CNP. "Membership Directory 2014," 3.

Meese, Singlaub, tax reform advocate Grover G. Norquist, anti-Islam Center for Security Policy (CSP) president and CEO Frank J. Gaffney, and Media Research Center (MRC) founder and president L. Brent Bozell. Raytheon and Lockheed Martin official David V. Trulio is listed as is Michael W. Grebe, at the time the president and CEO of The Lynde and Harry Bradley Foundation. The Bradley Foundation of Milwaukee is one of the leading conservative grantmaking foundations, contributing $16 million to Heritage.[437]

High-level administrators from more than a dozen conservative colleges and universities are found in the directory as well. Small and medium-sized business owners account for a large percentage of the CNP membership, in contrast to the transnational corporate and financial sector backgrounds of much of the Council on Foreign Relations membership. Each member has issues of interest noted in the directory, covering the economic, political, social, and international concerns of conservatives.[438] There is also a William F. Buckley Jr. Council for young conservatives, named in honor of the famous conservative author and commentator. One of those listed in this section is scandal-ridden Joshua J. (Josh) Duggar, who was affiliated with the FRC.[439]

An "In Memoriam" section in the 2014 directory provides some insight into the CNP's history. Joe Coors, Jerry L. Falwell, Daniel Graham, Jesse A. Helms, Larry McDonald, Howard J. Phillips, Edgar D. (Ed) Prince, Cleon Skousen, and Heritage co-founder Paul Weyrich are some of the

---

[437] Conservative Transparency. "Top Supporters of The Heritage Foundation."
[438] CNP. "Membership Directory 2014," 11-170.
[439] Ibid., 171-188.

familiar names to appear in this section.[440] One of several Republican leaders in Congress to have an affiliation with the CNP, Helms was a US senator from North Carolina for three decades and chairman of the Senate Committee on Foreign Relations in the 1990s.[441] Prince is the late father of Betsy DeVos and Erik D. Prince, founder of the private military company Blackwater. Phillips was the founder of The Conservative Caucus (TCC), a research and advocacy organization. Another deceased member is William E. Simon, who was Nixon's last secretary of the Treasury, president of the Olin Foundation, and a Heritage trustee.[442] Simon, like industrialist J. Peter Grace and a few other CNP members, became a member of the Council on Foreign Relations prior to the existence of the CNP and the rise to power of the conservative faction.[443]

LaHaye, Viguerie, and Phillips were instrumental in the creation of the Moral Majority, a political vehicle launched by Weyrich and television evangelist Falwell in 1979, which aimed to mobilize conservative Christians for the purpose of attaining Republican electoral victories. At a 1980 Christian right conference in Dallas, Weyrich told the audience: "I don't want everybody to vote. Elections are not won by a majority of people, they never have been from the beginning of our country and they are not now. As a matter of fact, our leverage in the elections quite candidly

---

[440] Ibid., 8-9.
[441] Joe Conason and Gene Lyons. *The Hunting of the President: The Ten-Year Campaign to Destroy Bill and Hillary Clinton* (New York: Thomas Dunne Books, 2000), 138.
[442] Ambinder.
[443] Internet Archive. "Collection of Membership Rosters on the CFR, Trilateral Commission, Bilderberg Group, and Rhodes Scholars": https://archive.org/details/2012BILDERBERGMEETINGSSPEC IALREPORT171

goes up as the voting populace goes down."[444] Reagan also spoke at this monumental gathering only months prior to winning the presidency.[445]

The CNP has maintained a low profile since its origins. Hunt, LaHaye and their associates recruited Reagan White House officials, conservative businessmen, and right-wing political and religious leaders. There were four hundred members by 1984.[446] Louis E. (Woody) Jenkins, a conservative Democrat and Louisiana state representative, ran the CNP from an antebellum mansion in Baton Rouge until 1985 when Washington was selected over Dallas for the location of the organization's permanent headquarters. In a CNP publication, he commented, "It is no secret that the Council for National Policy was modeled after the Council on Foreign Relations. Despite its wrong-headed philosophy, the CFR is the most influential single private organization in America today. Our greatest challenge is to have an even larger influence on public policy than has the CFR."[447] According to one CNP member, the efforts to remove George Shultz from his position as secretary of state were initiated at a Council meeting in 1985. Feulner, Weyrich, and Holland (Holly) Coors, ex-wife of Joe Coors, were executive committee members in the 1980s, and Holly Coors also served as a Heritage trustee. Infamous

---

444 peoplefor. "Paul Weyrich - 'I don't want everybody to vote'" [Video] (8 June 2007): https://www.youtube.com/watch?v=8GBAsFwPglw
445 Ronald Reagan, "Address by the Honorable Ronald Reagan to The Roundtable National Affairs Briefing (Dallas, Texas)": http://digitalcollections.library.cmu.edu/awweb/awarchive?type =file&item=684006
446 Bellant. *The Coors Connection*, 37.
447 Greg Garland, "North was member of private group once based in Baton Rouge," *The State-Times* (Baton Rouge) 8 January 1987, 1A: http://media.pfaw.org/Right/CNP-IRAN.txt

Lieutenant Colonel Oliver L. North joined the executive committee near the end of the decade.[448] By this time, each member of the CNP was paying two thousand dollars per year to be part of the organization.[449]

Over a decade later, in 2002, there were approximately five hundred CNP members. Supreme Court Justice Clarence Thomas was a keynote speaker at one of its 2002 conventions. In the wake of the CNP-supported Iraq invasion, Dick Cheney and Donald Rumsfeld attended a Council meeting and several Bush administration and campaign officials did likewise in 2004.[450] Trump addressed a CNP conclave as a presidential candidate in October 2015, as Bush had done in 1999.[451] While most of the other Republican presidential candidates also spoke at CNP conferences in 2015, including early favorite Rafael E. (Ted) Cruz, Trump's successful appearance began the gradual securing of support from the CNP and the conservative faction of the oligarchy.[452]

The CNP's history and direction of the Trump administration was explored in *Shadow Network*, a 2019 book written by journalist Anne Nelson, a member of the

---

448 Bellant. *The Coors Connection*, 37-38.
449 Ibid., 36.
450 David D. Kirkpatrick, "The 2004 Campaign: The Conservatives; Club of the Most Powerful Gathers in Strictest Privacy," *The New York Times* 28 August 2004: https://tinyurl.com/ycwyuqbn
451 Ambinder.
452 Jake Tapper and Stephen Collinson, "Conservatives in secretive group 'slow walk' Trump support," *CNN* 17 May 2016: https://www.cnn.com/2016/05/17/politics/conservatives-slow-walk-donald-trump-support/index.html

Council on Foreign Relations.[453] Nelson argues that the Trump administration has advanced the CNP's "harsh combination of plutocracy and theocracy."[454] In May 2017, Vice President Pence tweeted, "Joined the Council for National Policy, leaders in the conservative movement, who w/ @POTUS [Trump] are renewing the conservative vision in our time."[455] Steve Baldwin, a former executive director of the CNP, was obviously engaging in hyperbole when he remarked that "we control everything in the world," but the Trump administration has proven that the Council's membership is clearly a powerful political force.[456]

American Legislative Exchange Council and State Policy Network

The American Legislative Exchange Council (ALEC) and the State Policy Network (SPN), both based in Arlington, Virginia, are two organizations specializing in the formulation of policies at the state level. Co-founded in 1973 by Weyrich, ALEC is "America's largest nonpartisan, voluntary membership organization of state legislators dedicated to the principles of limited government, free markets and federalism."[457] Federalism refers to the partial restoration of the autonomy previously enjoyed by states, sometimes used synonymously with the term "states'

---

453 Columbia SIPA. "Anne Nelson":
https://sipa.columbia.edu/faculty-research/faculty-directory/anne-nelson
454 Anne Nelson. *Shadow Network: Media, Money, and the Secret Hub of the Radical Right* (New York: Bloomsbury Publishing, 2019), xv.
455 Vice President Mike Pence on Twitter (19 May 2017):
https://twitter.com/VP/status/865670477460656130
456 Ambinder.
457 ALEC. "About ALEC": https://www.alec.org/about

rights." Promoting federalism, the SPN was formed in 1992 and serves as an umbrella organization "to catalyze thriving, durable freedom movements in every state, anchored with high-performing independent think tanks" in order to achieve "lasting social change, personal freedom, and opportunity at the state and local level."[458] The Network believes "powerful elites are turning Washington, DC into an imperial city."[459] Its founder, the late Thomas A. Roe, was a South Carolina businessman and Heritage trustee, as well as a CNP member, who had a vision of creating Heritage-type think tanks at the state level.[460]

Dubbed a conservative "bill mill" by its critics, businesses pay substantial fees to attend ALEC sessions with state legislators where model legislation is drafted. These lawmakers then present versions of the bill to their own state legislatures. An average of one thousand new bills are created every year by ALEC, with about two hundred of them getting passed by state legislatures and enacted into law.[461] Areas of interest to the Council are tax reform, education, lawsuit reform, economic development, international trade, energy, transportation, health, privacy and security, and free speech, among many others.[462] In addition to a board of directors comprised of twenty-three state legislators, ALEC has a private enterprise advisory council consisting of almost twenty corporate representatives.[463] According to the CMD's *ALEC Exposed*

---

[458] SPN. "About State Policy Network": https://spn.org/state-policy-network-about
[459] Ibid.
[460] CNP. "Membership Directory 2014," 9.
[461] Mayer, 425-426.
[462] ALEC. "Issues Archive": https://www.alec.org/issue
[463] ALEC. "Leadership": https://www.alec.org/about/leadership

project, from 1998 to 2009 the Council was the recipient of $1.4 million from ExxonMobil. The Coors' Castle Rock Foundation, which merged into the Adolph Coors Foundation in 2011, was one of the grantmaking foundations that have helped finance ALEC.[464] As with Heritage, Scaife money was crucial early in the organization's existence, representing most of the Council's budget. Scaife donated approximately $500,000 to ALEC between 1973 and 1983.[465]

ALEC is an associate partner of the SPN. Heritage and the AEI are also associate partners of the Network.[466] The SPN's budget exceeded $83 million in 2011.[467] It has sixty-nine affiliated state-level think tanks with at least one in every state, bolstered by nearly one hundred associate partners.[468] "Core Programs" are listed as "Executive Leadership Program," "Policy Working Groups," "Training," and "Annual Meeting."[469] Although claiming that its members are "fiercely independent," SPN president and CEO Tracie J. Sharp told the attendees at the 2013 annual meeting that the Network's leadership would supply the resources for state think tanks to "customize" to their liking.[470] Donors Capital Fund (DCF) and affiliated Donors Trust (DT) have been the SPN's top donors since 2007.[471]

---

[464] CMD. "ALEC Exposed: What is ALEC?":
https://www.alecexposed.org/wiki/What_is_ALEC%3F
[465] Mayer, 109.
[466] SPN. "Directory": https://spn.org/directory
[467] Mayer, 425.
[468] SPN. "Directory."
[469] SPN. "Core Programs": https://spn.org
[470] Mayer, 425.
[471] Conservative Transparency. "State Policy Network":
http://conservativetransparency.org/recipient/state-policy-network

DT and DCF are designed to provide conservative donors anonymity regarding the recipients of their contributions. The Bradley Foundation, DeVos Foundation, and Charles Koch Foundation have reported funding DT and DCF. Both of these funds, as well as ALEC and the SPN themselves, have strong ties to the Koch network controlled by multi-billionaire brothers Charles G. Koch and David H. Koch until his death in 2019. They are widely considered part of the Koch network through personnel and co-hosted fundraising events.[472] The Charles Koch Institute, established in Arlington, Virginia in 2011 along with the Charles Koch Foundation, is an associate partner of the SNP. The Institute and Foundation are successors to the now defunct Charles G. Koch Charitable Foundation.

The Koch brothers have been recipients of ALEC's Adam Smith Free Enterprise Award.[473] Charles Koch saved ALEC with a $430,000 loan in 1997. In fact, the "Kochs were early financial angels of this state-focused activism."[474] Koch Industries, one of the largest privately-owned companies in the United States, was represented on ALEC's corporate board for nearly twenty years, during which time model legislation was crafted to further the oil interests of the Koch brothers' global conglomerate.[475] One of the first bills signed into law by Texas Governor George W. Bush was ALEC model legislation granting immunity to corporations if they reported their own environmental violations. ALEC bills, such as those promoting taxpayer-

---

472 Conservative Transparency. "State Policy Network."
473 Lisa Graves, "ALEC Exposed: The Koch Connection," *The Nation* 12 July 2011: https://www.thenation.com/article/alec-exposed-koch-connection
474 Mayer, 426.
475 Ibid., 426.

subsidized school vouchers, advance other areas of the Kochs' laissez-faire economic agenda as well.[476] A lobbyist for Koch Industries currently sits on ALEC's private enterprise advisory council.[477]

Headquartered in Wichita, Kansas, Koch Industries was co-founded as an oil refining company by Fred C. Koch, the father of Charles and David. Fred Koch was one of the founding members of the John Birch Society in Indianapolis, as was Harry L. Bradley, co-founder of The Bradley Foundation. Koch was actively involved in the far-right organization. Like all of its members, he feared communist infiltration in US politics and society. JBS members accused President Eisenhower himself of potentially being a communist agent. Koch's antipathy toward communism apparently stemmed from his experiences in the Stalin-era Soviet Union where his firm was contracted to build oil refineries. David Koch related being raised with "a fundamental point of view that big government was bad, and imposition of government controls on our lives and economic fortunes was not good."[478] Fred Koch and the JBS opposed desegregation, portraying it as a communist plot. Both he and the Society unwaveringly backed the presidential bid of Goldwater, who rejected the Civil Rights Act of 1964 and shared the same economic ideology. The Koch brothers were members of the JBS in the 1960s but did not adopt all of the Society's beliefs.[479]

In 1974, Charles Koch co-founded the libertarian Cato Institute in Washington and David Koch was the vice-

---

476 Graves.
477 ALEC. "Leadership."
478 Mayer, 46.
479 Ibid., 46-52.

presidential candidate for the Libertarian Party in the 1980 elections, but it was not until the early years of the new century that the brothers began to influence political processes through a massive undertaking. Their primary political vehicle is Arlington, Virginia-based Americans for Prosperity (AFP), an advocacy organization launched in 2004 that promotes "economic freedom."[480] Although the Kochs downplayed their involvement, AFP was a major sponsor of the Tea Party protests, providing training, speakers for rallies, and information on elected officials.[481] There was a definite populist component to the anti-tax Tea Party movement during the Obama era, but the support and leadership of AFP and Scaife-funded FreedomWorks were critical in its development as a political force.[482] Many right-wing causes have been the beneficiaries of Koch largesse. While David Koch claimed he was socially liberal, the Kochs' Freedom Partners donated almost $24 million to social conservative groups between 2010 and 2014.[483] Heritage has also received millions of dollars in total from the Koch family-controlled Charles R. Lambe Foundation and the Charles G. Koch Charitable Foundation.[484] Charles Koch was the recipient of an award from the CNP even though he is not a member.[485]

---

480 AFP. "About: Our Mission":
https://americansforprosperity.org/about
481 Mayer, 222-223.
482 Ibid., 223-224.
483 Irin Carmon, "Koch brother: I'm a social liberal," *MSNBC* 14 December 2014: http://www.msnbc.com/msnbc/koch-brother-im-social-liberal
484 Conservative Transparency. "Top Supporters of The Heritage Foundation."
485 Mayer, 287.

Financing political candidates has been a more direct route to political power for the Kochs. After Trump dismissed his Republican presidential contenders as "puppets" of the Kochs, the brothers focused their funding on congressional races, state elections, and even local contests. They achieved their main objective of retaining Republican control of the House of Representatives and the Senate, and secured overwhelming Republican dominance at the state level.[486] The Koch network's access to the Trump administration has been routine despite Trump's comments. David Koch attended his presidential victory party and Trump appointed Kansas Congressman Michael R. Pompeo, known as the "congressman from Koch" because of his reliance on Koch money, as his CIA director.[487] Vice President Pence was already "a trusted friend of the Koch network."[488] He was Charles Koch's choice for the presidency in 2012 and received $300,000 from David Koch for his gubernatorial campaigns in Indiana. Pence had to cancel a speaking engagement at a Kochs' donor summit after Trump selected him as his running mate.[489] Indeed, "the Kochs and their operatives have welcomed much of the fledgling administration's actions, including efforts to roll back federal regulations, the decision to pull out of the Paris global climate accord [. . .] and the appointment of Neil Gorsuch to the Supreme Court."[490]

---

[486] Ibid., xvii-xviii

[487] Ibid., 339.

[488] James Oliphant, "Once on the outside, conservative Koch network warms to Trump," *Reuters* 27 June 2017: https://tinyurl.com/y8463s2k

[489] Mayer, xiii.

[490] Oliphant.

MEDIA

Conservative faction media was undeveloped for many decades after World War II and, like the conservative power elite itself, struggled to challenge the dominance of the liberal faction. In spite of its tremendous growth in recent decades, it still does not possess the same influence at the national level in the United States. Nearly all of the major television networks and most of the leading newspapers are associated with the liberal power elite. However, the rise of the conservative faction of the oligarchy has been accompanied by an altered media landscape with the simultaneous rise of an affiliated media whose political views now reach a wide audience and shape the worldviews of much of the US population.

In the immediate postwar period, the weekly newspaper *Human Events* served as the principal conservative media outlet. Co-founded in 1944 by Henry Regnery and other "isolationists" with a donation of $3,000 from the vice president of Sun Oil Company (now Sunoco), it became the leading voice of the incipient conservative faction. In its vehement rejection of the New Deal, editor Frank Hanighen identified "man versus the state" as the most pressing issue of the epoch.[491] Beginning with only 117 subscribers, *Human Events* would develop into a major publication by the 1960s, strongly endorsing Goldwater in 1964 and moving from an anti-interventionist position in international relations to support an anti-communist foreign policy.[492]

---

[491] Diamond, 26.
[492] Ibid., 24-25

Human Events was purchased in 2019 by British alt-right activist and editor Raheem Kassam.[493] "U.S. Politics," "Foreign Affairs," "Tech," and "Culture" are the main sections of the now online-only publication.[494] It was previously owned by the Salem Media Group, which also owns Regnery Publishing.[495] Reagan named *Human Events* as his "favorite newspaper" and under Salem ownership it defended "the Reaganesque principles of free enterprise, limited government and, above all, a staunch, unwavering defense of American freedom."[496] Columnists included Patrick J. Buchanan, Ann H. Coulter, Newt Gingrich, Michelle Malkin, and George F. Will. Will, a "pragmatic conservative," also appeared in the liberal faction media and like renowned author William F. (Bill) Buckley was one of the few token conservative members of the Council on Foreign Relations.[497]

Disappointed in his inability to purchase *Human Events*, Buckley launched a new biweekly magazine called *National Review* in 1955. Buckley wrote *God and Man at Yale*, published by Regnery Publishing in 1951. In the book, he lambasted his secular and liberal education at the Ivy

---

[493] Erik Wemple, "Breitbart alum to resuscitate Human Events," *The Washington Post* 1 March 2019:
https://www.washingtonpost.com/opinions/2019/03/01/breitb
art-alum-resuscitate-human-events
[494] Human Events. "About HE":
http://humanevents.com/about-human-events
[495] Salem Media Group. "Businesses":
http://salemmedia.com/businesses
[496] Human Events. "About Human Events" (archived 16 January 2019):
https://web.archive.org/web/20190116131254/http://humaneve
nts.com/about-human-events
[497] Human Events. "Columnists" (archived 16 January 2019):
https://web.archive.org/web/20190116131254/http://humaneve
nts.com/about-human-events

League university.[498] Under Buckley's control, *National Review* fused different currents of conservative thought, uniting social conservatives with right-wing libertarians.[499] By the 1960s, Buckley and his publication sought to marginalize the JBS and racist and anti-semitic elements in conservative circles.[500] However, like the JBS, he opposed civil rights legislation and defended segregation. Staunchly anti-communist and pro-rollback in its foreign policy views, with a circulation of 70,000 at the time *National Review* intensely promoted Goldwater and his candidacy. Thereafter Reagan became the great hope for the right. He was a good friend of Buckley and a reader of the magazine. The president told *National Review* at its anniversary celebration in 1985: "You didn't just part the Red Sea -- you rolled it back, dried it up and left exposed, for all the world to see, the naked desert that is statism."[501] Even without Buckley, who died in 2008, *National Review* remains a widely read publication on the right, featuring a diversity of conservative ideologies.

Several other magazines are voices of the conservative power elite. *The American Spectator* has been a prominent one since the 1980s, attracting a broad readership in the 1990s when Scaife, financer of the monthly since 1970, used it as a vehicle in an attempt to sabotage Clinton's

---

[498] Diamond, 30.

[499] Jonah Goldberg, "Fusionism, 60 Years Later," *National Review* 5 November 2015:
https://www.nationalreview.com/2015/11/fusionism-conservatives-libertarians-success-national-review

[500] Brennan, 15-17.

[501] Douglas Martin, "William F. Buckley Jr. Is Dead at 82," *The New York Times* 27 February 2008:
http://www.nytimes.com/2008/02/27/business/media/27cnd-buckley.html

presidency through the "Arkansas Project."[502] Other major financial backers in the 1970s were South Carolina textile tycoon Roger Milliken and California oil magnate and Reagan advisor Henry Salvatori. Both men were CNP members and actively involved with The Heritage Foundation.[503] The Bradley Foundation later funded the magazine as well.[504] Alfred S. Regnery, the son of Henry Regnery, was the *Spectator*'s publisher and president from 2003 until 2012. During the 1980s, he served in the Reagan Justice Department.[505] The *Spectator* advocates "economic freedom, individual liberty, limited government, and traditional American values."[506] Its editor-in-chief, R. Emmett Tyrrell, played a key role in the anti-Clinton crusade.[507]

Some daily newspapers reached audiences in local markets. A few were associated with the ASC, such as the

---

[502] Washington Post Staff, "'Arkansas Project' Led to Turmoil and Rifts," *The Washington Post* 2 May 1999, A24:
https://www.washingtonpost.com/wp-srv/politics/special/clinton/stories/scaifeside050299.htm
[503] Jonathan M. Katz, "The Man Who Launched the GOP's Civil War: How a textile magnate turned the Party of Lincoln into the Party of Trump," *Politico Magazine* 1 October 2015:
https://www.politico.com/magazine/story/2015/10/roger-milliken-republican-party-history-213212
[504] Byron York, "The Life and Death of The American Spectator," *The Atlantic* November 2001:
https://www.theatlantic.com/magazine/archive/2001/11/the-life-and-death-of-the-american-spectator/302343
CNP. "Membership Directory 2014," 8-9.
[505] Michael W. Chapman, "Conservative Al Regnery Resigns as Publisher of The American Spectator," *CNSNews.com* 23 February 2012:
https://www.cnsnews.com/news/article/conservative-al-regnery-resigns-publisher-american-spectator
[506] Spectator. "About": https://spectator.org/about
[507] Washington Post Staff.

St. Louis Globe-Democrat and right-wing libertarian *The Detroit News*.[508] The *Chicago Tribune* had a similar libertarian editorial policy. Paleoconservative author and politician Pat Buchanan, who is a columnist for *Human Events* and has written for the *Spectator*, began his journalism career at the *St. Louis Globe-Democrat*. In 1970, Scaife acquired the small-market *Tribune-Review* in the Pittsburgh suburb of Greensburg, expanding into Pittsburgh in the early 1990s to create the new *Pittsburgh Tribune-Review*. Its editorial position reflected Scaife's right-wing politics. One of its journalists, Christopher W. Ruddy, would found multiplatform Newsmax Media in 1998 assisted by an investment from Scaife and build it into one of the nation's leading conservative media outlets.[509] Ruddy sat on the CNP board of governors in 2014.[510]

In 1982, the launch of *The Washington Times* changed the media landscape in the nation's capital. The newspaper was established by Unification Church leader Reverend Sun Myung Moon as a subsidiary of his News World Communications corporation. Moon's committed anti-communism made him a natural ally of the conservative power elite. He proclaimed that communism was "satanic" in his sermons. In *Our Times*, a book from Regnery Publishing edited by Lee Edwards, *The Washington Times* columnist Arnold Beichman observed that from "the very first day, the *Times* dared to speak in what Washington

---

[508] Turner, 203.
[509] Newsmax Wires. "Ruddy: Dick Scaife Had 'Zeal and Dedication' for America," *Newsmax* 2014 July 4: https://www.newsmax.com/Newsfront/Chrisotpher-Ruddy-Dick-Scaife/2014/07/04/id/580896
[510] CNP. "Membership Directory 2014," 7.

liberal elites regarded as a discordant voice."[511] Reagan, a daily reader of the newspaper during his tenure, stated in 1997: "The American people know the truth. You, my friends at *The Washington Times*, have told it to them. It wasn't always the popular thing to do. But you were a loud and powerful voice. Like me, you arrived in Washington at the beginning of the most momentous decade of the century. Together, we rolled up our sleeves and got to work. And--oh, yes--we won the Cold War."[512] The newspaper's opinion editor, David A. Keene, was listed as a CNP member in the 2014 directory, having just completed his term as president of the NRA.[513]

It was not until 1996 that a permanent conservative presence on US television was established when Australian-American media mogul Rupert Murdoch created the Fox News Channel. Murdoch characterized CNN as too liberal when he launched his news network.[514] His vast media holdings in the United States, Britain, and Australia promote his right-wing views. One of Murdoch's former editors for UK's *The Sunday Times* accurately described Fox News when he wrote, "Rupert expects his papers to stand broadly for what he believes: a combination of right-wing Republicanism from America mixed with undiluted Thatcherism from Britain [. . .] the resulting potage is a radical-right dose of free market economics, the social agenda of the Christian Moral

---

[511] Arnold Beichman, "Washington's Conscience," in Lee Edwards (ed.). *Our Times: The Washington Times* (Washington, DC: Regnery Publishing, 2002), 172.
[512] John Gorenfeld, "Dear Leader's Paper Moon," *The American Prospect* 19 June 2005: http://prospect.org/article/dear-leaders-paper-moon
[513] CNP. "Membership Directory 2014," 90.
[514] Robert Manne (ed.). *Do Not Disturb: Is the Media Failing Australia?* (Melbourne, Australia: Black Inc., 2005), 71.

Majority and hard-line conservative views on subjects like drugs, abortion, law and order and defence."[515] When Murdoch's News Corporation purchased *The Wall Street Journal* in 2007, his second US newspaper after buying the *New York Post* in 1976, he acquired control over a daily with one of the highest circulations in the United States and one that had long espoused the economic policies embraced by the conservative faction.[516]

Fox News has supplied an outlet for members of the conservative power elite. Oliver North, Newt Gingrich, and Steve Forbes are among the many individuals who have made regular appearances on the network. Sean P. Hannity, Laura A. Ingraham, and Tucker S. Carlson are Fox News' current stars. Heritage showcases Hannity's endorsement on its website: "No organization on earth is a better supplier of innovative, conservative ideas grounded in founding principles than Heritage."[517] Of all of the major news networks, Fox News has been the only one to provide Trump with favorable coverage.[518] Murdoch and Trump have been friends for years and have remained in close contact since Trump won the presidency. They met through Roy Cohn, their mutual attorney and mentor.[519] In

---

[515] Ibid., 72.
[516] WorldAtlas. "The 10 Most Popular Daily Newspapers In The United States" (updated 1 August 2017):
http://www.worldatlas.com/articles/the-10-most-popular-daily-newspapers-in-the-united-states.html
[517] Heritage. "About Heritage: Impact":
http://www.heritage.org/about-heritage/impact
[518] Thomas E. Patterson, "News Coverage of Donald Trump's First 100 Days," *Harvard Kennedy School Shorenstein Center* 18 May 2017: https://tinyurl.com/kel4lwf
[519] Lucia Graves, "Donald Trump and Rupert Murdoch: inside the billionaire bromance," *The Guardian* 16 June 2017:
www.theguardian.com/us-news/2017/jun/16/donald-trump-rupert-murdoch-friendship-fox-news

recent years, Fox News has faced some competition on the right. Newsmax TV was launched in 2014 and is available on cable as well as on the Internet where it is streamed live for free.[520]

The phenomenon of conservative talk radio, arising in the late 1980s after the elimination of the Fairness Doctrine by the US Federal Communications Commission (FCC), has contributed significantly to the dissemination of right-wing views in the United States. Rush H. Limbaugh and Glenn L. Beck are famous conservative radio personalities whose shows are nationally syndicated and reach millions of Americans. Soros, Obama, and the Clintons are popular targets on conservative radio talk shows. Many of Trump's strongest backers in the general public, his "base," are listeners.[521] The Trump administration hosted a marathon event in July 2017 in which nineteen conservative radio hosts from the Salem Media Group broadcasted from the White House.[522] Trump himself participated in interviews with conservative radio personalities a few months later.[523] Trump's 2015 guest appearance on the *Infowars* program

---

[520] Rebecca Savransky, "Trump friend: 'Bizarre' Fox News so 'closely aligned' with Trump," *The Hill* 9 November 2017: http://thehill.com/homenews/media/359623-trump-friend-bizarre-fox-news-so-closely-aligned-with-trump
[521] Sabrina Tavernise, "Conservative Talk Radio Stands by Trump Despite Turmoil," *The New York Times* 15 February 2017: https://www.nytimes.com/2017/02/15/us/conservative-talk-radio-trump.html
[522] Jennifer Harper, "Trump media: 19 talk radio hosts broadcast live from the White House on Tuesday," *The Washington Times* 24 July 2017: https://www.washingtontimes.com/news/2017/jul/24/inside-the-beltway-19-talk-radio-hosts-broadcast-f
[523] Inside Radio. "Trump Momentarily Returns To Key Ally: Conservative Radio" (18 October 2017): https://tinyurl.com/yb8kqo2c

hosted by alt-right radio host Alexander E. (Alex) Jones reached a receptive audience, and according to Jones, Trump called to thank him after winning the presidency.[524]

Diverse media platforms, from newspapers and magazines to television networks and radio programs, have been established by the conservative faction since World War II to influence society and realize its political agenda. As conservative media extended its reach, power at the national level became obtainable. Yet it was Reagan's victory and subsequent Reagan Revolution that acted as the major catalyst for conservative media growth. In fact, the common element uniting today's "media figures and venues into a conservative media establishment is their embrace of the tenets of Reagan conservatism."[525]

CONCLUSION

Through its think tanks, grantmaking foundations, and media, the conservative faction of the oligarchy has risen from its weak post-WWII position vis-à-vis the liberal faction. The right-wing transformation of the Republican Party beginning in the 1960s and the plutocratic funding surge in the 1970s culminated in the Reagan Revolution of the 1980s. Post-Cold War decline was overcome by the Republican Revolution in Congress during the 1990s and in the new century the conservative power elite has sustained a serious rivalry with its liberal counterpart,

---

[524] Shane Goldmacher, "Alex Jones says Trump called to thank him," *Politico* 14 November 2016: https://www.politico.com/story/2016/11/trump-thanked-alex-jones-231329

[525] Kathleen H. Jamieson and Joseph N. Cappella. *Echo Chamber: Rush Limbaugh and the Conservative Media Establishment* (Oxford, UK: Oxford University Press, 2008), xi.

reaching new heights with Trump. While his election and presidency have polarized the general public, at the highest level of power the oligarchy has also entered a period of acute factional conflict in the Trump era.

CHAPTER 4
ANTI-COMMUNIST ALLIES: THE INTERNATIONAL CONNECTIONS OF THE CONSERVATIVE FACTION

As is the case with its liberal counterpart, the conservative power elite was active in an international network during the Cold War. In contrast to the liberal faction's transnational network, however, none of these organized connections were initiated by the conservative faction. Rather, European and Asian hardline anti-communists established Le Cercle and the World Anti-Communist League (WACL), respectively. Americans were recruited by these groups and then became indispensable to their anti-communist campaigns. This alliance also incorporated fascist elements from several continents.

LE CERCLE

Highly confidential, the Cercle has been even more publicity shy than the Bilderberg Group. It is "a right-wing think-tank set up at the height of the Cold War for senior politicians, diplomats and intelligence agents which is one of the most influential, secretive, and, it goes without saying, exclusive political clubs in the West."[526] Organized in 1952-1953 by French Prime Minister Antoine Pinay and

---

[526] Chris Blackhurst, "Aitken dropped by the Right's secret club," *The Independent* 28 June 1997:
http://www.independent.co.uk/news/aitken-dropped-by-the-rights-secret-club-1258522.html

his compatriot Jean Violet, it was also referred to as Le Cercle Pinay with Pinay serving as the chairman. He would soon become a regular Bilderberg attendee. Violet, a Parisian lawyer, worked as an agent for France's foreign intelligence agency. West German chancellor Konrad H. Adenauer and federal minister Franz Josef Strauss of Bavaria co-founded the Cercle. The promotion of French-German reconciliation after World War II was given priority.[527] Violet "played an historically key role between 1957 and 1961 in bringing about this [Franco-German] rapprochement, which is the real core of the European Community [. . .] The Pinay Cercle was a natural offshoot of Jean Violet's Franco-German activities."[528]

A long-term ambition of Cercle members was the realization of a Catholic-dominated Europe. French statesman J.B. Robert Schuman and diplomat Jean O. Monnet, two of the founding fathers of the European Union (EU), were Cercle members along with Otto von Habsburg, the last crown prince of Austria-Hungary. Within a short time, government officials from Italy, the Netherlands, Belgium, and Luxembourg joined the forum. Together with France and West Germany, these countries were the signatories of the Treaty of Rome in 1957 which created the European Economic Community (EEC). The religious character of the early Cercle membership persisted, with a large number of Opus Dei and Sovereign

---

[527] Adrian Hänni, "A Global Crusade against Communism: The Cercle in the 'Second Cold War,'" in Luc van Dongen, Stéphanie Roulin, and Giles Scott-Smith (eds.). *Transnational Anti-Communism and the Cold War: Agents, Activities, and Networks* (New York: Palgrave Macmillan, 2014), 161.
[528] David Teacher. *Rogue Agents: The Cercle and the 6I in the Private Cold War 1951-1991* (December 2015), 21.

Military Order of Malta (SMOM or Knights of Malta) members attending Cercle meetings over the years.[529]

David Rockefeller was the first American to participate in the Cercle. Then-national security advisor Kissinger attended the Cercle's Washington gatherings. In *Memoirs*, Rockefeller recounted his membership in the group, beginning in 1967 when Italian tycoon Carlo Pesenti invited him. Rockefeller noted the commitment to European integration but also the preoccupation with the communist threat, identifying Violet and Habsburg among others: "Using an overhead projector, Violet displayed transparency after transparency filled with data documenting Soviet infiltration of governments around the world and supporting his belief that the threat of global Communist victory was quite real. While all of us knew the Soviets were behind the 'wars of national liberation' in Asia, Africa, and Latin America, I was not personally convinced the Red Menace was quite as menacing as Maître Violet portrayed it to be, but my view was a minority one in that group." After an undisclosed amount of time, Rockefeller terminated his Cercle membership: "Even though I found some of the discussions fascinating, the ultraconservative politics of some participants were more than a bit unnerving. My Chase associates, who feared my membership could be construed as 'consorting with reactionaries,' eventually prevailed upon me to withdraw."[530]

In the 1970s, the Cercle expanded its membership geographically by incorporating British persons.

---

[529] Hänni, 161-162.
[530] David Rockefeller. *Memoirs* (New York: Random House, 2002), 412-413.

Australian-born Brian R. Crozier became the most active British figure in the forum. A militant anti-communist, he worked for both US and British intelligence. Crozier, a columnist for *National Review* in the United States for eighteen years, was recruited to the Cercle by Violet in 1971.[531] In 1970, he had founded the Institute for the Study of Conflict (ISC) in London while running the CIA's Forum World Features (FWF) press service.[532] Richard Scaife legally owned FWF and donated $100,000 per year to the ISC in the 1970s.[533] In the mid-1970s, the Cercle and the ISC "unleash[ed] a propaganda offensive against the [UK] Labour government and its union supporters."[534] Margaret H. Thatcher's rise to the leadership of the Conservative Party and the country was facilitated by this right-wing offensive.[535] Another prominent British member of the Cercle was H. Julian Amery, a Conservative member of parliament who would assume the chairmanship upon Pinay's retirement in 1980, the same year Violet transferred the forum's organizational responsibilities to Crozier.[536]

British and American men were the largest contingent in the Cercle by the 1980s as the forum developed a distinctly transatlantic character. The delegation from the United States "counted among its ranks an impressive number of senior officials from the key bodies which planned and implemented US foreign and security policy."[537] These

---

[531] John O'Sullivan, "Brian Crozier, Cold Warrior, R.I.P.,"
National Review 7 August 2012:
http://www.nationalreview.com/corner/313341
[532] Hänni, 163.
[533] Teacher, 37.
[534] Ibid., 82.
[535] Ibid., 82-83.
[536] Hänni, 163.
[537] Hänni, 165.

included officials from the CIA, National Security Council, and Defense Department, as well as veteran intelligence officers.[538] Former CIA Director William E. Colby attended the December 1979 convention.[539] He was a regular member along with Bill Casey, Reagan's CIA director.[540] Colby's ex-deputy, Vernon A. Walters, was a Cercle member and would serve as UN ambassador in Reagan's second term.[541] Former president Richard Nixon was in attendance at an early 1983 Cercle meeting along with Richard V. Allen, Reagan's first national security advisor.[542] Fred C. Iklé, under-secretary of defense for policy in the Reagan administration, attended the February 1985 meeting in Washington with his deputy, General Richard Stilwell.[543] Stilwell and Admiral Thomas Moorer, an ex-chairman of the Joint Chiefs of Staff, were two directors of the American Security Council at this assembly.[544] Reagan's first ambassador to the Vatican, SMOM member William A. Wilson, acted as the president's "personal link" with the Cercle.[545]

Other figures in the conservative power elite, particularly ones affiliated with The Heritage Foundation, also attended Cercle conferences and were thus referred to as "members" by the forum. Ed Feulner, Heritage president since 1977, participated in the December 1979 assembly in Washington.[546] Heritage co-founder Paul Weyrich attended the 1982 conclave in Wildbad Kreuth, Germany and the

---

[538] Ibid., 165.
[539] Teacher, 184.
[540] Blackhurst.
[541] Hänni, 164.
[542] Teacher, 266.
[543] Ibid., 269.
[544] Ibid., 273.
[545] Hänni, 165.
[546] Teacher, 255.

"Cercle's strong transatlantic connections to the American section of WACL and the Heritage Foundation would continue at its July 1983 meeting in Bonn in the person of veteran right-wing multi-functionary Lee Edwards."[547] Heritage analyst Jeffrey B. Gayner participated in several gatherings, including the one in July 1984 again in Bonn and the February 1985 meeting in Washington.[548] As the conservative faction of the US oligarchy rose to a position of power in the late 1970s and 1980s, the Cercle's European leadership sought out its substantial involvement whereas previously there was only minimal and short-lived US representation, namely liberal faction luminaries Rockefeller and Kissinger.

In 1976, Pesenti had created an inner circle or "executive staff" of Cercle leaders. Its purpose was "to enlarge the sphere of action of the Cercle and study methods of influence," establishing some of the Cercle's priorities without input from the rest of the forum.[549] The inner circle met periodically during the 1980s. At its 1980 meeting in Zurich directed by Violet, Crozier and Stilwell were among the participants. Others present were J. Nicholas Elliott, former station chief of the UK's foreign intelligence service MI6, retired CIA senior officer Donald (Jamie) Jameson, and Hans Graf Huyn, a retired diplomat who at the time was a member of the Bundestag, Germany's parliament. Huyn was an active member of WACL as well. One of the inner circle's plans was to influence developments in apartheid South Africa "from a European Conservative viewpoint."[550]

---

[547] Ibid., 263, 268.
[548] Ibid., 268-269.
[549] Hänni, 164.
[550] Ibid., 164.

South Africa played a central role in the Cercle throughout the 1980s, both in terms of participation and funding. Along with European companies and a few other sources, the South African Department of Foreign Affairs financed the forum until the early 1990s. South Africa's government was the only one to select an official delegation to attend Cercle meetings, composed of senior officials and ambassadors. A few South African businessmen also attended Cercle gatherings. The Cercle and the apartheid regime collaborated on a campaign to improve the image of the country, initiated in the 1970s. In a display of its appreciation, the South African government arranged a visit of Cercle members to the country in 1988.[551]

The Reagan Doctrine benefited from Cercle and South African assistance in its rollback strategy. Crozier and others were convinced that the Soviet Union had to be destroyed and rollback was the means to achieving this objective. Crozier prepared "The Case for a Roll-Back in the 1980s," a memorandum he shared with US national security advisor William P. Clark, who in turn examined it with Reagan. Crozier subsequently discussed it at the White House and CIA in December 1982. Prime Minister Thatcher was also supplied with a copy. It argued for intervention against Soviet-friendly countries in the Global South. Amery, the Cercle chairman, declared at a February 1986 Cercle meeting in Washington: "The principle of supporting anti-Soviet Freedom Fighters has thus been accepted. We need now to ensure that help is given to them on a sufficient scale. It is urgent that this should be done if we are to deter the Soviet Union."[552] With South African military and intelligence cooperation, Marxist-Leninist

---

[551] Ibid., 165-167.
[552] Ibid., 167.

governments in Angola and Mozambique were targeted for rollback. Anti-government forces in Afghanistan, another country on the rollback list, were connected to the Cercle through Fatima Gailani, the daughter of a Mujahideen-affiliated leader.[553] In 1991, Reagan wrote to Crozier: "we were allies in the fight against the evil Communism and it looks like we scored."[554]

Despite the Cercle's obsession with communism and the Soviet Union, the end of the Cold War did not render the forum obsolete. Post-Cold War, "the confidential talking shop for about 70 politicians, businessmen, polemicists and personnel from the diplomatic and security services" continued with its mission of "advocating right-wing causes round the world."[555] The US section was led by Theodore G. (Ted) Shackley, a former deputy director of covert operations for the CIA who was involved in some of the most sensitive and contentious operations in the agency's history. Nicknamed "the blond ghost," Shackley had attended the Cercle in the 1980s.[556] He registered The Atlantic Cercle, Inc. to his home address in Miami in 1994.[557] The corporation's assets and his estate were donated to the Association of Former Intelligence Officers (AFIO) upon his death in 2002.[558]

Since the mid-1990s, all Cercle chairmen have been British. The most recent confirmed chairman is Nadhim

---

[553] Ibid., 167-168.
[554] Ibid., 170.
[555] Blackhurst.
[556] Teacher, 189.
[557] The Atlantic Circle. "Le Cercle: A Statement on Origin and Function":
http://web.archive.org/web/20010428032018/http://www.atla
nticcircle.com:80
[558] Teacher, 391.

Zahawi, a Conservative member of parliament who backed the pro-Brexit campaign for the UK's withdrawal from the EU.[559] Previous chairman Michael Ancram (Marquess of Lothian), a Conservative member of the House of Lords, argued that Brexit would prevent "sell[ing] ourselves out of national existence."[560] Ancram succeeded former Chancellor of the Exchequer Norman S. Lamont in 2010. Lord Lamont served as Cercle chairman for thirteen years.[561] More information is extremely difficult to obtain because the Cercle's secrecy has remained intense. One UK newspaper was told by a Cercle member that he could not discuss the group "even off, off the record."[562]

WORLD ANTI-COMMUNIST LEAGUE

The East Asian origins of WACL were the result of the post-WWII communist takeover of China and the stalemate of the Korean War. Taiwan and South Korea "were desperately seeking anti-communist allies throughout the world. An organization in which conservative leaders from the United States and Europe could meet with their Asian counterparts seemed a good avenue for this."[563]

---

[559] John Johnston, "Top Tories face questions over links to secretive foreign affairs group," *PoliticsHome* 22 July 2019: https://www.politicshome.com/news/article/excl-top-tories-face-questions-over-links-to-secretive-foreign-affairs-group
[560] Michael Ancram, "After 40 years of being lied to, it's time to leave the EU," *The Telegraph* 25 April 2016: https://www.telegraph.co.uk/news/2016/04/25/after-40-years-of-being-lied-to-its-time-to-leave-the-eu
[561] Teacher, 459.
[562] Blackhurst.
[563] Scott Anderson and Jon Lee Anderson. *Inside the League: The Shocking Exposé of How Terrorists, Nazis, and Latin American Death Squads Have Infiltrated the World Anti-Communist League* (New York: Dodd, Mead and Company, 1986), 47.

Established in 1954, the Asian Peoples' Anti-Communist League (APACL), the forerunner of WACL, was formed by Chiang Kai-shek's Kuomintang regime in Taiwan and South Korean intelligence.[564] The APACL "was born out of the desire of these two nations to cement ties with potential friends in other parts of the world, as well as to justify their own dictatorships."[565] Philippines president Elpidio R. Quirino assisted in its creation and South Vietnam was the next country to join the League.[566]

Although the APACL was co-organized by the South Korean state under the presidency of Syngman Rhee, dictator Park Chung-hee is credited with raising the stature of the Korean chapter and the APACL in the 1960s. Park hired US professor David Rowe to revamp the chapter. High-ranking military officers and presidential advisors started to participate in the organization's activities as "the new ruling elite of South Korea could meet, confer, and negotiate informally with influential military officers and parliamentarians from throughout the world."[567] Both South Korea and Taiwan were highly dependent on US government assistance in the 1950s and former US intelligence officers have suggested that APACL and WACL funding was supplied covertly by US government agencies. Chiang's backers in the US "China lobby," comprised of congressmen and businessmen who focused their anti-

---

[564] Ibid., 47.
[565] Ibid., 51.
[566] Pierre Abramovici, "The World Anti-Communist League: Origins, Structures and Activities," in Luc van Dongen, Stéphanie Roulin, and Giles Scott-Smith (eds.). *Transnational Anti-Communism and the Cold War: Agents, Activities, and Networks* (New York: Palgrave Macmillan, 2014), 117.
[567] Anderson and Anderson, 53.

communist campaign on East Asia, also supported the APACL's formation.[568]

Another founding organization of WACL, in this case originally based in Eastern Europe, was a group named the Anti-Bolshevik Bloc of Nations (ABN). It was created in 1943 near the peak of World War II by Ukrainian nationalists who had fought under German command in the Nazi invasion of the Soviet Union. Yaroslav Stetsko would not only serve as chairman of the ABN from its inception until his death in 1986, he also headed Stepan A. Bandera's wing of the Organization of Ukrainian Nationalists (OUN-B) beginning in 1968. Together with its Ukrainian Insurgent Army (UPA) paramilitary arm, the OUN-B was responsible for the barbaric ethnic cleansing of Poles in Nazi-occupied Poland from 1943 to 1944. After the war, emigrant groups from Soviet republics and every country of the Eastern Bloc, many of them established by Nazi collaborators living in exile in the West, joined the ABN and it adopted a formal structure. Of the eleven members of the ABN central committee in 1980, a minimum of seven were accused war criminals.[569] An admirer of Chiang's ruthless anti-communism, Stetsko attended APACL conferences in the 1950s and 1960s and traveled to Taiwan numerous times, laying the groundwork for WACL.[570]

Stetsko was present in Mexico City at the World Anti-Communist Congress in 1958, an early attempt to unite various regional anti-communist outfits.[571] Delegates from five continents attended the conference. In 1960 and 1961,

---

[568] Abramovici, 117.
[569] Anderson and Anderson, 35-36.
[570] Ibid., 20.
[571] Ibid., 21.

French political scientist Suzanne Labin organized international conferences in Paris and Rome, another effort to integrate the regional bodies.[572] One of the attendees was Le Cercle founder Antoine Pinay.[573] The American Security Council was represented at the conclaves and Labin subsequently published a long article in the ASC's *Washington Report*, detailing plans for an international organization "to counteract Soviet political warfare."[574] She identified the APACL as a model. A few years later, at the annual APACL congress in Seoul, South Korea in 1966, WACL was finally founded. Its original assembly was held in Taipei, the Taiwanese capital, in September 1967 and representatives from sixty countries participated, including the US China lobby. The League would be structured around national and regional chapters as well as non-governmental organizations, notably ones with a right-wing Christian orientation.[575]

In addition to the presence of the APACL and ABN, Latin America had significant representation in WACL from the outset. Its leading organization in the initial years was the Mexican Anti-Communist Federation (FEMACO).[576] FEMACO was a front for the pro-Nazi Tecos secret society based at the Autonomous University of Guadalajara. At the annual WACL conference in 1972 in Mexico City, the Latin American Anti-Communist Confederation (CAL) was established "as a joint initiative of several groups

---

[572] Abramovici, 119.
[573] Teacher, 28.
[574] Abramovici, 120.
[575] Ibid., 120-121.
[576] Fernando López. *The Feathers of Condor: Transnational State Terrorism, Exiles and Civilian Anticommunism in South America* (Newcastle upon Tyne, UK: Cambridge Scholars Publishing, 2016), 286.

connected with various national intelligence services, internal security services and armed forces."[577] Like the APACL and ABN, CAL had its own publication and the three of them exchanged and reprinted articles.[578] The president of FEMACO became the CAL chairman.[579] He also served as an executive board member of WACL.[580] The first US chapter of the League, the American Council for World Freedom (ACWF), uncovered the neo-Nazism of the Tecos but did little to combat it, eventuating in turmoil within WACL as the head of the UK chapter then used the findings in an unsuccessful attempt to expose the extremism of League members.[581]

The ACWF was established in 1970 through the endeavors of conservative faction stalwart Lee Edwards, who would become its first secretary. ASC head John Fisher was the ACWF's first chairman.[582] Among the membership were conservative congressmen and such right-wing figures as future CNP member Reed J. Irvine, founder of the Scaife-funded media watchdog Accuracy in Media (AIM).[583] Pro-segregation South Carolina Senator J. Strom Thurmond addressed a League conference in the early 1970s as did the ASC's Admiral John McCain in 1974.[584] Stefan T. Possony, a member of the advisory council behind the SDI or "Star Wars" project adopted by Reagan, undertook the process for the ACWF's application for admission to WACL. It was Possony who would soon conduct the confidential

---

577 Abramovici, 121.
578 López, 286.
579 Abramovici, 121-123.
580 Anderson and Anderson, 79.
581 Ibid., 85-89.
582 Bellant. *Old Nazis*, 65.
583 CNP. "Membership Directory 2014," 8.
584 Teacher, 339.

investigation on the Mexican chapter's virulent anti-semitism. Despite the ACWF's relative passivity on the subject, CAL viewed the US chapter as an enemy because of Possony's report. In 1974, the ACWF hosted WACL's annual convention in Washington, introducing a motion against anti-semitism and extremism. Due at least in part to the reaction of CAL and a lack of support from the WACL leadership, the following year the ACWF withdrew from the League.[585]

However, the Council on American Affairs (CAA) would be launched in 1975 and join WACL as the new US chapter in 1976. Its founder, UK-born anthropologist Roger Pearson, had much in common with these League members. He had a background in the promotion of racial eugenics, first as the head of the Northern League in Europe and then as an editor for the magazine of the far-right Liberty Lobby in the United States while also writing books for its publishing arm. After several academic appointments, Pearson settled in Washington and started the CAA as well as its publication, *The Journal of Social, Political, and Economic Studies (JSPES)*, still published today with Pearson as the general editor.[586] A defense of apartheid South Africa as vital to the anti-communist cause appeared in *JSPES*. Senator Jesse Helms and conservative Congressman Jack F. Kemp authored articles for the journal.[587] Other authors or co-authors were Lieutenant General Daniel Graham and Ray Cline of the ASC, and Ed

---

[585] Anderson and Anderson, 83-90.

[586] Ibid., 92-95.
JSPES. "About The Journal for Social, Political, and Economic Studies": http://www.jspes.org/about.html

[587] Haroon Kharem. *A Curriculum of Repression: A Pedagogy of Racial History in the United States* (New York: Peter Lang Publishing, 2006), 133.

Feulner and Jeffrey Gayner of Heritage.[588] *National Review* writer Ernest van den Haag, a Dutch-born sociologist known for his pro-segregation views, was also affiliated with both Heritage and *JSPES*. In turn, Pearson sat on the editorial board of Heritage's *Policy Review* and on the board of the ASC's American Foreign Policy Institute while editing its *Journal of International Relations*.[589]

As the host of the 1978 WACL congress in Washington, Pearson became the League's chairman for one year. Impressed with the anti-communist extremism of most WACL chapters, "Pearson saw the weak link was in Western Europe."[590] He set out to transform the relatively moderate European branch (EUROWACL). Fascists, many with Nazi ties, were recruited by Pearson through the Northern League and the followers of Swedish fascist Per C. Engdahl. At the convention, Western European Nazi collaborators and fascists were among the delegates. The older Western European chapters protested their inclusion and threatened to end their own participation in the League.[591]

The negative publicity from a 1978 article in *The Washington Post* proved detrimental to Pearson's aspirations. It described the "fascist specter" behind WACL, detailing the background of Pearson and his League associates.[592] After it appeared, Pearson was asked to resign from the editorial board at Heritage, but he

---

588 Teacher, 267.
589 Bellant. *Old Nazis*, 61-63.
590 Anderson and Anderson, 96.
591 Ibid., 96-100.
592 Paul W. Valentine, "The Fascist Specter behind the World Anti-Red League," *The Washington Post* 28 May 1978, C1.

maintained his positions with the ASC.[593] In 1980, the WACL executive board requested his resignation in order to resolve the League's internal conflict.[594] Pearson would continue his publishing and political work. He received a letter from President Reagan in 1982 acknowledging his "substantial contributions to promoting and upholding those ideas and principles that we value at home and abroad."[595] The White House refused to renounce Pearson or the letter when journalists discovered it in 1984.[596] During this time, Stetsko and other leaders from the ABN would be welcomed by Reagan at the White House.[597]

A third US chapter would soon be established. In 1981, Major General John Singlaub of the ASC and CNP attended the annual WACL conclave as an observer. League leaders asked him to form a new chapter and loaned him money to organize it. Another early financier was Joe Coors.[598] Named the United States Council for World Freedom (USCWF), Singlaub invited associates with national security and foreign policy experience and created "a body of powerful and respected American conservatives the likes of which the League had never seen."[599] The USCWF formed the North American regional unit of WACL (NARWACL) together with the Canadian Freedom Foundation (CFF).[600]

---

[593] Bellant. *Old Nazis*, 61.
[594] Anderson and Anderson, 102.
[595] Ibid., 92.
[596] Bellant. *Old Nazis*, 60.
[597] Ibid., 76.
[598] Bellant. *The Coors Connection*, 76.
[599] Anderson and Anderson, 152.
[600] Bellant. *Old Nazis*, 67.

Daniel Graham, an ex-director of the US military's Defense Intelligence Agency (DIA), took up the position of vice chairman. Besides serving on the ACWF board, Graham had been a speaker at a WACL executive committee meeting in 1977 at Pearson's request. On the USCWF's advisory board were other familiar names like Ray Cline, John Fisher, and Howard Phillips. Cline had been associated with the APACL since the late 1950s when he was the CIA station chief in Taiwan, Fisher had been the chairman of the ACWF, and Phillips was a CNP member and chairman of The Conservative Caucus.[601] Lawyer J. Fred Schlafly, the husband of anti-feminist author Phyllis Schlafly and a CNP member himself, sat on the board as well.[602] Fred Schlafly had been an officer of the ACWF along with Possony, who also joined this new chapter. Several former military and intelligence officials were appointed to the board. WACL's "fascist specter" did not dissuade these individuals from joining the League.[603]

Through WACL, the USCWF and ASC forged a close working relationship with the Latin American section, specifically CAL's paramilitary death squad leaders from Central America. CAL conferences were an opportunity for networking, coordinating strategies, and securing various forms of assistance. Italian neofascist terrorist Stefano Delle Chiaie traveled to the 1980 CAL convention in Buenos Aires from Bolivia where he was working for that country's particularly brutal military regime.[604] The Confederation was an integral component of Operation Condor, a network of cooperation between Latin American intelligence agencies for the repression of their own

---

[601] Anderson and Anderson, 55.
[602] CNP. "Membership Directory 2014," 9.
[603] Anderson and Anderson, 152-154.
[604] Ibid., 147.

citizens through kidnapping, torture, and murder.[605] At CAL gatherings, Central American members met officials from the Argentine military junta, infamous for their tens of thousands of "dirty war" forced disappearances, and the junta sent officers to Central America to train the local armed forces in these counterinsurgency methods.[606] The wider WACL contacts were equally important, as the League reportedly contributed $8 million to this mission.[607] In addition, the Taiwanese government supplied major military aid and training to Central American officers both in their home countries and Taiwan.[608]

Mario Sandoval Alarcón of Guatemala's National Liberation Movement (MLN) political party and Roberto D'Aubuisson Arrieta of El Salvador's Nationalist Republican Alliance (ARENA) party were two of CAL's most notorious members. Sandoval's MLN organized the Mano Blanca death squad as its paramilitary wing to target not only guerrillas but unarmed communists and other "subversives," a wide range of individuals including proponents of land reform, human rights activists, unionists, and moderate political reformers. Supplementing the kidnappings and assassinations by government forces, the Mano Blanca tortured and killed thousands of Guatemalan civilians in a partnership with the military and landowners. Sandoval was the country's vice president and president of Congress in the 1970s, the peak of Mano Blanca activity. In September 1980, an ex-

---

[605] López, 288.

[606] J. Patrice McSherry. *Predatory States: Operation Condor and Covert War in Latin America* (Lanham, MD: Rowman and Littlefield Publishers, 2005), 212.

[607] Ibid., 214.

[608] Anderson and Anderson, 170-171.

press secretary for the country's interior minister, then in exile, alleged that Sandoval had worked for the CIA.[609] Sandoval's proximity to the center of power in Washington was on display in January 1981 when he was a guest at Reagan's inaugural ball.[610] While unsuccessfully running for president in 1985, Sandoval proclaimed: "If I have to get rid of half of Guatemala so the other half can live in peace, I'll do it."[611]

The US conservative faction supported the state forces engaged in repression. In December 1979, an ASC delegation led by Singlaub and Graham traveled to Guatemala and reassured the military regime of Fernando Lucas García that, if elected, Reagan would resume the military aid which had been suspended by President Carter, who was regarded as a communist sympathizer by right-wing Guatemalans and WACL for his human rights policy. Singlaub subsequently justified death squad violence committed by those "dedicated to retaining the free enterprise system."[612] In 1980, as Reagan campaigned for the presidency, more delegations from the United States followed. Representatives from Heritage, the Moral Majority, and Phillips' TCC all visited Guatemala on "fact finding" missions. The public relations firm Deaver and Hannaford supervised Reagan's campaign and counted WACL members from Guatemala and Taiwan among its clients that year.[613] Once in office, Reagan met with Guatemalan dictator J. Efraín Ríos Montt during a Central

---

609 Ibid., 162-186.
610 Ibid., 177.
611 Ibid., 184.
612 Ibid., 174-175.
613 Jonathan Marshall, Peter Dale Scott, and Jane Hunter. *The Iran-Contra Connection: Secret Teams and Covert Operations in the Reagan Era* (Boston: South End Press, 1987), 54-55.

America trip in 1982 and pledged to "support his efforts to restore democracy and to address the root causes of this violent insurgency," lauding him as "a man of great personal integrity" despite reports of massacres by the armed forces during his rule.[614] Ríos Montt would be convicted of genocide by a Guatemalan court in 2013.[615]

D'Aubuisson, Sandoval's Salvadoran protégé, also developed a relationship with the USCWF, the ASC, Heritage, and the Reagan administration. Although barred from visiting the United States during Carter's presidency, he managed to enter the country in 1980 only months after the assassination of Archbishop Óscar A. Romero, for which the US embassy and later the UN Truth Commission on El Salvador would implicate him as the person giving the order.[616] In Washington, he met with Heritage officials and was an honored guest at an ASC conference.[617] According to Robert E. White, Carter's ambassador to El Salvador, the new Reagan administration ignored the embassy's findings and "granted D'Aubuisson a visa to enter the United States, made him an honored guest at our Embassy and saw to it that he met regularly with high-ranking Administration officials and visiting Senators and Congressmen."[618] Aides to Senator Helms traveled to El

---

[614] Ronald Reagan, "Remarks in San Pedro Sula, Honduras, Following a Meeting With President Jose Efrain Rios Montt of Guatemala" (4 December 1982): https://tinyurl.com/y7ru2wr3
[615] HRW. "Guatemala: Rios Montt Convicted of Genocide," *HRW* 10 May 2013:
https://www.hrw.org/news/2013/05/10/guatemala-rios-montt-convicted-genocide
[616] Equipo Nizkor. *Report of the UN Truth Commission on El Salvador*:
http://www.derechos.org/nizkor/salvador/informes/truth.html
[617] Anderson and Anderson, 203.
[618] Ibid., 207-208.

Salvador to assist D'Aubuisson in building his ARENA party, and conservative faction leaders and groups such as Weyrich, Phillips, and the Moral Majority sent him a letter of support in 1983.[619] As one would expect, Singlaub and the USCWF collaborated with D'Aubuisson as well, one photo from El Salvador showing the two men examining a military map together.[620]

Reagan sent a letter conveying his "warm greetings" to the participants of the 1984 WACL convention in San Diego, presided over by Singlaub as League chairman.[621] The head of the Nicaraguan Contras and members of six other anti-communist guerrilla groups from Asia and Africa attended the conclave. WACL would act as a conduit for material assistance to these insurgents.[622] The Reverend Moon's Unification Church played a pivotal role in these operations and in WACL through its Japanese branch.[623] There are common elements with the seemingly disparate League participants. During the Cold War, the violent methods employed by WACL associates shared many similarities, for example the creation of paramilitary forces and the perpetration of large-scale forced disappearances and killings. This modus operandi can be traced to the unconventional warfare practiced by the Nazis.[624] The victims were communists and perceived communists, the latter an extremely broad category.

---

[619] Ibid., 211.
[620] Bellant. *Old Nazis*, 85.
[621] Ibid., 68.
[622] Abramovici, 125.
[623] Anderson and Anderson, 105-106.
[624] USHMM. "Night and Fog Decree": https://www.ushmm.org/wlc/en/article.php?ModuleId=100074 65

As with the Cercle, the collapse of the Soviet Union and conclusion of the Cold War did not lead to the folding of WACL, but it did necessitate an altered focus, demonstrated by a change in the League's name to the World League for Freedom and Democracy (WLFD). Still based in Taipei, the League has maintained a similar structure with national and regional units. The APACL was renamed the Asian Pacific League for Freedom and Democracy (APLFD), the NARWACL became the North American Federation for Freedom and Democracy (NAFFD), and the other regional affiliates also included freedom and democracy in their new names.[625] The last known chairperson of the US chapter of the WLFD was Michael D. (Mike) Huckabee, a former governor of Arkansas.[626] He also hosted the show *Huckabee* on Fox News before making a short-lived bid for the presidency. Huckabee was an early backer of Trump's candidacy, inviting the president as the first guest on his new show on the Christian-oriented Trinity Broadcasting Network (TBN) in October 2017.[627] His daughter, Sarah E. Sanders, was Trump's White House press secretary for two years.[628]

OTHER GROUPS

Besides the Cercle and WACL, another organization that merits attention is the Mont Pelerin Society (MPS).

---

[625] WLFD. "Structure":
http://wlfdroc.org.tw/2019/02/24/structure
[626] "Governor Huckabee Responds," *Christian Headlines* 18 January 2008:
https://www.christianheadlines.com/news/governor-huckabee-responds-11565039.html
[627] TBN. "Huckabee: Episodes":
https://www.tbn.org/programs/huckabee/episodes
[628] White House. "Press Briefings":
https://www.whitehouse.gov/search/?s=sanders

Established by Austrian economist Friedrich A. von Hayek in Mont Pèlerin, Switzerland in 1947, the Society is a gathering for proponents of laissez-faire economics. It was conceived as an international forum for those who "believed that freedom was under serious threat, either from socialism or from Keynesian ideas."[629] The MPS has overlapping membership with The Philadelphia Society, founded in the United States in 1964 and modelled on the MPS. Individuals from approximately fifty countries on every continent are members of the MPS, including Americans Charles Koch, Ed Feulner, and Edwin Meese.[630] Feulner was the Society's president from 1996 to 1998.[631] Bill Buckley and Henry Regnery are deceased ex-members.[632] Before his death, State Policy Network founder Thomas Roe asked the MPS and The Philadelphia Society to sue the trustees of his Roe Foundation if they ever failed to uphold its conservative mission.[633] Another

---

[629] Niels Bjerre-Poulsen, "The Mont Pèlerin Society and the Rise of a Postwar Classical Liberal Counter-Establishment," in Luc van Dongen, Stéphanie Roulin, and Giles Scott-Smith (eds.). *Transnational Anti-Communism and the Cold War: Agents, Activities, and Networks* (New York: Palgrave Macmillan, 2014), 201.

[630] Mont Pelerin Society Directory - 2010: https://tinyurl.com/y8fkj809

[631] MPS. "Past Presidents": https://www.montpelerin.org/past-presidents-2

[632] William F. Buckley Jr. *Let Us Talk of Many Things: The Collected Speeches* (New York: Basic Books, 2008), 223. James Bowman, "A New Kind of Right," *The New York Sun* 25 March 2008: http://www.nysun.com/arts/new-kind-of-right/73550

[633] Stephen Foley, "Ambitious Wealth: Heirs will be heirs," *Financial Times* 3 May 2016: https://www.ft.com/content/7ed82b5e-0230-11e6-99cb-83242733f755

late member of the MPS is former Cercle regular Otto von Habsburg.[634]

Together with these two societies, The Heritage Foundation, American Enterprise Institute, American Legislative Exchange Council, State Policy Network, and Americans for Prosperity, all reviewed in chapter 3, are partners in the Washington-based Atlas Network, a globe-spanning organization with hundreds of partners dedicated to the promotion of laissez-faire policies.[635] The MPS and The Philadelphia Society are vaguely similar to the liberal faction's more secretive Pilgrims Society of Great Britain and the United States, created in 1902 to foster Anglo-American relations "as one of the principal custodians of what has come to be known as the Special Relationship."[636]

CONCLUSION

The international connections of the conservative power elite were based on anti-communist cooperation for most of the post-WWII period. Le Cercle and the World Anti-Communist League, founded in the decades after the war, were the main forums for this massive undertaking. For the conservative faction of the oligarchy, international ties strengthened its domestic advances. Unsurprisingly, Reagan's presidency engendered the most active and influential time for this right-wing transnational network.

---

[634] Al Scheck, "Obituary: Otto von Habsburg," *Vision* 29 July 2011: http://www.vision.org/visionmedia/biography-otto-vonhabsburg/46881.aspx

[635] Atlas Network. "Global Directory: United States": https://www.atlasnetwork.org/partners/global-directory/united-states

[636] Pilgrims. "The Pilgrims of Great Britain": http://www.pilgrimsociety.org/index.php

With the demise of the Soviet Union and the weakened state of global communism in more recent decades, these organizations and the conservative faction itself extended their efforts to other right-wing causes.

CHAPTER 5
US HEGEMONY BY FACTION: CASES OF FOREIGN INTERVENTION

US intervention in the Global South, commonly referred to as the "Third World," has been an enduring feature of US foreign policy since World War II. While these interventions have occasionally been overt in nature, involving the deployment of military forces, more frequently they have involved CIA operations and covert assistance, as in the cases reviewed in this chapter. The motivations of policymakers have often revolved around the protection and expansion of economic investments and the acquisition of resources, but during the Cold War interventions were attributed to the communist threat. However, as one might anticipate from the analysis in the preceding chapters, a factional approach reveals that the liberal power elite was driven more by transnational corporate interests in its interventions whereas the conservative power elite's ideological anti-communism dictated its course of action in the 1980s.

LIBERAL FACTION INTERVENTIONS

The two interventions in this section built on a long history of US involvement in Latin American affairs. The Monroe Doctrine of 1823 stipulated that any European interference in the Americas would be viewed by the US government as a hostile act justifying a US response. A widespread belief in American exceptionalism or "manifest destiny" served as the foundation for US expansion abroad beginning in the late nineteenth century. Given their geographical proximity, Central and South America were perceived by US policymakers as the "backyard" of the United States, its immediate sphere of influence. As such, intervention in these areas was perceived as legitimate in order to safeguard vital national interests.[637]

In addition to the backyard argument, the Cold War conflict served as the principal rationale for liberal faction interventions, but the cases examined here indicate corporate and personal interests as the most critical factors in the decision-making process. Leading members of the liberal power elite were the architects of the interventions. They occurred two decades apart in Central and South America, respectively, Guatemala in the first half of the 1950s and Chile in the early 1970s. Both operations deposed democratically-elected civilian governments committed to social and economic reform. In each case, military dictatorship and mass repression followed in the aftermath of the CIA action. These interventions were preceded by the CIA's Operation Ajax, codename for the 1953 overthrow of Mohammad Mosaddegh in Iran after he nationalized the nation's oil industry, previously under the control of the UK's Anglo-Iranian Oil Company (AIOC). As in Guatemala and Chile, the Mosaddegh government implemented many reforms, some of which threatened foreign corporate interests.[638]

---

[637] Grace Livingstone. *America's Backyard: The United States and Latin America from the Monroe Doctrine to the War on Terror* (London: Zed Books, 2009), 8-22.
[638] Bethany Allen-Ebrahimian, "64 Years Later, CIA Finally Releases Details of Iranian Coup," *Foreign Policy* 20 June 2017: http://foreignpolicy.com/2017/06/20/64-years-later-cia-finally-releases-details-of-iranian-coup-iran-tehran-oil

Guatemala

Until 1944, Guatemala was ruled by a series of authoritarian governments since its independence from Spain in 1821. In the presidential election of 1944, the first open elections in the nation's history, philosophy professor Juan J. Arévalo won a landslide victory. For the first time Guatemalans enjoyed fundamental civil liberties during his presidency. Decidedly anti-communist, Arévalo envisioned a regulated capitalism along the lines of Roosevelt's New Deal. Investments in education and health care included the construction of new schools and hospitals, and suffrage was extended to all men and literate women. A new constitution in 1945 and a far-reaching labor code in 1947 improved labor conditions, provided workers' benefits, and allowed union organizing in factories and on large plantations.[639] This last provision impinged on the operations of the Boston-based United Fruit Company (UFCO), Guatemala's largest landowner.[640]

Arévalo was succeeded by his minister of national defense, Jacobo Árbenz Guzmán, who won the 1950 election and commenced his presidency in March 1951. The Guatemalan Party of Labor (PGT), a communist political party, was legalized during Árbenz's tenure and a small number of communists were appointed to lower-level government positions. Nevertheless, "there was no evidence that Árbenz himself was anything more than a

---

[639] Paul J. Dosal. *Power in Transition: The Rise of Guatemala's Industrial Oligarchy, 1871-1994* (Westport, CT: Praeger Publishers, 1995), 91.
[640] Stephen Schlesinger, "Ghosts of Guatemala's Past," *The New York Times* 3 June 2011: http://www.nytimes.com/2011/06/04/opinion/04schlesinger.ht ml?_r=0

European-style democratic socialist."[641] Of the Soviet bloc countries, Guatemala only had relations with Czechoslovakia.[642] Árbenz deepened Arévalo's reforms, seeking to ameliorate Guatemala's vastly unequal land ownership. Decree 900 was promulgated in 1952, an agrarian reform law permitting the expropriation of idle land on large estates for redistribution to landless peasants. Árbenz offered the UFCO compensation according to the value declared by the company for tax purposes. UFCO officials opposed this method since they had undervalued the land to reduce payments.[643]

At the Council on Foreign Relations, a study group was convened on Political Unrest in Latin America in the autumn of 1952, concluding in 1953. Although no publications resulted from this group, some basic information is available. It was led by Spruille Braden, a former assistant secretary of state for Western Hemisphere affairs and a UFCO consultant. Guatemala was the subject of the first meeting, and UFCO assistant vice president John C. McClintock acted as the discussion leader. By the time of Eisenhower's inauguration, a CFR consensus in favor of intervention had already developed.[644] Since communist influence was greater in Latin American countries of more strategic importance for the United States, the "takeover of United Fruit land was probably the

---

[641] Ibid.
[642] Stephen Schlesinger and Stephen Kinzer, "Bitter Fruit: The Untold Story of the American Coup in Guatemala," in Michael J. LaRosa and Frank O. Mora (eds.). *Neighborly Adversaries: Readings in U.S.-Latin American Relations* (Lanham, MD: Rowman and Littlefield Publishers, 2007), 157.
[643] Livingstone, 26.
[644] Laurence H. Shoup and William Minter. *Imperial Brain Trust: The Council on Foreign Relations and United States Foreign Policy* (New York: Monthly Review Press, 1977), 196.

decisive factor pushing the Americans into action."[645] Its "implementation was to be in the hands of men closely tied with the Council on Foreign Relations. Most important were President Eisenhower himself, the CIA head Allen Dulles, who continued on the Council's board of directors at the same time, and Frank Wisner, another Council member who was the CIA's deputy director for plans (the man in charge of clandestine operations)."[646]

There was no shortage of UFCO connections to the CFR and Eisenhower administration. In fact, with respect to the Guatemala intervention, there existed a "triangular relationship of interlocks among the government officials involved, the Council, and the United Fruit Company."[647] CFR chairman John McCloy was on the UFCO's board of directors in the 1950s.[648] Other UFCO directors among the Council's membership were Under Secretary of State General Walter B. Smith and Lehman Brothers CEO Robert O. Lehman. CFR director Whitney H. Shepardson was an officer of the UFCO-owned International Railways of Central America (IRCA). Among CFR members who were also high-ranking government officials, the Dulles brothers were at the forefront in terms of foreign policy. They both had ties to the UFCO through their law firm, Sullivan and Cromwell. Secretary of State John Foster Dulles had negotiated a contract for the UFCO in Guatemala.[649] CIA Director Allen Dulles sat on the board of directors of Schroder Bank, an IRCA stockholder. John M.

---

[645] Schlesinger and Kinzer, 149.
[646] Shoup and Minter, 196.
[647] Ibid., 198.
[648] Kai Bird. *The Chairman: John J. McCloy and the Making of the American Establishment* (New York: Simon and Schuster, 1992), 483.
[649] Shoup and Minter, 198-199.

Cabot, assistant secretary of state for Western Hemisphere affairs in the lead-up to the intervention, and UN Ambassador Henry C. Lodge were both UFCO stockholders.[650] Of the twelve key decision makers on the intervention, Cabot and Lodge were among the eight who were either CFR members at the time or would soon join the Council.[651]

Codenamed Operation PBSUCCESS, many months of destabilization efforts authorized by Eisenhower culminated in a CIA-sponsored invasion to overthrow Árbenz. A group of 480 Guatemalans and Central American mercenaries organized by CIA asset Carlos Castillo Armas received CIA training and weapons in neighboring countries to launch an invasion into Guatemala. Under CIA direction and with air support from the agency, these forces invaded, forcing Árbenz's resignation and exile in June 1954. National Liberation Movement leader Castillo Armas usurped power, bringing an end to ten years known as the "Guatemalan Spring."[652] He reversed the reforms of Arévalo and Árbenz, including Decree 900. Lists of "Communists and collaborators" compiled by the CIA prior to the invasion were used by the new dictatorship to kill hundreds of Guatemalans.[653] Allen Dulles and the CIA would unsuccessfully attempt to replicate PBSUCCESS by staging the Bay of Pigs Invasion to overthrow Cuba's Fidel Castro in 1961.[654]

---

[650] Schlesinger and Kinzer, 157.
[651] Shoup and Minter, 198.
[652] Nick Cullather. *Secret History: The CIA's Classified Account of Its Operations in Guatemala, 1952-1954* (Stanford, CA: Stanford University Press, 2006), 74-123.
[653] NSARCHIVE. "CIA and Assassinations: The Guatemala 1954 Documents" (edited by Kate Doyle and Peter Kornbluh): https://nsarchive2.gwu.edu//NSAEBB/NSAEBB4/index.html
[654] Schlesinger and Kinzer, 149.

Guatemala was subsequently ruled by a series of military-controlled authoritarian regimes backed by the US government, its armed forces and police trained by US advisors. A guerrilla insurgency and thirty-six-year civil war began in 1960, claiming the lives of more than 200,000 people, the vast majority of them indigenous Guatemalans. Military and associated forces were responsible for most of the violence. The repression of even peaceful anti-government activity through abductions and assassinations in both urban and rural areas was routine throughout the armed conflict.[655] Guatemala transitioned to civilian rule in the mid-1980s and peace accords were finally signed in 1996. During a visit to the country in 1999, President Clinton issued an apology for the US government's "support for military forces and intelligence units which engaged in violence and widespread repression."[656]

Chile

Unlike Guatemala, Chile had a contemporary history of constitutional democracy, uninterrupted from 1932 until the 1973 coup d'état that ushered in a military dictatorship. Several political parties competed in congressional and presidential elections, notably the National Party on the right, the centrist Christian Democratic Party, and the

---

[655] HRDAG. *Guatemala: Memory of Silence (Report of the Commission for Historical Clarification: Conclusions and Recommendations)*, 17-22: https://hrdag.org/wp-content/uploads/2013/01/CEHreport-english.pdf
[656] John M. Broder, "Clinton Offers His Apologies To Guatemala," *The New York Times* 11 March 1999: http://www.nytimes.com/1999/03/11/world/clinton-offers-his-apologies-to-guatemala.html

Socialist Party on the left. In 1964, fearing the success of Socialist presidential candidate Salvador Allende Gossens, the CIA heavily funded the campaign of Christian Democrat Eduardo Frei Montalva. Frei won fifty-seven percent of the vote in the election and served one six-year term as president, as per the Chilean constitution. He undertook some modest reforms, but land occupations and labor strikes escalated during his tenure.[657]

Allende ran again in the 1970 election, and this time he emerged victorious by a small margin in his fourth attempt at the presidency. Since no candidate received an absolute majority of votes, election rules required congress to select between the two top candidates in the popular vote. On the three previous occasions when congress had selected the winner, the legislative body had chosen the candidate with the most votes. Bowing to precedent, congress overwhelmingly confirmed Allende as president. His "peaceful transition to socialism" agenda included the nationalization of copper mines, agrarian reform, and wealth redistribution. Allende's nationalization program alarmed US corporations with Chilean investments.[658] Indeed, "the very name of Allende was anathema to the extreme Right in Chile, to certain powerful corporations (notably ITT, Pepsi Cola and the Chase Manhattan Bank) which did business in Chile and the United States, and to the CIA."[659] As evidenced by the number of key players in the Chile intervention holding membership in the Council on Foreign Relations, one should add the CFR to the list of anti-Allende institutions. Upon learning of Allende's election, Edward M. Korry, the US ambassador to Chile

---

[657] Livingstone, 51-52.
[658] Ibid., 51-53.
[659] Christopher Hitchens. *The Trial of Henry Kissinger* (London: Verso, 2001), 55.

and a CFR member, exclaimed, "Once Allende comes to power we shall do all within our power to condemn Chile and all Chileans to utmost deprivation and poverty."[660]

Before Allende's election, David Rockefeller enlisted US government officials in a campaign to prevent the socialist leader from attaining the presidency. In 1962, President Kennedy had apparently requested that Rockefeller "start an organization of businessmen as cover for [CIA] Latin American operations."[661] Rockefeller eventually founded this organization, the Council of the Americas, through which he developed a friendship with Agustín Edwards Eastman, the proprietor of the leading Chilean newspaper *El Mercurio* and the CIA's main contact in Chile. In his *Memoirs*, Rockefeller wrote about his indispensable role in the orchestration of anti-Allende operations. Rockefeller related Edwards' distress over Allende prior to the 1970 election: "[Edwards'] concerns were so intense that I put him in touch with Henry Kissinger. I later learned that [Edwards'] reports confirmed the intelligence already received from official intelligence sources, which led the Nixon administration to increase its clandestine financial subsidies to groups opposing Allende."[662] The source of this intelligence was, in fact, Edwards himself as well as his associates.[663]

---

[660] Laurence H. Shoup. *Wall Street's Think Tank: The Council on Foreign Relations and the Empire of Neoliberal Geopolitics, 1976-2014* (New York: Monthly Review Press, 2015), 169.
[661] Joseph J. Trento. *Prelude to Terror: The Rogue CIA and the Legacy of America's Private Intelligence Network* (New York: Carroll and Graf Publishers, 2005), 367.
[662] David Rockefeller. *Memoirs* (New York: Random House, 2002), 432.
[663] Peter Dale Scott. *The Road to 9/11: Wealth, Empire, and the Future of America* (Berkeley: University of California Press, 2007), 41.

Rockefeller's involvement went deeper. He allowed his Chase Manhattan Bank to be used in the CIA's Chilean operations.[664] His influence even extended to the appointment of relevant government personnel. Charles A. Meyer, assistant secretary of state for Western Hemisphere affairs and an active COA member, "told a private [COA] luncheon that he had been 'chosen' for the post 'by David Rockefeller.'"[665] After Allende's election victory, meetings with Rockefeller and PepsiCo CEO Donald M. Kendall, a CFR member, prompted Kissinger as the national security advisor to join with CIA Director Richard Helms in convincing President Nixon of the urgency of preventing Allende's confirmation by the Chilean congress.[666] Helms' notes from this meeting with Nixon reveal that a minimum of $10 million was made available and the US embassy in Santiago was not to participate in the operations. "Make the economy scream" appeared in the notes. A special covert-operations group was established for the implementation of a two-track policy, one diplomatic, the other "a strategy of destabilization, kidnap and assassination, designed to provoke a military coup."[667] When this Track II strategy, codenamed Project FUBELT, failed to block Allende's congressional approval, Rockefeller and the administration then sought the removal of Allende after he assumed the presidency.

Officials from other US businesses with investments in Chile also requested the intervention of the CIA and Nixon administration. International Telephone and Telegraph

---

[664] Trento, 62.
[665] Seymour M. Hersh. *The Price of Power: Kissinger in the Nixon White House* (New York: Summit Books, 1983), 266.
[666] CFR. *AR 2016*, 55.
[667] Hitchens, 56.

(ITT) president and CEO Harold S. Geneen, another CFR member, offered the CIA $1 million to depose Allende. ITT had already channeled $350,000 through the CIA to one of Allende's election opponents.[668] The company was reprising its role in an earlier US intervention in Brazil after that country's reformist president, João B. Goulart, nationalized its subsidiary. In the Brazilian case, the Johnson administration and CIA undertook covert action to foment a military coup in 1964.[669] Later that year, Rockefeller informed a discussion group at a West Point conference on Latin America that "it had been decided quite early that Goulart was not acceptable to the US banking community, and that he would have to go."[670] A twenty-one year military dictatorship ensued in Brazil.

US copper mining corporations Anaconda and Kennecott suffered their own losses to the policy of nationalization in Chile. In 1971, Rockefeller brokered a meeting between Kissinger and John B. Place, the new president and CEO of Anaconda.[671] Rockefeller knew Place from Chase Manhattan where he had been the vice chairman before joining Anaconda. Rockefeller's personal and corporate interests were at stake as the copper company owed $250 million to a consortium of banks led by Chase

---

[668] Livingstone, 52.
[669] NSARCHIVE. "Brazil Marks 40th Anniversary of Military Coup: Declassified Documents Shed Light on U.S. Role" (edited by Peter Kornbluh): https://nsarchive2.gwu.edu//NSAEBB/NSAEBB118/index.htm
[670] Jan Knippers Black. *United States Penetration of Brazil* (Philadelphia: University of Pennsylvania Press, 1977), 78.
[671] NSARCHIVE. "Document 8: 'Chile', Memorandum of Conversation with Anaconda Copper Executives, 17 August 1971, White House, memoranda and letters attached, Confidential": https://nsarchive2.gwu.edu/NSAEBB/NSAEBB193/hak-8-17-71.pdf

Manhattan.[672] Overall, the bank's Chilean interests were even more substantial than those of PepsiCo.[673] Rockefeller's contacts with Anaconda were not limited to banking. Anaconda's previous CEO, C. Jay Parkinson, served as a member of the COA's executive committee along with Kendall and Geneen. The COA liaised with the CIA through the agency's Enno Hobbing, who would later work for the COA as its principal operations officer.[674]

Events accelerated in Chile in the second half of 1972. A truckers' strike lasting nearly four weeks critically disrupted Chile's economy. An abortive coup was staged in June 1973, and then another long strike by truckers beginning in July had "catastrophic" consequences for the Chilean economy. Agriculture suffered significantly, industrial production declined, and commodity supplies "reached 'a crucial point.'" Allende's minister of national policy interpreted it as "a political strike aimed at overthrowing the Government, with the help of imperialism."[675] The CIA did finance the previous 1972 strike, with its organizers "heavily subsidized" by the agency. Direct subsidies were also distributed by the CIA to various middle-class strikers in 1973. In total, more than 250,000 Chileans participated in strikes over a period of eighteen months, creating conditions that perhaps "made a violent overthrow inevitable."[676]

---

[672] P.D. Scott, 291.
[673] Ibid., 42.
[674] Hersh, 260.
[675] Marvine Howe, "Chile Calls Truck Strike 'Catastrophic,'" *The New York Times* 18 August 1973:
http://www.nytimes.com/1973/08/18/archives/chile-calls-truck-strike-catastrophic-chile-says-strike-is.html
[676] Seymour M. Hersh, "C.I.A. Is Linked to Strikes In Chile That Beset Allende," *The New York Times* 20 September 1974:
https://tinyurl.com/y9bnovys

Institutional opposition to Allende also increased and became more vocal. A congressional resolution was passed by the chamber of deputies in August 1973, supported by Christian Democratic and National Party deputies, accusing the Allende government of seeking from the outset "to conquer absolute power with the obvious purpose of subjecting all citizens to the strictest political and economic control by the state."[677] The armed forces were informed of their "duty to put an immediate end to all situations herein referred to that breach the Constitution and the laws of the land."[678] The following day, the resignation of constitutionalist General Carlos Prats González as the army's commander-in-chief, replaced by General Augusto Pinochet Ugarte, removed the final obstacle to a military takeover.

On September 11, the widely anticipated military coup occurred. The military seized control of most television and radio stations and bombed the others. All branches of the Chilean armed forces participated in the coup and any Allende loyalists were prevented from interfering. Allende falsely assumed Pinochet's loyalty to constitutional government. The navy captured the strategically important coastal city of Valparaíso while the air force heavily bombarded the presidential palace, resulting in Allende's suicide. His final speech on live radio proclaimed: "Go forward knowing that, sooner rather than later, the great avenues will again be opened through which will pass free

---

[677] Chilean Chamber of Deputies. "Agreement of the Chamber of Deputies of Chile, 22 August 1973" (translated by José Piñera): https://en.wikisource.org/wiki/Agreement_of_the_Chamber_of _Deputies_of_Chile
[678] Ibid.

men to construct a better society. Long live Chile! Long live the people! Long live the workers!"[679]

The precise role of the US government in the coup itself remains unknown to researchers and the public. For decades it has been a contentious subject. Some documents from government agencies have been declassified over the years, including ones related to Project FUBELT, but they do not shed light on the question of US involvement in the events of "Chile's 9/11."[680] A CIA report in 2000 denied any direct responsibility but admitted, "Although CIA did not instigate the coup that ended Allende's government on 11 September 1973, it was aware of coup-plotting by the military, had ongoing intelligence collection relationships with some plotters, and--because CIA did not discourage the takeover and had sought to instigate a coup in 1970-- probably appeared to condone it."[681] Interestingly, the agency's legendary covert action specialist Ted Shackley, later the leader of Le Cercle's US section, ran the CIA's Western Hemisphere division at the time of the coup.

The Church Committee, chaired by Senator Frank F. Church in 1975, investigated the CIA's clandestine activities in Chile. While acknowledging the Chilean

---

[679] Salvador Allende, "Salvador Allende's Last Speech" (11 September 1973):
https://en.wikisource.org/wiki/Salvador_Allende%27s_Last_Sp eech
[680] NSARCHIVE. "Chile and the United States: Declassified Documents Relating to the Military Coup, September 11, 1973" (edited by Peter Kornbluh):
https://nsarchive2.gwu.edu//NSAEBB/NSAEBB8/nsaebb8i.ht m
[681] CIA. *CIA Activities in Chile* (18 September 2000):
https://www.cia.gov/library/reports/general-reports-1/chile/index.html#6

government's expanded relations with the Soviet Union and Cuba under Allende, the senate committee reported that "Allende was charting an independent nationalistic course, both within the hemisphere and internationally. Allende was, in short, committed to a policy of non-alignment."[682] It noted that the CIA launched "an extensive covert action program in Chile" and expanded it in the early 1970s.[683] The committee's report determined that the Nixon administration "moved finally to advocating and encouraging the overthrow of a democratically elected government."[684] The report concluded, "Given the costs of covert action, it should be resorted to only to counter severe threats to the national security of the United States. It is far from clear that that was the case in Chile."[685]

In the wake of the coup, a military junta headed by Pinochet seized power. The US-backed Pinochet regime imprisoned and tortured Allende supporters and leftists, dissolved congress, censored the media, burned "subversive" books, and suspended all political activity. As in other Latin American countries, thousands were disappeared and killed. In 1991, the official *National Commission for Truth and Reconciliation Report* documented "3,428 cases of disappearance, killing, torture and kidnapping" in the post-coup years.[686] A subsequent report from the National Commission on Political

---

[682] AARC Public Library. "Church Committee Reports Volume 7: Covert Action," 193:
http://www.aarclibrary.org/publib/church/reports/vol7/html/ChurchV7_0101b.htm
[683] Ibid., 198.
[684] Ibid., 198.
[685] Ibid., 203.
[686] USIP. "Truth Commission: Chile":
https://www.usip.org/publications/1990/05/truth-commission-chile-90

Imprisonment and Torture was based on testimony from nearly 30,000 recognized victims, the majority of cases occurring in the months immediately following the coup. It concluded that "Torture and detention were used as a tool for political control by State authorities [. . .] Torture by members of the Armed Forces and Carabineros (paramilitary police) was a generalized practice on a national scale."[687]

The junta formed a new intelligence agency, the National Intelligence Directorate (DINA), which became a core unit of the transnational Operation Condor apparatus. The "gestapo-like" DINA orchestrated the high-profile assassinations of Carlos Prats in Buenos Aires and Orlando Letelier del Solar in Washington. Letelier was a minister in Allende's government and a steadfast opponent of the Pinochet regime. His US colleague was also killed in the attack. These assassinations were committed by American Michael V. Townley, who was accused by DINA officials of actually working as an operative for the CIA.[688] An attempted assassination of exiled Christian Democrat Bernardo Leighton Guzmán in Rome was perpetrated by neofascist Stefano Delle Chiaie, a World Anti-Communist League attendee.[689] Delle Chiaie was also suspected of contributing his lethal services for bomb attacks in Italy linked to NATO's Operation Gladio.[690]

---

[687] USIP. "Commission of Inquiry: Chile":
https://www.usip.org/publications/2003/09/commission-inquiry-chile-03
[688] J. Patrice McSherry. *Predatory States: Operation Condor and Covert War in Latin America* (Lanham, MD: Rowman and Littlefield Publishers, 2005), 5-7.
[689] Ibid., 43.
[690] Daniele Ganser. *NATO's Secret Armies: Operation Gladio and Terrorism in Western Europe* (London: Frank Cass, 2005), 108-109.

Following a 1988 referendum and general elections in 1989, civilian rule and democratic government were restored in Chile, ending seventeen years of military dictatorship. In 1998, Spanish judge Baltasar Garzón Real indicted Pinochet for human rights violations under the principle of universal jurisdiction, a landmark in the history of international law. Pinochet was arrested and detained in London for seventeen months. The UK government allowed him to return to Chile, but his legal troubles continued in his home country. The Chilean courts revoked his immunity from prosecution and he was placed under house arrest. In 2006, Pinochet was charged with multiple counts of kidnapping, torture, and murder. He died later that year before he could be convicted of any crimes.[691]

Kissinger faced his own legal concerns in Chile. A Chilean judge investigating the death of US journalist Charles E. Horman shortly after the coup, frustrated with Kissinger's lack of cooperation, considered requesting his extradition to Chile in 2002 so that he could testify as a witness regarding "CIA involvement in the coup, whether US officials passed lists of leftwing Americans in Chile to the military and whether the US embassy failed to assist Americans deemed sympathetic to the deposed government."[692] Declassified documents reveal Kissinger

---

[691] Monte Reel and J.Y. Smith, "A Chilean Dictator's Dark Legacy," *The Washington Post* 11 December 2006: http://www.washingtonpost.com/wp-dyn/content/article/2006/12/10/AR2006121000302.html
[692] Jonathan Franklin and Duncan Campbell, "Kissinger may face extradition to Chile," *The Guardian* 12 June 2002: https://www.theguardian.com/world/2002/jun/12/chile.pinoch et

fearing that Allende's "'model' effect can be insidious" and as secretary of state telling Pinochet in 1976: "We want to help, not undermine you. You did a great service to the West in overthrowing Allende."[693]

In his autobiography, David Rockefeller preferred to emphasize the "economic side of the story" in which economists trained at the University of Chicago, his alma mater, and funded by the Ford and Rockefeller foundations, used Chile as a laboratory for their neoliberal experiment in the mid-1970s.[694] This economic model would be replicated throughout Latin America and in many other countries, including the United States and United Kingdom beginning in 1979. Rockefeller described Pinochet's rule as "a reign of terror" and did mention his "abhorrence of the excesses committed."[695] Nevertheless, the liberal oligarch was "concerned first and foremost for U.S. corporate property" despite the regime's "excesses" and he did not express any remorse even though his "hidden instigation of the Allende overthrow is amply acknowledged in his own *Memoirs*."[696]

CONSERVATIVE FACTION INTERVENTIONS

In contrast to the liberal power elite, the conservative faction of the oligarchy was motivated less by specific corporate interests than by the global crusade against

---

[693] NSARCHIVE. "Kissinger and Chile: The Declassified Record" (edited by Peter Kornbluh):
https://nsarchive2.gwu.edu/NSAEBB/NSAEBB437
[694] Inderjeet Parmar. *Foundations of the American Century: The Ford, Carnegie, and Rockefeller Foundations in the Rise of American Power* (New York: Columbia University Press, 2012), 181.
[695] Rockefeller, 433.
[696] P.D. Scott, 40.

communism in its interventions. It was not until the Reagan administration that the conservative power elite could successfully campaign for a rollback of Soviet-aligned and left-wing governments in the Global South by assisting insurrectionary forces. This policy shift from containment and détente occurred due to a number of factors, particularly "the effects of the Vietnam War, the rise of the conservative right, and, most significantly, the election victory of Ronald Reagan in 1980."[697] The Reagan Doctrine was applied to several "Third World" countries in the 1980s, with the president declaring in his 1986 State of the Union address: "America will support with moral and material assistance your right not just to fight and die for freedom, but to fight and win freedom -- in Afghanistan; Angola; Cambodia and Nicaragua."[698] In the African case covered in this section, Angola, a communist government held power, while in Nicaragua a socialist government supported by the Soviet Union and Cuba led the Central American nation.

Angola

After a protracted guerrilla war, Angola achieved its independence from Portugal in 1975. Three separate groups, the National Union for the Total Independence of Angola (UNITA), the Popular Movement for the Liberation of Angola (MPLA), and the National Liberation Front of Angola (FNLA) all fought the Portuguese armed forces in this war for independence. These three organizations and

---

[697] James M. Scott. *Deciding to Intervene: The Reagan Doctrine and American Foreign Policy* (Durham, NC: Duke University Press, 1996), 15.
[698] Patrick E. Tyler and David B. Ottaway, "The Selling of Jonas Savimbi: Success and a $600,000 Tab," *The Washington Post* 9 February 1986: https://tinyurl.com/yckjpj8x

the Portuguese government signed the Alvor Agreement in January 1975, which marked the end of colonial rule in Angola and the commencement of a civil war between the armed groups. The MPLA formed the new government while UNITA continued its armed struggle, this time fighting against the nation's Soviet and Cuba-backed government. Cuba's government made a major military commitment, deploying tens of thousands of troops to the Southern African country.[699]

Following a power struggle between the conservative faction and the Department of State, Angola became an exemplar of the Reagan Doctrine in President Reagan's second term. The diplomatic approach pursued by Secretary of State George Shultz in Reagan's first term was supplanted by covert assistance for UNITA insurgents. The conservative faction, led by The Heritage Foundation, undertook a "UNITA project" beginning in 1983. These "individuals and groups maintained that the State Department's policy was ineffective, anti-Western, and hostile to President Reagan's desires."[700] They campaigned for the repeal of the Clark Amendment, an amendment to the US Arms Export Control Act (AECA) of 1976 outlawing aid to private groups engaged in armed conflict in Angola. Leading supporters from inside the administration included CIA Director Bill Casey, Oliver North, Fred Iklé, Pat Buchanan, and John M. Poindexter, Reagan's national security advisor. Jesse Helms headed the congressional contingent backing the repeal. In July 1985, these efforts secured their objective as Congress voted to repeal the

---

[699] Stephen J. Solarz, "Next Stop, Angola," *New Republic* 2 December 1985: https://newrepublic.com/article/79546/next-stop-angola-reagan-doctrine-communism-intervention
[700] James Scott, 127.

amendment, allowing for the application of the Reagan Doctrine to Angola.[701]

Over the next few months, Heritage and the American Security Council advocated for the provision of assistance to UNITA and its leader Jonas M. Savimbi, referred to as "freedom fighters" by Reagan and the conservative power elite. A Heritage board member reportedly organized a conference at UNITA's main base in Angola for anti-communist insurgents from Afghanistan, Cambodia, Laos, and Nicaragua.[702] Savimbi traveled to Washington in February 1986, where he visited the White House and State Department as well as Capitol Hill and media offices. He was represented on Capitol Hill by the lobbying firm Black, Manafort, Stone and Kelly.[703] The firm's principals included Paul J. Manafort and Roger J. Stone, both of whom would achieve mass notoriety decades later working for President Trump's campaign. Savimbi was also a guest at a Heritage luncheon.[704] A seminar at the American Enterprise Institute and a meeting sponsored by the Center for Strategic and International Studies were part of the itinerary.[705]

Through cooperation with administration officials, the decision to supply aid to UNITA was reached at the time of Savimbi's trip to Washington.[706] For the next five years,

---

[701] Ibid., 126-127.
[702] George V. Wright, "Reagan, Bush and Southern Africa," *African Studies Journal* 1989 (Vol. 11), 39.
[703] Tyler and Ottaway.
[704] James Scott, 137.
[705] Bernard Gwertzman, "Angolan Rebel Sees Top U.S. Officials," *The New York Times* 30 January 1986: https://www.nytimes.com/1986/01/30/world/angolan-rebel-sees-top-us-officials.html
[706] Tyler and Ottaway.

Savimbi's UNITA received a total of $163 million in aid from the Reagan and Bush administrations.[707] Rollback was not realized in Angola, however, as the MPLA government remained in power. Nonetheless, the Reagan Doctrine contributed to a regional agreement in 1988 entailing the withdrawal of Cuban troops from Angola and South African troops from Namibia.[708] Heritage analyst Michael Johns and Howard Phillips of The Conservative Caucus visited Angola in 1989 to meet with Savimbi, who was displeased with the agreement as it terminated South African assistance to UNITA.[709] US government assistance to UNITA finally ended in 1991 with the collapse of the Soviet Union eliminating the justification for the Reagan Doctrine.

Savimbi returned to Washington in 1989 and delivered a lecture at Heritage headquarters. He opened by stating: "When we come to the Heritage Foundation, it is like coming back home. We know that our success here in Washington in repealing the Clark Amendment and obtaining American assistance for our cause is very much associated with your efforts. This foundation has been a source of great support. The UNITA leadership knows this, and it is also known in Angola."[710] Savimbi concluded: "My last word for The Heritage Foundation is that you have been for us a source of great support. No Angolan will

---

[707] James Scott, 34-35.
[708] Ibid., 150.
[709] 101st Congress. "Savimbi's Elusive Victory in Angola -- Hon. Dan Burton (Extension of Remarks - October 26, 1989): https://tinyurl.com/ybsw59ak
[710] Jonas Savimbi, "The Coming Winds of Democracy in Angola," *The Heritage Lectures #217* 5 October 1989, 1: http://www.heritage.org/africa/report/the-coming-winds-democracy-angola

forget your efforts."[711] As a leading think tank of the conservative faction of the oligarchy, Heritage was as responsible as any organization, public or private, for the application of the Reagan Doctrine to Angola.

Nicaragua

For most of the twentieth century, Nicaraguans were subjected to dictatorship and repeated US intervention. US Marines occupied the country from 1912 to 1925, and then again beginning in 1926 when a civil war erupted after a US-supervised election. The Marines remained after a US-brokered peace settlement in 1927 and battled the guerrilla army of Augusto C. Sandino, a revolutionary who demanded sovereignty for Nicaragua and the removal of US soldiers. In 1933, the Marines were withdrawn from the country, but Sandino would be assassinated the next year by the US-organized National Guard acting under the command of Anastasio Somoza García. Somoza would soon become the Nicaraguan president and exercise dictatorial control over the nation until his death in 1956. The US-supported Somoza dynasty would continue to rule Nicaragua for decades through Anastasio's two sons, first Luis Somoza Debayle and then Anastasio Somoza Debayle.[712]

During the 1970s, opposition to the Somoza regime intensified. The Sandinista National Liberation Front (FSLN), named after Sandino, waged a guerrilla war against the National Guard. A turning point occurred in the aftermath of a devastating earthquake in 1972 which caused thousands of deaths and massive destruction in the

---

[711] Ibid., 4.
[712] Livingstone, 16.

capital city of Managua. Somoza and his associates pilfered the foreign aid for disaster relief and monopolized government contracts for rebuilding and the provision of supplies.[713] Disaffected middle-class Nicaraguans and business owners not connected to the Somoza family consequently joined the resistance to the Somoza dictatorship with other urban sectors. By 1979, the FSLN had won important victories and weakened the National Guard. In July of that year, the Sandinista guerrillas defeated the National Guard, entered Managua, and seized power in a revolutionary takeover of the country.

Three of the five members of the new Council of National Reconstruction government were members of the FSLN. The Sandinista-led government promoted a mixed economy and prioritized education, healthcare, housing, and land reform. A massive literacy program dramatically reduced illiteracy and more than seven hundred schools were built in the first two years of the new government, earning Nicaragua the United Nations Educational, Scientific and Cultural Organization (UNESCO) literacy award in 1980. Preventive health programs were implemented and the United Nations International Children's Emergency Fund (UNICEF) lauded Nicaragua for "one of the most dramatic improvements in child survival in the developing world."[714] A social security institute was created, responsible for the construction of foster homes and senior care facilities. Somoza land holdings and other properties were expropriated and

---

[713] Wayne King, "The Wealth of Anastasio Somoza," *The New York Times* 22 July 1979: https://tinyurl.com/y7vwuwlu
[714] Mark Major, "The Sandinista Revolution and the 'Fifth Freedom,'" *MR Online* 15 August 2005: https://mronline.org/2005/08/15/the-sandinista-revolution-and-the-fifth-freedom

converted into state farms and cooperatives. More land was redistributed to peasants than in all other Central American countries combined in their entire history. While GDP per capita declined in neighboring countries in the early 1980s, Nicaragua's increased by seven percent. The new constitution guaranteed not only civil liberties but also socio-economic rights, and a participatory political system and democratic institutions were established.[715]

The FSLN-controlled government maintained a close relationship with Cuba and relations with the Soviet Union were initiated in 1980. The USSR provided both economic and military assistance to Nicaragua, increasing at a significant rate during the first half of the 1980s after US economic assistance was suspended by President Carter in his final week in office. Soviet military aid peaked in the middle of the decade. Thousands of Cubans and hundreds from the Soviet Union served in Nicaragua as advisors. Beyond the support from these communist states, the Sandinistas adopted Marxist tenets and a position of anti-imperialism vis-à-vis the foreign policy of the United States.[716] For the incoming Reagan administration and the conservative power elite, the Nicaraguan Revolution posed an intolerable left-wing threat to US hegemony in the hemisphere.

The Heritage Foundation published a *Backgrounder* entitled "U.S. Policy and the Marxist Threat to Central America" only weeks before the 1980 US elections, prepared by a former senior CIA officer. He criticized the Carter administration for "project[ing] an image of support to the left and hostility to the right" and urged that "actions

---

[715] Ibid.
[716] James Scott, 154-155.

by the U.S. in the next six months must be taken to project the correct image to all parties in the conflict, including the Soviets, to preclude their attempting dangerous and perhaps irreversible maneuvers."[717] Furthermore, he recommended a "well orchestrated program targeted against the Marxist Sandinista government."[718] The new administration proved highly receptive to these arguments.

In fact, it was in Nicaragua that the "most publicized and controversial application of the Reagan Doctrine occurred."[719] The doctrine was applied to Nicaragua only months into Reagan's presidency. In its first stage, the administration formulated a policy of aiding counter-revolutionary forces known as the Contras, armed insurgents led by former members of the National Guard. The administration enlisted the financial assistance of Rupert Murdoch and Richard Scaife in a CIA "perception management" campaign to publicly vilify the Sandinista government and extol the Contra war.[720] Its purpose was "to generate public and congressional support for the insurgency and to prepare for the possibility that the paramilitary operation, and the U.S. role in it, might become public."[721]

---

[717] Cleto DiGiovanni, "U.S. Policy and the Marxist Threat to Central America," *Backgrounder* 15 October 1980, 1: https://www.heritage.org/americas/report/us-policy-and-the-marxist-threat-central-america
[718] Ibid., 5.
[719] James Scott, 152.
[720] Robert Parry, "Murdoch, Scaife and CIA Propaganda," *Consortium News* 31 December 2014: https://consortiumnews.com/2014/12/31/murdoch-scaife-and-cia-propaganda
[721] James Scott, 161-162.

President Reagan authorized a covert aid program of $20 million in late 1981. The CIA supplied aid and training to the Contras, originally through Argentine and Honduran military surrogates, and then directly. Contra operations subsequently became more sophisticated and targeted infrastructure and government personnel. These attacks included the sabotage of roads and bridges, the killing of education and health workers, and the destruction of buildings and crops.[722] International human rights organizations documented Contra atrocities, with the International Human Rights Law Group identifying a "pattern of brutality against largely unarmed civilians, including rape, torture, kidnappings, mutilation and other abuses."[723]

Shultz's Department of State pursued a diplomatic path at odds with the strictly confrontational approach of the conservative power elite and its hardliners in the administration. Through their representatives in the administration, the oligarchic factions struggled for control over Reagan's Nicaragua policy. The State Department viewed the Contras as leverage in negotiations with the Nicaraguan government, ultimately for the purpose of reaching a diplomatic settlement, but "Each time the State Department opened a diplomatic initiative, these hardliners within the administration cooperated to scuttle it."[724] The hardliners, fully committed to the rollback of the Sandinista government, succeeded in their quest to dictate administration policy toward Nicaragua by 1983.

---

[722] Ibid., 161.
[723] Doyle McManus, "Rights Groups Accuse Contras: Atrocities in Nicaragua Against Civilians Charged," *Los Angeles Times* 8 March 1985: http://articles.latimes.com/1985-03-08/news/mn-32283_1_contras
[724] James Scott, 162.

Congress, however, presented a major obstacle to their rollback plans. Beginning in late 1982, Democratic members of Congress obstructed the administration's Nicaragua policy. In a letter, thirty-seven members of Congress warned Reagan of the possible illegal nature of CIA operations in Central America. One congressman commented, "Congress intended to prohibit the administration from trying to take paramilitary action against Nicaragua, but they have ignored it."[725] The expansion of the Contras to seven thousand fighters, revealed by Bill Casey to the House Intelligence Committee, greatly exceeded the five hundred-member force Congress had authorized. The committee supported a ban on assistance to the Contras after the House Foreign Affairs Western Hemisphere Subcommittee voted for an end to aid for the insurgents.[726]

In a series of amendments from 1982 to 1984, collectively named the Boland Amendment for their sponsorship by Representative Edward P. Boland of Massachusetts, Congress increasingly restricted assistance to the Contras. The first amendment, to the 1983 Department of Defense Appropriation Act, prohibited "the CIA or Defense Department to use funds of the bill to furnish military equipment, military training or advice, or other support for military activities, to any group or individual, not part of a country's armed forces, for the purpose of overthrowing the government of Nicaragua or provoking a military exchange between Nicaragua and Honduras."[727] One year

---

[725] Ibid., 164.
[726] Ibid., 164.
[727] 97th Congress. *H.Amdt.974 to H.R. 7355*: https://www.congress.gov/amendment/97th-congress/house-amendment/974

later an amendment was passed to the Intelligence Authorization Act for Fiscal Year 1984 "to prohibit covert assistance for military operations in Nicaragua."[728] Finally, the most restrictive amendment, adopted for the 1985 fiscal year, read, "No funds available to the Central Intelligence Agency, the Department of Defense or any other agency or entity of the United States involved in intelligence activities may be obligated or expended for the purpose or which would have the effect of supporting, directly or indirectly, military or paramilitary operations in Nicaragua by any nation, group, organization, movement or individual."[729]

The hardliners in the administration and the conservative faction more broadly would not desist from their active support for the Contras in spite of the congressional ban. A fundraising network organized by Oliver North, John Poindexter, and other administration officials, but without the support of the liberal faction-aligned State Department, was created to finance the Contras. North, a staff member of Reagan's National Security Council, informed Council for National Policy members of "the Contras' needs."[730] Through CIA Director Bill Casey, Joe Coors met with North in 1985 and transferred $65,000 to a Swiss bank account controlled by North for the purchase of a small airplane for the Contras. Reagan was the keynote speaker at a 1985 Contra fundraising dinner hosted by the Nicaraguan

---

[728] 98th Congress. *H.Amdt.461 to H.R.2968*:
https://www.congress.gov/amendment/98th-congress/house-amendment/461
[729] "Iran-Contra Hearings; Boland Amendments: What They Provided," *The New York Times* 10 July 1987:
http://www.nytimes.com/1987/07/10/world/iran-contra-hearings-boland-amendments-what-they-provided.html
[730] Bellant. *The Coors Connection*, 37.

Freedom Foundation (NFF), a conduit for funds to the guerrillas established by *The Washington Times*. Jeane Kirkpatrick and William Simon sat on the NFF board, and Coors and other CNP members like Nelson Bunker Hunt donated to the NFF. Pat Robertson's Christian Broadcasting Network was one of the largest donors, contributing millions of dollars and holding a fundraising telethon for the Contras in 1985.[731] US ambassador to Costa Rica Lewis A. Tambs, a CNP member, supervised a secret airstrip that was part of North's Contra supply network.[732]

At the same time, the CNP-linked United States Council for World Freedom led by John Singlaub organized a fundraising drive for the Contras with backing from administration officials. Although prohibited by its tax-exempt status, the USCWF claimed to have raised $300,000 for the Contras.[733] Singlaub reported his Contra fundraising to North and Casey beginning in 1984, relying on his relationships with World Anti-Communist League affiliates in Taiwan and Latin America.[734] Singlaub acquired more than $10 million for non-lethal supplies partly through the USCWF and WACL. In an interview, Singlaub stated that he eventually arranged a $5 million arms shipment to the Contras in 1985. The shipment of

---

[731] Ibid., 76-77.

[732] Greg Garland, "North was member of private group once based in Baton Rouge," *The State-Times* (Baton Rouge) 8 January 1987, 1A: http://media.pfaw.org/Right/CNP-IRAN.txt

[733] James Barron, "Outspoken General: A Fast Friend to Contras, *The New York Times* 8 October 1986: https://www.nytimes.com/1986/10/08/world/outspoken-general-a-fast-friend-to-contras.html

[734] Jonathan Marshall, Peter Dale Scott, and Jane Hunter. *The Iran-Contra Connection: Secret Teams and Covert Operations in the Reagan Era* (Boston: South End Press, 1987), 21.

rifles, grenade launchers, and ammunition from overseas suppliers arrived in Honduras, where the Contras were based.[735] The Heritage Foundation contributed to North's clandestine network as well, facilitating a donation of $100,000 to the Contras.[736]

Funding for the Nicaraguan insurgents was ultimately obtained through the "Enterprise" operation involving the sale of weapons to Iranian officials in violation of an arms embargo, resulting in the Iran-Contra scandal. Congressional investigations and the Reagan-appointed Tower Commission did not find evidence that the president himself had knowledge of the Iran-Contra operations but Reagan praised the Contras as "freedom fighters" and "the moral equal of our Founding Fathers" in a 1985 speech at the annual Conservative Political Action Conference (CPAC).[737] A congressional investigation found that "The Enterprise, functioning largely at North's direction, had its own airplanes, pilots, airfield, operatives, ship, secure communications devices, and secret Swiss bank accounts."[738] Following the investigations, US aid to the insurgents ended.[739] In 1990, after the Sandinistas lost power in national elections the Contra war drew to a close.

---

[735] Benjamin Weiser and Joe Pichirallo, "3 Groups Channeled Arms to Contras After Ban," *The Washington Post* 26 February 1987: https://tinyurl.com/yb6stzfo
[736] Bellant. *The Coors Connection*, 79.
[737] Ronald Reagan, "Remarks at the Annual Dinner of the Conservative Political Action Conference" (1 March 1985): https://www.presidency.ucsb.edu/documents/remarks-the-annual-dinner-the-conservative-political-action-conference
[738] 100th Congress. *Report of the Congressional Committees Investigating the Iran-Contra Affair* (November 1987), 4: https://archive.org/stream/reportofcongress87unit#page/n7/mode/2up/search/oliver
[739] James Scott, 34-35.

Both the Angola and Nicaragua interventions, and the Reagan Doctrine itself, were motivated by the fierce anti-communism of the conservative power elite. Reagan's presidency in the 1980s afforded the first opportunity for the conservative faction to implement its rollback strategy. Rather than directly confronting the Soviet Union, however, the Reagan Doctrine was applied with some success to Soviet-backed and left-wing governments in the "Third World." By the conclusion of the decade, the conservative faction of the oligarchy was claiming credit for the collapse of the Soviet Union. In a 1997 lecture to The Heritage Foundation, Reagan's "political soulmate" Margaret Thatcher described the Reagan Doctrine as "a rejection of both containment and detente. It proclaimed that the truce with communism was over. The West would henceforth regard no area of the world as destined to forego its liberty simply because the Soviets claimed it to be within their sphere of influence. We would fight a battle of ideas against communism, and we would give material support to those who fought to recover their nations from tyranny."[740]

CONCLUSION

The cases of US foreign intervention explored in this chapter reflect the divergent foreign policy goals of the liberal and conservative factions of the oligarchy during the Cold War. While the liberal power elite was committed to the containment of communism, US corporate interests figured most prominently in its interventions in Latin America. For the conservative power elite, ideological

---

[740] Margaret Thatcher, "Lecture to the Heritage Foundation: The Principles of Conservatism" (10 December 1997): https://www.margaretthatcher.org/document/108376

opposition to communism and socialism propelled the Reagan Doctrine interventions in the 1980s. President Trump reiterated this right-wing foreign policy position at the United Nations General Assembly in 2017 in reference to Venezuela's socialist Bolivarian Revolution, asserting, "From the Soviet Union to Cuba, Venezuela -- wherever socialism or communism has been adopted, it has delivered anguish, devastation, and failure."[741] These different foreign policy motivations of the two factions stem from their distinct political views and objectives. Conflict between them was inevitable with the conservative faction's rise to power.

---

[741] Kyle Feldscher, "Trump: Venezuela in crisis because 'socialism has been faithfully implemented,'" *Washington Examiner* 19 September 2017: https://tinyurl.com/y793f84l

CHAPTER 6
A "VAST RIGHT-WING CONSPIRACY": FACTIONAL CONFLICT FROM THE 1990s TO THE PRESENT

Through the Iran-Contra affair and discord between the State Department and Reagan administration conservative hardliners, antagonism between the two oligarchic factions manifested itself in the 1980s. The Clinton administration of the 1990s was accompanied by an escalation in factional conflict, as elements of the conservative power elite devised the "Arkansas Project" and other initiatives to stage an offensive against a presidency strongly supported by the liberal power elite. Hillary Clinton famously referred to it as a "vast right-wing conspiracy" against her husband in a 1998 interview on NBC's *Today* show.[742] She reiterated this view during her presidential campaign in 2016.[743] Since the 2016 elections, factional conflict has intensified, but this time the liberal faction of the oligarchy through its associated media and most prominent living oligarch has sought to delegitimize a presidency firmly backed by the conservative faction of the oligarchy.

---

[742] Who2TV. "Vast Right Wing Conspiracy" [Video] (27 January 2010): https://www.youtube.com/watch?v=EwtkorQKGFE
[743] Stephanie Condon, "Hillary Clinton: The 'vast, right-wing conspiracy' is 'even better funded' now," *CBS News* 3 February 2016: https://www.cbsnews.com/news/hillary-clinton-the-vast-right-wing-conspiracy-is-even-better-funded-now

THE CONSERVATIVE FACTION VERSUS CLINTON

Early in President Clinton's tenure, a group of right-wing political actors funded by conservative plutocrat Richard Scaife developed a plan to discredit Clinton with the apparent aim of effecting his removal from the White House. The origins of the anti-Clinton campaign can be found in a fishing trip during October 1993. Emmett Tyrrell, founder of *The American Spectator*, was accompanied by Scaife's senior aide Richard M. Larry, public relations consultant David W. Henderson, and attorney Steven S. Boynton. Both Henderson and Boynton claimed to know individuals in Arkansas who could expose misdeeds by the president when he was the state's governor. Henderson's contact was David Hale, a Little Rock municipal judge who accused Clinton of pressuring him into granting a fraudulent $300,000 loan to the Clintons' partner in the Whitewater real estate development.[744] Boynton was friends with Parker Dozhier, the owner of a bait shop who despised Clinton and alleged corruption at the Arkansas Game and Fish Commission (AGFC) during Clinton's governorship. The group of men agreed that the *Spectator* should seek a Scaife foundation grant to allow Boynton to pursue Dozhier's story. At the time, *Spectator* journalist David Brock was separately working on a story involving allegations from Arkansas state troopers that they arranged sexual liaisons for Governor Clinton.[745]

---

[744] Washington Post Staff, "'Arkansas Project' Led to Turmoil and Rifts," *The Washington Post* 2 May 1999, A24:
https://www.washingtonpost.com/wp-srv/politics/special/clinton/stories/scaifeside050299.htm
[745] Byron York, "The Life and Death of The American Spectator," *The Atlantic* November 2001:

Henderson and Boynton met with Hale in Little Rock and secured his assistance in their Whitewater investigation. The two men also attended a meeting at the office of a law firm in Washington, hosted by senior partner Theodore B. (Ted) Olson, an influential conservative figure and friend of Tyrrell. Others were present, including *Spectator* publisher Ronald Burr. They reportedly discussed ideas for using the magazine and Scaife money to probe into the Clintons' past in Arkansas.[746] Boynton's AGFC story, for which the publication received a Scaife grant, was soon overshadowed by the more serious Whitewater scandal and other investigations. The wide-ranging Arkansas Project was born, and in Tyrrell's opinion, "I thought by early '94 we really had a hell of a lot of scandal to reveal."[747]

Although neither was a journalist, their important connections within the conservative faction and in Arkansas placed Henderson and Boynton in a key position.[748] They were given full control of the confidential Arkansas Project and not even *Spectator* staff were privy to their work.[749] Paid by the American Spectator Educational Foundation, they traveled regularly to Arkansas to consult with Hale, who was a "living road map" to Whitewater according to Henderson. By 1995, their inquiries had expanded to Mena in western Arkansas, home to a landing strip rumored to be the site of CIA-sponsored drug

---

https://www.theatlantic.com/magazine/archive/2001/11/the-life-and-death-of-the-american-spectator/302343
[746] Joe Conason and Gene Lyons. *The Hunting of the President: The Ten-Year Campaign to Destroy Bill and Hillary Clinton* (New York: Thomas Dunne Books, 2000), 109.
[747] York.
[748] Conason and Lyons, 110.
[749] Ibid., 160.

trafficking and illegal arms shipments for funding the Nicaraguan Contras in the 1980s. Collaborating with Tyrrell, a state trooper was again used as the source for the Mena story, but Tyrrell's attempt at an exposé linking Clinton to the operations was largely ignored in Washington. However, it did create internal dissension at the magazine.[750]

Already funding the *Spectator* through his foundations since 1970, Scaife provided an additional $2.3 million to the magazine exclusively for the Arkansas Project.[751] From the outset, Scaife had "an intense, almost obsessive enmity for Clinton."[752] According to one of his good friends he obviously "disliked Clinton's liberal politics."[753] Scaife also hired *New York Post* writer Christopher Ruddy in 1994 at his *Pittsburgh Tribune-Review* to report on the July 1993 death of Deputy White House Counsel Vincent W. (Vince) Foster. Examining the case, Ruddy disputed the official finding that Foster, a friend of the Clintons from Arkansas, had committed suicide. His book fueled speculation that Foster was killed by the Clintons to conceal their role in illegal dealings related to Whitewater and other ventures. Joseph F. Farah, a governor of the Council for National Policy in 2014 and the founder and editor of right-wing *WorldNetDaily* (WND), later reprinted Ruddy's articles in *The Washington Times* as a series of fifty ads.[754] The Carthage Foundation, another Scaife foundation, partly

---

[750] York.
[751] Robert G. Kaiser and Ira Chinoy, "Scaife: Funding Father of the Right," *The Washington Post* 2 May 1999, A1: http://www.washingtonpost.com/wp-srv/politics/special/clinton/stories/scaifemain050299.htm
[752] Conason and Lyons, 109.
[753] Ibid., 108.
[754] CNP. "Membership Directory 2014," 6.

financed the undertaking along with other right-wing foundations.[755] Foster's death became the most controversial component of the Arkansas Project. It remains a topic of discussion among right-wing opponents of the Clintons. In 2016, for example, Donald Trump referred to the circumstances surrounding his death as "very fishy."[756]

A scathing review of Ruddy's book was published in the *Spectator* in 1997, which provoked an irate Scaife into withdrawing all support for the magazine. An article in *The New York Times* questioned whether the money spent by Henderson and Boynton in Arkansas had actually delivered any tangible benefits for the plutocrat.[757] Scaife and the *Spectator* would soon find themselves in legal trouble after the liberal-left website *Salon* published "The Road to Hale," an article charging the billionaire and the magazine with paying Hale, using Dozhier as an intermediary, to influence his testimony against Clinton in Independent Counsel Kenneth W. (Ken) Starr's investigation of Whitewater. The story appeared shortly after Hillary Clinton's comments on NBC. The Clinton Justice Department subsequently recommended an investigation to Starr. Scaife, Henderson, Boynton, and Dozhier were all

---

[755] Political Research Associates. "Western Journalism Center - Joseph Farah":
http://www.publiceye.org/conspire/clinton/Clintonculwar8-06.html#
[756] Glenn Kessler, "No, Donald Trump, there's nothing 'fishy' about Vince Foster's suicide," *The Washington Post* 25 May 2016: https://tinyurl.com/ybr765gb
[757] Neil A. Lewis, "Almost $2 Million Spent in Magazine's Anti-Clinton Project, but on What?," *The New York Times* 15 April 1998: https://tinyurl.com/yc37ocpw

called to testify before a grand jury in Arkansas in 1998.[758] Ultimately none of them were prosecuted due to "insufficient credible evidence" but it brought Scaife considerable notoriety in the national media.[759]

Interestingly, the Clintons would reconcile with Scaife and Ruddy in the years following the Clinton presidency. Bill Clinton even delivered a eulogy at Scaife's memorial service in 2014. According to Scaife's *Pittsburgh Tribune-Review*, "Clinton recalled how, after his presidency, he built a 'counterintuitive friendship' with the conservative billionaire."[760] Scaife donated more than $100,000 to the Clinton Foundation after visiting the ex-president at the foundation in 2007 and his newspaper endorsed Hillary Clinton over Barack Obama in the 2008 Pennsylvania Democratic primary. Ruddy, who asked Clinton to speak at the memorial, admitted that Scaife "was the bete noire of the Clinton administration during those years, sort of like what the Kochs are to the Obama administration today."[761]

Another right-wing effort simultaneously targeting President Clinton was the 1994 film *The Clinton Chronicles*, covering most of the same allegations as the Arkansas Project. Jerry Falwell promoted it on his television program "as if it were *The Ten Commandments*."[762] The Council for National Policy bulk-

---

[758] John Mintz, "Anti-Clinton Billionaire Goes Before Grand Jury," *The Washington Post* 29 September 1998: http://www.washingtonpost.com/wp-srv/politics/special/clinton/stories/scaife092998.htm
[759] York.
[760] Kenneth P. Vogel, "Clinton eulogizes Scaife," *Politico* 2 August 2014: https://www.politico.com/story/2014/08/bill-clinton-richard-mellon-scaife-eulogy-109670
[761] Ibid.
[762] Conason and Lyons, 143.

ordered copies for its membership, with approximately 150,000 copies sold in total and hundreds of thousands of bootlegs produced for distribution.[763] In *The New York Times Magazine,* the film was described as "a hodgepodge of sometimes-crazed charges that are thrown off with an air of knowingness but little documentation."[764] An article in *The Washington Post* referred to it as a "bizarre and unsubstantiated documentary."[765]

The most consequential of the Arkansas Project stories proved to be Brock's investigation of the troopers' allegations, specifically the sexual misconduct by Clinton involving Arkansas state employee Paula C. Jones. It was during a deposition taken under oath resulting from the Jones revelations that Clinton denied having sexual relations with White House intern Monica S. Lewinsky, leading to impeachment articles for perjury and obstruction of justice. Brock eventually renounced his own reporting for the Arkansas Project and his service to the conservative power elite in his book *Blinded by the Right,* which unsurprisingly "received glowing reviews from the heart of the liberal literary establishment," in Brock's words, while *"The Washington Times* and the *New York Post* took a pass" and "conservative television and radio

---

[763] Ibid., 145.
[764] Philip Weiss, "The Clinton Haters: Clinton Crazy," *The New York Times Magazine* 23 February 1997:
https://www.nytimes.com/1997/02/23/magazine/clinton-crazy.html
[765] Lois Romano, "A Core Collection of Clinton Enemies," *The Washington Post* 2 March 1998:
https://www.washingtonpost.com/wp-srv/politics/special/clinton/stories/enemies030298.htm?noredirect=on

outlets virtually blacked me out."[766] Henderson wrote an insider account defending the Arkansas Project in 2016, denouncing Brock as engaging in "the dirty act of protecting Hillary [Clinton] from exposure of her criminal activities" and accusing the former First Lady of "politicizing the Department of Justice and the FBI" in the 1990s.[767]

In the Clintons' estimation, the "vast right-wing conspiracy" continues to exist. Bill Clinton told NBC's *Meet the Press* in 2009 that President Obama was under attack from the same right-wing elements.[768] Journalist Jane Mayer soon identified the Koch brothers as the plutocrats "waging a war against Obama."[769] As a presidential candidate, Hillary Clinton was asked for her opinion during a televised town hall in 2016. Now "even better funded" in her judgement, Clinton elaborated, "At this point it's probably not correct to say it's a conspiracy because it's out in the open." She referenced the Kochs: "They've brought in some new multibillionaires. They want to control our country. They want to rig the economy so they can get richer and richer." Clinton further stated,

---

[766] David Brock. *Blinded by the Right: The Conscience of an Ex-Conservative* (New York: Three Rivers Press, 2003), xii-xiii.
[767] David W. Henderson. *The Arkansas Project: From the United States Jaycees to the United States Justice Department and Whitewater* (Olive Branch, MS: R. Glenn Kelly Publications, 2016), iii-iv.
[768] "Bill Clinton: 'Vast right-wing conspiracy' as 'virulent' as ever," *CNN* 27 September 2009: http://www.cnn.com/2009/POLITICS/09/27/clinton.conspiracy/index.html
[769] Jane Mayer, "Covert Operations: The billionaire brothers who are waging a war against Obama," *The New Yorker* 30 August 2010: https://www.newyorker.com/magazine/2010/08/30/covert-operations

"They salve their consciences by giving money to philanthropy, but make no mistake, they want to destroy unions, they want to go after any economic interest they don't believe they can control."[770] When she lost the election to President Trump, it was the liberal power elite's turn to wage a campaign against a sitting president.

THE LIBERAL FACTION VERSUS TRUMP

The liberal faction's rejection of Trump during his presidential candidacy did not subside when he won the election in November 2016. Through its affiliated media, which constitutes most of the major media, the liberal power elite has vehemently opposed Trump and his administration from the outset, and the president's tweets have provided it plenty of ammunition. The enormous influence of this media greatly exceeds that of the conservative faction media during the Clinton era, and it continues to be more powerful than its conservative counterpart, albeit to a lesser extent than in the twentieth century. Another source of powerful opposition to the president has been billionaire financier George Soros and his network of associates, just as Scaife had endeavored to undermine the Clinton presidency.

Trump's relationship with the liberal faction media is similar to the media's coverage of Barry Goldwater, another conservative faction favorite, during his 1964 presidential run: "The liberal press played a pivotal role in establishing the image of Goldwater as an extremist by almost continuously questioning his credentials and even his sanity. Only a handful of newspapers endorsed Goldwater, with an overwhelming majority supporting

---

[770] Condon.

Johnson. Goldwater was partly responsible for this lack of support from the media, however, since he made only a few real attempts to gain media backing and often treated the press as the enemy."[771] As for Trump, "When he announced his presidential candidacy, journalists embraced him, and he returned the favor [. . .] Only after he had secured the Republican nomination did the press sharpen its scrutiny and, as his news coverage turned negative, Trump turned on the press."[772] Certainly, by the time of the election, the liberal faction media had fully turned against Trump.

Trump has directly and publicly confronted the establishment media whereas other presidents backed by the conservative faction took an indirect approach. They either privately fought or circumvented the national media: "Nixon worked largely behind the scenes, threatening to take away broadcasters' licenses if they didn't shape up. Ronald Reagan created what amounted to a White House news service, feeding stories directly to local news outlets in order to bypass the national press."[773] Trump's hostility has undoubtedly contributed to the media's treatment of him, but much of the president's antagonism has been a reaction to consistently negative coverage of his administration thus far. Trump has made it clear that he is referring to the liberal faction media in his disparaging remarks about the media. One of his many tweets about "fake news" stated, "So they caught Fake News CNN cold, but what about NBC, CBS & ABC? What about the failing

---

[771] Mary C. Brennan. *Turning Right in the Sixties: The Conservative Capture of the GOP* (Chapel Hill: The University of North Carolina Press, 1995), 96.
[772] Thomas E. Patterson, "News Coverage of Donald Trump's First 100 Days," *Harvard Kennedy School Shorenstein Center* 18 May 2017: https://tinyurl.com/kel4lwf
[773] Ibid.

@nytimes & @washingtonpost? They are all Fake News!"[774] Conversely, Trump has been laudatory of conservative faction media, tweeting, "Congratulations to @FoxNews for being number one in inauguration ratings. They were many times higher than FAKE NEWS @CNN - public is smart!"[775]

An analysis from Harvard Kennedy School's Shorenstein Center on Media, Politics and Public Policy reveals the overwhelmingly negative news coverage of Trump's early presidency. News reports from all of the television networks in the study, except for Fox News Channel, were deemed to be more than ninety percent negative in the tone of their coverage of Trump. Reporting on the president from *The New York Times* and *The Washington Post*, the two main liberal faction newspapers, was well over eighty percent negative in tone. These numbers were far worse for Trump than the previous three presidents included in the study. Furthermore, the coverage was exceedingly negative on virtually every issue studied, although Trump's missile strikes on a Syrian air force base received praise. Contrary to the others, Fox News balanced positive and negative coverage, with *The Wall Street Journal* offering thirty percent favorable coverage of Trump.[776] A different study from the Pew Research Center confirmed this "polarized media environment."[777]

---

[774] Donald J. Trump on Twitter (27 June 2017): https://tinyurl.com/y78zt3tl

[775] Donald J. Trump on Twitter (24 January 2017): https://tinyurl.com/y9ag9pvf

[776] Patterson.

[777] Amy Mitchell et al., "Covering President Trump in a Polarized Media Environment," *Pew Research Center* 2 October 2017: http://www.journalism.org/2017/10/02/covering-president-trump-in-a-polarized-media-environment

Rather than providing mixed coverage of the president and his administration, Fox News is widely viewed as serving as Trump's media arm. A typical example was published in *The New York Times* in July 2018 under the title "Fox News Once Gave Trump a Perch. Now It's His Bullhorn." Reflecting on Trump's relationship with the network since his first appearance in 2011, the article states that Fox News "commentators resolutely defend the president's agenda" and notes that "Several former Fox News employees said they did not recall the channel so rigorously supporting a sitting president's agenda." Trump's friendships with the network's founder Rupert Murdoch and its star Sean Hannity have drawn attention, as Fox News commentators "both parrot and help shape the president's narratives." In addition, the administration has hired personnel from the network.[778]

While Fox News has the highest ratings of any cable news network, the establishment media of the liberal power elite still maintains a greater collective presence. Thus, its anti-Trump position has made it a formidable foe of the administration. Its reporting on "Russiagate" demonstrated this media's unwavering opposition to his presidency. Allegations of Russian government interference in the 2016 elections and collusion with the Trump campaign featured in the liberal faction media on a daily basis following Trump's election victory. In contrast, Fox News gave it less than half the coverage of the other media outlets in the Trump presidency's first one hundred days.[779] As Jack F. Matlock, the last US ambassador to the

---

[778] Michael M. Grynbaum, "Fox News Once Gave Trump a Perch. Now It's His Bullhorn," *The New York Times* 1 July 2018: https://www.nytimes.com/2018/07/01/business/media/fox-news-trump-bill-shine.html
[779] Patterson.

Soviet Union and a special assistant to the president for national security, acknowledged in 2018, "in our print and electronic media it has been accepted as a 'fact' that 'Russia' 'interfered' in the 2016 election."[780]

Matlock, who noted that he did not vote for Trump and like many believes the results of "the 2016 presidential and congressional elections pose an imminent danger to the republic," nevertheless criticized the Russiagate "hysteria" of "much of our 'responsible media.'" He listed seven facts, some of which were uncovered by Special Counsel Robert S. Mueller's Russia investigation, such as Russians purchasing Facebook advertisements before and after the elections, both pro- and anti-Trump, constituting considerably less than one percent of all Facebook ads bought at the time. None of Matlock's seven facts amounted to anything remotely close to the stealing of the 2016 elections by the nationalist-oriented Russian government and he "consider[ed] the charges that Russian actions 'interfered' in the election, or--for that matter-- damaged the 'quality of our democracy' *ludicrous, pathetic, and shameful*."[781] After reading the January 2017 report issued by part of the intelligence community, Matlock lamented that "Prominent American journalists and politicians seized upon this shabby, politically motivated, report as proof of 'Russian interference' in the US election without even the pretense of due diligence."[782]

---

[780] Jack F. Matlock, "Musings ... 'Russiagate' Hysteria," *JackMatlock.com* 2 June 2018: http://jackmatlock.com/2018/06/musings-russiagate-hysteria
[781] Ibid.
[782] Jack F. Matlock, "Musings II ... The 'Intelligence Community,' 'Russian Interference," and Due Diligence," *JackMatlock.com* 29 June 2018: http://jackmatlock.com/2018/06/musings-ii-the-intellience-community-russian-interference-and-due-diligence

Independent journalists and other former US government officials likewise rejected the Russiagate narrative. In the opinion of the late Robert (Bob) Parry, an investigative journalist who helped expose the Iran-Contra scandal for The Associated Press, "Trump's opponents turned to the Russia-gate investigation as the vehicle to create the conditions for somehow nullifying the election, impeaching Trump [which "Ukrainegate" eventually accomplished], or at least weakening him sufficiently so he could not take steps to improve relations with Russia." Regarding the media, "the drive for 'another Watergate' to oust an unpopular - and to many insiders, unfit - President remains at the center of the thinking among the top mainstream news organizations as they have scrambled for Russia-gate 'scoops' over the past year even at the cost of making serious reporting errors."[783] Retired CIA analyst Raymond (Ray) McGovern offered a critical assessment of both Mueller's investigation and omissions in the major media's Russiagate reporting.[784]

Mueller's probe concluded in 2019. He did not find any evidence of collusion between Trump campaign officials and the Russian government.[785] Dissenting from the liberal

---

[783] Robert Parry, "The Foundering Russia-gate 'Scandal,'" *Consortium News* 13 December 2017: https://consortiumnews.com/2017/12/13/the-foundering-russia-gate-scandal
[784] Ray McGovern, "Still Waiting for Evidence of a Russian Hack," *Consortium News* 7 June 2018: https://consortiumnews.com/2018/06/07/still-waiting-for-evidence-of-a-russian-hack
[785] Robert Mueller. *The Mueller Report: The U.S. Special Counsel's Report on the Investigation into Russian Interference in the 2016 Presidential Election* (Washington, DC: U.S. Department of Justice, March 2019).

faction narrative, Princeton professor emeritus Stephen F. Cohen argued, "Russiagate was initiated by political actors, but the elite establishment media gave it traction, inflated it, and promoted it to what it is today," producing "one of the worst episodes of media malpractice in the history of American journalism." He adds, "Russiagaters rarely if ever mention the potentially apocalyptic consequences of war between these two nuclear superpowers."[786] McCarthyism in the 1950s featured a right-wing senator and his equally right-wing chief counsel, who would later serve as a lawyer for Trump and Murdoch, attacking the establishment liberal faction and the State Department in particular. Bob Parry contended that Russiagate was fomenting "Establishment McCarthyism," a role reversal others have dubbed "Neo-McCarthyism."[787] At minimum, the liberal power elite utilized its major media to cast doubt on the legitimacy of the Trump presidency based on Russiagate.

Not unlike Clinton with Scaife, Trump is also facing an oppositional campaign from a billionaire, only more openly, although in this case the president is a billionaire himself. On the eve of the presidential inauguration, liberal plutocrat George Soros referred to Trump as "an impostor and a con man and a would-be dictator," perhaps inadvertently lending credence to accusations that he sponsored anti-Trump protests in the weeks following the

---

[786] Stephen F. Cohen, "'Russiagate' Is Revealing Alarming Truths About America's Political-Media Elites," *The Nation* 21 February 2018: http://www.thenation.com/article/russiagate-is-revealing-alarming-truths-about-americas-political-media-elites
[787] Robert Parry, "Russia-gate Breeds 'Establishment McCarthyism,'" *Consortium News* 26 October 2017: https://consortiumnews.com/2017/10/26/russia-gate-breeds-establishment-mccarthyism

2016 election.[788] Trump attended the World Economic Forum for the first time in January 2018, but according to a column in *The New Yorker* he was "upstaged" by Soros, a returning WEF participant. The two men did not cross paths in Davos: "As the President was hosting a dinner for various business leaders, Soros was across town, talking about the various threats facing Western democracies, a category in which he included the Trump Administration."[789] Soros delivered "a searing attack on Donald Trump."[790] Later in 2018, the global financier told an interviewer that Trump is a "narcissist" who is "willing to destroy the world."[791] By mid-2018, Soros had already contributed almost $10 million to support liberal candidates in the 2018 election cycle.[792]

Soros has pitted himself against not only the Trump administration and the conservative power elite in the United States, but also against governments and movements in Europe similarly espousing some form of

---

[788] Jeff Cox, "George Soros calls Trump a 'would-be dictator' who 'is going to fail,'" *CNBC* 19 January 2017:
www.cnbc.com/2017/01/19/george-soros-calls-donald-trump-a-would-be-dictator-who-is-going-to-fail.html
[789] John Cassidy, "How George Soros Upstaged Donald Trump at Davos," *The New Yorker* 25 January 2018:
https://www.newyorker.com/news/our-columnists/how-george-soros-upstaged-donald-trump-at-davos
[790] Maya Oppenheim, "Davos 2018: George Soros launches blistering attack on Trump - 'The survival of our entire civilisation is at stake,'" *The Independent* 26 January 2018:
https://tinyurl.com/y8nzgmdf
[791] Post Staff Report, "Trump is 'willing to destroy the world': George Soros," *New York Post* 9 June 2018:
https://nypost.com/2018/06/09/trump-is-willing-to-destroy-the-world-george-soros
[792] Center for Responsive Politics. "Top Individual Contributors: All Federal Contributions":
https://www.opensecrets.org/overview/topindivs.php

right-wing nationalism. Hungarian Prime Minister Viktor M. Orbán, a proponent of "illiberal democracy," repeatedly denounced Soros for allegedly encouraging Muslim migration to Europe. Soros' Open Society Foundations subsequently closed its office in Budapest, Hungary.[793] The Hungarian parliament passed legislation named "Stop Soros" in 2018, making it illegal to help undocumented migrants seek asylum in the country if they are not legally entitled to protection.[794] Soros has also been vocal in opposing Russian President Vladimir V. Putin.[795] He publicly challenged the UK's withdrawal from the EU, financially backing the anti-Brexit group Best for Britain and promoting its campaign for a second referendum.[796]

CONCLUSION

Factional conflict within the US oligarchy has been a reality since the conservative faction built itself into a serious competitor for power at the national level. In the 1990s, this took the form of the Scaife-funded Arkansas Project targeting Bill Clinton, a president favored by the liberal faction. Between the Clinton and Trump presidencies, the post-9/11 era of President George W. Bush was

---

[793] Reuters Staff, "Soros foundations to quit Hungary amid political hostility," *Reuters* 19 April 2018: https://tinyurl.com/y77mp4vj
[794] Eszter Zalan, "Hungary to push ahead with 'Stop Soros' law on NGOs," *EUobserver* 20 June 2018: https://euobserver.com/political/142134
[795] George Soros, "Wake Up, Europe," *The New York Review of Books* 20 November 2014: https://www.nybooks.com/articles/2014/11/20/wake-up-europe
[796] Magdaline Duncan, "George Soros: Campaign for second Brexit referendum about to start," *Politico Europe* 29 May 2018: https://www.politico.eu/article/second-brexit-referendum-george-soros-campaign-about-to-start

characterized by general oligarchic unity with an administration inclusive of both factions. After the election of Donald Trump, factional conflict has been evident in the establishment media's wholesale opposition to a presidency endorsed by the conservative faction and specifically in its coverage of Russiagate. Concurrently, Soros is playing an anti-Trump role reminiscent of Scaife's earlier anti-Clinton crusade. At the 2019 United Nations General Assembly, Trump announced his opposition to the liberal power elite by insisting, "The future does not belong to globalists, the future belongs to patriots."[797] This profound oligarchic discord will shape the future of the United States.

---

[797] Reuters Staff, "Trump calls on nations to reject globalism, embrace nationalism," *Reuters* 24 September 2019: https://tinyurl.com/yxm9k2lr

CONCLUSION

In the preceding pages, an investigation of the post-WWII US oligarchy or power elite has been undertaken. Two rival factions, labelled liberal and conservative in this study, have comprised the oligarchy, with the latter faction rising over decades to eventually challenge the establishment liberal faction for national power. While the oligarchy has not been a pure plutocracy, billionaires have played dominant roles in both factions. The differentiated power elite has vied for control of the main political parties, government institutions and agencies, and public discourse. With some noteworthy exceptions, the Democratic and Republican parties are presently guided by the liberal and conservative factions, respectively.

The first two chapters examined the liberal power elite, both its domestic composition and its international network. Domestically, the faction's major think tanks, foundations, and media were reviewed, revealing an integrated power network that has ruled the United States since World War II. At its core has been the leadership and membership of the Council on Foreign Relations. This power elite has enjoyed plenty of international reinforcement, affiliations built through various organizations and conferences beginning with the Bilderberg Group in the 1950s. Its monopoly on power was lost by the 1960s but its hegemony within the oligarchy persisted into the new century, hence "the establishment" remains an accurate description of the faction.

Chapters three and four focused on the postwar rise of the conservative power elite and its international connections, culminating in the Reagan Revolution. Again, the faction's principal think tanks were explored as well as their extensive links to key grantmaking foundations. The massive growth of its associated media was delineated. These interlocking components revealed another integrated power network. International groups such as Le Cercle have bolstered the domestic trajectory of the conservative power elite. With the current presidency of Donald Trump and strong influence in Congress, this right-wing faction has obtained its greatest amount of national power, exceeding the level of the Reagan era.

Foreign intervention by the US oligarchy was the subject of the fifth chapter. Four cases from the Cold War epoch were analyzed, two of them organized by the liberal faction and another two orchestrated by the conservative faction. Economic interests were of paramount importance in the former whereas ideological anti-communism drove the latter. The Nicaragua intervention in the 1980s also exposed serious factional conflict, the theme of the sixth chapter. Today's liberal faction opposition to the Trump administration recalls the concerted anti-Clinton campaign by conservative faction elements in the 1990s. Leading plutocrats from both factions have been central figures in these efforts to delegitimize sitting presidents.

Conversely, oligarchic unity has been witnessed at other times, and can be seen in the familiar names with ties to both factions. George H.W. Bush, Dick Cheney, Bill Casey, Jeane Kirkpatrick, and many neoconservatives are only some of the individuals who developed solid inter-factional affiliations. The now liberal faction-dominated Center for Strategic and International Studies, once the domain of the conservative power elite, opened itself to the inclusion of the liberal power elite beginning with Henry Kissinger. The Brookings Institution and the American Enterprise

Institute have sponsored joint projects.[798] The precise nature of the relations between the factions is difficult to ascertain. These links may be used to prevent factional conflict from fatally damaging the oligarchy. Still, the vast majority of the oligarchy is loyal to only one power elite network, enabling the prevailing divisions that preclude unity and undermine oligarchic rule. By weakening the oligarchy, factional conflict in the Trump era enhances the potential for democratic change.

Oligarchy does not permit substantive democracy. In an oligarchic society, power and control are top down, with the general population endorsing one of the ruling factions through elections and governments representing the interests of one or more factions. As demonstrated here with respect to the United States, factions are focused on the accumulation of their own political power to the detriment of the public interest. The US case is an illustration of democratic form concealing oligarchic substance. Perhaps much of the population is willing to passively accept the rule of the oligarchy, such as voting for the "lesser evil" in elections contested by candidates primarily responsive to oligarchic interests. Nonetheless, popular support for the oligarchy and its factions, active or passive, does not translate into substantive democracy.

What are the prospects for genuine democratic rule in the United States? The 2020 presidential election will be contested by two oligarchic candidates, with Democratic nominee Joseph R. (Joe) Biden representing the liberal faction. Bernard (Bernie) Sanders' presidential campaigns highlighted the US oligarchy's disdain for a democratic political project. However, constructing a third,

---

[798] AEI. "AEI-Brookings": http://www.aei.org/tag/aei-brookings

"democratic" faction on the left side of the oligarchy to compete with the two factions on the right would be a contradiction since any form of oligarchy is incompatible with democratic rule. A third faction representing the public interest might be viable in the short term, but in the long term it would likely transform into another faction serving private interests. Likewise, while growing a third party can be seen as an important first step, either faction of the oligarchy might attempt to destroy, corrupt, or capture it if the party begins to enjoy electoral success. Only a powerful democratic movement, which would disperse instead of concentrate power, can sustain such a party and ensure the longevity of a substantive democracy functioning in the public interest.

Such a movement would need to concern itself with a wide range of issues. At the moment, tens of millions of Americans live in poverty and income inequality is at the same level as in Russia.[799] Wealth disparity is even more extreme than the income gap. Three men, Warren E. Buffett, William H. (Bill) Gates, and Jeffrey P. (Jeff) Bezos collectively hold greater wealth than the poorest half of Americans.[800] The COVID-19 lockdown in 2020 has dramatically exacerbated this inequality. From March 18 to June 4, when 42.6 million Americans filed for unemployment, the cumulative wealth of US billionaires increased $565 billion.[801] Rising economic disparity has

---

[799] CBS/AP, "Report: America's income inequality is on par with Russia's," *CBS News* 15 December 2017:
https://www.cbsnews.com/news/report-americas-income-inequality-is-on-par-with-russias
[800] Inequality.org. "Wealth Inequality in the United States":
https://inequality.org/facts/wealth-inequality
[801] Chuck Collins, "As 42.6 Million Americans File for Unemployment, Billionaires Add Half a Trillion Dollars to Their

been a reality for the past three to four decades, the same period the neoliberal economic model has been promoted by both ruling factions.

Replacing these policies with a more ethical model would need to take precedence for social and environmental reasons. Another priority could be more funding for the civilian economy and less for military industry, entailing a significant reduction in military spending and closing a large number of the approximately eight hundred US military bases abroad.[802] It would allow for greater expenditure on infrastructure and public services including a comprehensive health care system. A new non-interventionist foreign policy would reject wars of choice and regime change. Perhaps public ownership of vital natural resources and utilities would be part of the agenda. A democratic movement might also act as catalyst for the formation of cooperatives throughout the private sector, extending the democratization process to the economy.

Ellen H. Brown's *The Public Bank Solution* proposes the creation of financial institutions that work in the public interest.[803] Public banks are government-owned banks at the local, state, and national levels. According to the Public Banking Institute (PBI), founded and chaired by Brown, "Publicly-owned banks operate in the public interest by law. That means they must support the real, wealth-producing economy. Bank profits generated from the credit

---

Cumulative Wealth," *Inequality.org* 4 June 2020: https://inequality.org/great-divide/billionaire-bonanza-update
[802] David Vine. *Base Nation: How U.S. Military Bases Abroad Harm America and the World* (New York: Metropolitan Books, 2015), 6-7.
[803] Ellen H. Brown. *The Public Bank Solution* (Baton Rouge: Third Millennium Press, 2013).

of the public are returned to the public." The PBI maintains, "The advantages of public over private banking are not rocket science. A government that owns its own bank can keep the interest and reinvest it locally, resulting in potential public savings of 35 percent to 40 percent. Costs can be reduced across the board; taxes can be cut or services increased; and market stability can be created for governments, borrowers and consumers."[804] There are many public banks operating throughout the world. In the United States, however, the only financial institution of this type is the Bank of North Dakota (BND). Established in 1919, it offers affordable credit to residents of the state and supports local governments. All state revenues are deposited in the bank, which this century "has reported record profits year after year, allowing it to return several hundred million dollars to the state's general fund."[805] The BND and public banks in other countries could serve as a model for democratization of the banking system.

The environmental crisis merits considerable attention. Biodiversity loss through species extinction caused by human activity is occurring at a record rate. The world is currently in an extinction crisis unprecedented in human history.[806] Ocean dead zones, so named because of the death of most marine life in these areas, have quadrupled since 1950 due to fossil fuel burning, fertilizer usage, and sewage. Large-scale extinction events in the planet's history have been associated with these oceanic

---

[804] PBI. "Intro to Public Banking":
https://www.publicbankinginstitute.org/intro-to-public-banking
[805] Ibid.
[806] Center for Biological Diversity. "Halting the Extinction Crisis":
https://www.biologicaldiversity.org/programs/biodiversity/elements_of_biodiversity/extinction_crisis

conditions.[807] In the United States, they are most common along the East Coast and in the Gulf of Mexico. Dead zones also exist in other large bodies of water like the Great Lakes. The US National Oceanic and Atmospheric Administration (NOAA) states that the "second largest dead zone in the world is located in the U.S., in the northern Gulf of Mexico."[808] Beyond climate change, other urgent environmental issues are ocean plastics pollution, soil erosion, resource depletion, and freshwater scarcity including in certain regions of the United States.[809] The Flint water crisis has demonstrated the danger of contaminated drinking water resulting from aging infrastructure throughout the country.[810]

Both factions of the oligarchy have been grossly negligent in combating environmental degradation, although the conservative faction has been especially dismissive of all concerns related to the environment. During his presidential campaign, Trump claimed that he would abolish the Environmental Protection Agency.[811] His

---

[807] Damian Carrington, "Oceans suffocating as huge dead zones quadruple since 1950, scientists warn," *The Guardian* 4 January 2018: https://www.theguardian.com/environment/2018/jan/04/oceans-suffocating-dead-zones-oxygen-starved
[808] NOAA. "What is a dead zone?": https://oceanservice.noaa.gov/facts/deadzone.html
[809] Shannyn Snyder, "Water Scarcity - The U.S. Connection," *The Water Project*: https://thewaterproject.org/water-scarcity/water_scarcity_in_us
[810] M.B. Pell and Joshua Schneyer, "The thousands of U.S. locales where lead poisoning is worse than in Flint," *Reuters* 19 December 2016: https://www.reuters.com/investigates/special-report/usa-lead-testing
[811] Kyle Feldscher, "Trump says he'd eliminate 'Department of Environment Protection,'" *Washington Examiner* 3 March 2016: https://tinyurl.com/ya86jlkv

administration has prioritized deregulation at home, eliminating dozens of environmental rules.[812]

Democratization of the political process would require the proliferation of democratic media to supplant the oligarchic media. Mass media defending the public interest and disseminating critical views rarely presented in today's major media would democratize public discourse. The Internet has been extremely useful for this purpose, but grassroots media still reaches less of the public than oligarchic media on the most crucial issues, and the output of this dominant media is uncritically absorbed by much of the population. Even if democratic media continues to expand and becomes more influential, public apathy or daily commitments, a divided population, and the aspirations of some Americans to join oligarchic circles will still present immense obstacles to overcome. As Occupy Wall Street protesters learned, through control of government agencies the oligarchy has access to the vast surveillance apparatus built after 9/11.[813] Given these realities, one can only conclude that the oligarchy will likely rule for the foreseeable future.

Earlier this century, political theorist Sheldon S. Wolin had already analyzed the increasing "inverted totalitarianism" in the contemporary United States. According to Wolin, this form of totalitarianism differs in some important

---

[812] Nadja Popovich et al., "78 Environmental Rules on the Way Out Under Trump," *The New York Times* 28 December 2018: https://www.nytimes.com/interactive/2017/10/05/climate/tru mp-environment-rules-reversed.html
[813] Lisa Graves, "How the Government Targeted Occupy," *PRWatch* 21 May 2013: https://www.prwatch.org/news/2013/05/12120/how-government-targeted-occupy

respects from classical totalitarianism but shares core characteristics, such as the promotion of fear.[814] The climate of fear permits an expansion of governmental power and enables control of the population. COVID-19 and the global lockdown are now set to transform the United States and the world across social, economic, and political realms in accordance with oligarchic plans for the so-called new normal.[815] Other events may also contribute to this totalizing process. Despite this appalling global trajectory, a neo-totalitarian future can still be averted by democratic resistance from all people who value liberty in the United States and throughout the world.

---

[814] Sheldon S. Wolin. *Democracy Incorporated: Managed Democracy and the Specter of Inverted Totalitarianism* (Princeton: Princeton University Press, 2008).
[815] GlobalResearchTV. "The COVID-19 Lockdown: Economic & Social Impacts – Peter Koenig – The Global Research Report" [Video] (15 July 2020): https://www.youtube.com/watch?time_continue=1&v=1a7J-Nz7jVo&feature=emb_logo;
Scott W. Atlas et al., "The COVID-19 shutdown will cost Americans millions of years of life," *The Hill* 25 May 2020: https://thehill.com/opinion/healthcare/499394-the-covid-19-shutdown-will-cost-americans-millions-of-years-of-life

ADDENDUM:
NOTABLE DEVELOPMENTS
(FEBRUARY 2022)

Events in Canada and other Western countries in early 2022 are finally revealing meaningful resistance against the advancement of global totalitarianism.

The Freedom Convoy of Canadian truckers and supporters occupying the capital city of Ottawa, with border blockades in other locations, marked the first significant acts of coordinated opposition to totalitarian policies imposed under the guise of COVID-19 measures. Similar protests have followed in Australia, New Zealand, Israel, France, and other European countries. In the United States, a truck convoy is traveling from California to Washington, DC. For its part, most of the "left" has exhibited contempt for the working-class movement, preferring to regurgitate government and establishment media propaganda as an appendage of the liberal faction of the oligarchy.

A discussion of the World Economic Forum in chapter 2 emphasized its key role in the transnational network of the liberal faction, including involvement in events related to COVID-19 as well as plans for "The Great Reset." The Liberal regime in Canada, which invoked the draconian Emergencies Act to forcefully end the nonviolent protests, is closely aligned with the WEF. Deputy Prime Minister and Finance Minister Chrystia Freeland concurrently sits on the WEF board of trustees.[816] Many members of the ruling party are Young Global Leaders of the WEF, a

---

[816] WEF. "Leadership and Governance":
https://www.weforum.org/about/leadership-and-governance

program which has included Angela Merkel of Germany and Vladimir Putin of Russia according to WEF executive chairman Klaus Schwab. At Harvard University in 2017, Schwab boasted, "So, yesterday, I was at a reception for Prime Minister Trudeau, and I know that half of his cabinet, or even more than half of his cabinet, are actually Young Global Leaders of the World Economic Forum."[817]

As the destruction of rights and liberties accelerates globally through the implementation of technological and other forms of control, various events are likely to affect the neo-totalitarian process in the United States. The liberal power elite is in command of the Biden administration, but its agenda is deeply unpopular in many areas of the country. A critical factor in determining the future may be the strength of the resistance at the state and local levels. Ultimately, the United States is likely to serve as the setting for the culmination of the globalist totalitarian project, or its defeat, over the coming months and years.

---

[817] JHOC. "Klaus Schwab/HARVARD Talk/Trudeau Cabinet & others "penetrated." [Video] (26 January 2022): https://www.youtube.com/watch?v=b4cDNyvrP4o

INDEX